NATIONAL
LITERATURE IN
MULTINATIONAL
STATES

NATIONAL LITERATURE IN MULTINATIONAL STATES

EDITED BY
ALBERT BRAZ & PAUL D. MORRIS

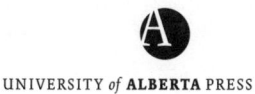

UNIVERSITY of ALBERTA PRESS

Published by

University of Alberta Press
1–16 Rutherford Library South
11204 89 Avenue NW
Edmonton, Alberta, Canada T6G 2J4
amiskwaciwâskahikan | Treaty 6 |
Métis Territory
uap.ualberta.ca | uapress@ualberta.ca

Copyright © 2022 University of Alberta Press

LIBRARY AND ARCHIVES CANADA
CATALOGUING IN PUBLICATION

Title: National literature in multinational states
   / edited by Albert Braz and Paul D. Morris.
Names: Braz, Albert, 1957– editor. | Morris, Paul
   Duncan, 1961– editor.
Description: Includes bibliographical references.
Identifiers: Canadiana (print) 20220260044 |
   Canadiana (ebook) 2022026015X |
   ISBN 9781772126075 (softcover) |
   ISBN 9781772126747 (EPUB) |
   ISBN 9781772126754 (PDF)
Subjects: LCSH: Nationalism and literature. |
   LCSH: Nationalism in literature. |
   LCSH: National characteristics in literature. |
   LCSH: Comparative literature.
Classification: LCC PN51 .N38 2022 |
   DDC 809/.933581—dc23

First edition, first printing, 2022.
First printed and bound in Canada by Houghton
Boston Printers, Saskatoon, Saskatchewan.
Copyediting and proofreading by Joanne Muzak.

All rights reserved. No part of this publication
may be reproduced, stored in a retrieval
system, or transmitted in any form or by any
means (electronic, mechanical, photocopying,
recording, or otherwise) without prior written
consent. Contact University of Alberta Press
for further details.

University of Alberta Press supports copyright.
Copyright fuels creativity, encourages diverse
voices, promotes free speech, and creates a
vibrant culture. Thank you for buying an authorized edition of this book and for complying
with the copyright laws by not reproducing,
scanning, or distributing any part of it in any
form without permission. You are supporting
writers and allowing University of Alberta Press
to continue to publish books for every reader.

University of Alberta Press is committed to
protecting our natural environment. As part of
our efforts, this book is printed on Enviro Paper:
it contains 100% post-consumer recycled fibres
and is acid- and chlorine-free.

This book has been published with the help of
a grant from the Canadian Federation for the
Humanities and Social Sciences, through the
Awards to Scholarly Publications Program,
using funds provided by the Social Sciences
and Humanities Research Council of Canada.

University of Alberta Press gratefully acknowledges the support received for its publishing
program from the Government of Canada,
the Canada Council for the Arts, and the
Government of Alberta through the Alberta
Media Fund.

Most nations are not states; most states are not nations.
—*JONATHAN KERTZER*, Worrying the Nation

Contents

The Nation and Its Literature(s) IX
Representing People, Representing a People
PAUL D. MORRIS & ALBERT BRAZ

1 **Reticent Nations** 1
Governor General's Award–Winning Fiction and the Representation of Canada
PAUL D. MORRIS

2 **Cultural Memory, National Identity** 21
The Changing Paradigms of Acadian Literature
MATTHEW CORMIER

3 **Literary Resistance** 43
Situating a Métis National Literature
MATTHEW TÉTREAULT

4 **Intersections of Nationhood, Multiculturalism, and Globalization in South Asian Canadian Fiction** 65
A Study of Anita Rau Badami's Can You Hear the Nightbird Call?
SABUJKOLI BANDOPADHYAY

5 **Canadian Literature in Heritage Languages and the Politics of Canon Formation** 89
ASMA SAYED

6   "No Nation Now but the Imagination" 109
    No Caribbean Nation without the Dutch Caribbean
    DORIS HAMBUCH

7   Rediscovering the Republic 129
    The Work of Joan Daniel Bezsonoff
    JERRY WHITE

8   A Multinational Narrative in a Case Study of Translating an Eastern Christian Play 147
    CLARA A.B. JOSEPH

9   Nigeria's Other Civil War 167
    Ken Saro-Wiwa and Ogoni Nationalism
    ALBERT BRAZ

10   "Write Only the Truth" 185
    (Re)contesting the Nigerian Nation in Chimeka Garricks's Tomorrow Died Yesterday *and Helon Habila's* Oil on Water
    UCHECHUKWU PETER UMEZURIKE

Contributors 203

The Nation and Its Literature(s)
Representing People, Representing a People

PAUL D. MORRIS & ALBERT BRAZ

THE PAIRED CONCEPTS contained in the title of this volume—national literature and multinational states—harbour a single contradiction that is rarely addressed because it is rarely acknowledged. The power of literature both to create and reflect understandings of collective belonging has long been acknowledged as one of its central attributes. Assembled into a tradition identified as *national*, the literary works of a national literature are habitually accorded status as the privileged sign and progenitor of the nation-state, a fact attested to in forms as simple as the shelving of literature in bookstores and the arrangement of literature departments in universities. A moment's reflection, however, reveals the tension inherent in the lived experience of the nation and its literature(s). For although literature is amenable to the creation of a sense of the national collective, very few nation-states are reducible to representation in a homogeneous cultural narrative. Most countries comprise complex, multinational polities formed of a plurality of cultural communities (in many countries, accruing), each laying claim to the privileges and prerogatives of (literary) representation; *le récit national* is almost always a story of many, usually contested, narratives. The Romantic nation(-state) and the ideal of a corresponding national literature have struggled with this simple reality since the shared historical moment of their inception. Each chapter of *National Literature in Multinational States* addresses the persistent and yet always imperfect link between literature and nation. It is neither the goal nor the effect of the collection to disqualify the notions of either nation or national literature, but rather to address some of the practical and theoretical limitations of their manifestations and, secondly, to illustrate particular instances where the two related notions exist in tension. Literary studies have long been occupied with the multiple intersections of literature and nation (Bhabha; Horton and Baumeister; Szeman). Likewise, the responsibility of the nation(-state) to acknowledge the place of subnational communities has been discussed, if infrequently, as a question of *politico-administrative* representation (Kymlicka; A. Smith, "Ethnic Nationalism"; R. Smith). As a matter of *literary* representation, however, the problems—cultural and political—of adequately portraying the diversity of multinational states within a unified national literature have not received adequate attention. *National Literature in Multinational States* is intended to offer diverse points of reflection upon this very lacuna.

In preparation for the individual discussions of literature and the nation presented in this book, the following introduction will seek to provide a contextualizing overview of the conceptual terrain, the cluster of concepts and processes that the contributors to *National Literature in Multinational States* return to in their separate ways. Key here is the very idea of the nation and its attendant ideology, nationalism. A formative construct in organizing social and political life since the latter half of the eighteenth century, the nation is a surprisingly difficult concept to capture in definitional specificity due to the competing and evolving visions of its historical sources and sociopolitical character. One of its finest theoreticians, Anthony Smith, has suggested that the idea of the nation has at best "appeared sketchy and elusive, at worst absurd and contradictory" (*National Identity* 17). The differences of definition that plague the term are of relevance for a variety of reasons, not the least because they signal significant differences regarding the origins and composition of the nation and, following from this, its claims to legitimacy as the primary claimant to the symbolic and political powers of the state. A further matter of overarching concern is the identification of the sources of the fissure complicating identification of a nation(-state) with its national literature. What was long understood as insoluble—the symbiotic relation between nation and national literature—has become the basis of a contestation that emerges from two broad directions. The first and most frequent derives from subnational cultural communities disputing the adequacy of the national narrative and thus demanding revisions to, and inclusion in, an altered national story. A second more general but equally persistent challenge derives from alternative, usually supranational, constructs that challenge the nation's primacy as the privileged source of collective and individual identity. Central to both of these broadly conceived forms of contention is representation—literary and political—a topic that *National Literature in Multinational States* returns to repeatedly whether in affirmation of an evolving understanding of the nation or in the service of a contestatory vision of its composition and legitimacy.

Emerging from the collective effort of the book is the realization that both literature and the nation encompass interdependent and yet non-identical impulses. Both are grounded in the social; both assume a form of culture (Gilbert 198); both are instantiated through representation; and both find articulation in narrative. Yet each, ultimately, has a separate telos. Literature may be entrusted with the representation of *a people* as a portion of a nationalist project reified in a national literature; its first and broader allegiance, however, remains to represent *the people* who individually and collectively comprise all identity-bearing entities. Neither the nation nor national literatures are likely to disappear; their capacity to affirm a sense of collective belonging as the basis for the provisioning of material and spiritual needs remains too strong, too important to social life (Kymlicka and Straehle 224–29). Nonetheless, a common thread in most if not all of the chapters of this collection is a sense of dissatisfaction, a *ressentiment* born of imperfect representation within the national narrative, the national literature. The collective effort of *National Literature in Multinational States* suggests that any resolution to the conflicts lodged in the book's title, any effort to heal the fractures of the nation will require expansion of "our senses of peoplehood" (R. Smith 19). The better representation of both people and peoples will remain the imperative of both national literatures and their associated systems of social and political life.

The Nation: Origins, Definitions, Implications

National Literature in Multinational States appears at a time of one of the most startling developments of the twenty-first century—the pronounced resurgence of thinking about the nation and the still more vociferous resurgence of nationalism. A concept conventionally thought to have receded from prominence due to its supposed superseding by supranational organizations (Mathews) and its associations with some of the greatest crimes in human history has re-emerged as a driving force in the organization of political and cultural life around the globe. The undeniable—and to many, troubling—reappearance of the nation poses a host of both theoretical and practical questions that demand reflection even prior to considerations of how politics and the aesthetic interact in the shaping of national literatures.

What, for example, is a nation?[1] According to one reading, the nation exists prior to specific political considerations as a collective sharing a geographical space, a sense of common historical experience, unifying cultural and linguistic practices, and a psychological bond manifested in an ongoing commitment to a common destiny (Connor 379–80). Anthony Smith adjoins political and administrative dimensions to define an "ideal type" of nation as "a named community of history and culture, possessing a unified territory, economy, mass education system and common legal rights" ("Origins" 342). Stymied in the present, commentators frequently reach for explicative purchase in the past, appealing to accounts of the historical "rise" of the nation and nationalism. Historically understood, the nation is frequently conceived as having its roots in an *ethnie* (345), pre-modern peoples who shared a sense of cultural belonging and lineage but who remained subject to the political control exercised by supranational authorities, such as ecclesiastic, monarchical or imperial/colonial organizations. In this reading, a central shift occurred in the late eighteenth and early nineteenth centuries with the displacement of political control and the increasing self-awareness of nations as themselves constituent forces of the social and political order (Wimmer, *Waves of War*). The nation understood as a people becomes itself a font of political power and authority, an arm of an expanding understanding of democracy. Rather than a monarch or an elite retaining the unquestionable prerogative to guide the collective—*l'état c'est moi*—it is "we the people," the nation, that is sovereign, invested through the democratic process with the power to confer authority to a national assembly or monarch. A further elaboration of the story of the nation's emergence in the modern era emphasizes nationalism's fostering of nations as a prelude to the provision of the centralized bureaucracies, common languages, codified legal frameworks, educated workforce, and so on needed by industrial societies (Kramer 12–13). Ernest Gellner's claim that "it is nationalism which engenders nations, and not the other way round" (55) provides famous expression to an influential theory of the constructedness of the nation, whereby various tools of modernity—including literary—are used in the creation of an "imagined community."

Important consequences derive from the choice to locate the nation in the deep cultural roots of an *ethnie* or, conversely, to theorize it as an "imagined" artifact of nationalism and the demands of modernizing, industrializing societies. Anthony Smith in *Myths and Memories of the Nation* outlines four dominant paradigms for understanding the nation and nationalism: the *primordialist*, the *perennialist*, the *modernist*, and the model advanced by Smith himself, the *ethnosymbolic* (3–19). According to the primordialist view, the nation exists outside of or prior to history as a fact of nature, the foundational basis of all aspects of human life. As the Abbé Sieyès famously expressed it on the eve of the French Revolution, "The nation exists before all; it is at the source of all. Its will is always legal; it is itself the law…A nation never leaves the state of nature" (53, 55).[2] The perennialist conception holds that the nation is a product of human culture rather than a component of the natural order and that nations emerge and recede historically as the basis of identifiable communities of cultural belonging whose roots run deep in shared territorial spaces and cultural practices. The third and perhaps reigning conception of the nation is the modernist. For the above-referenced Ernest Gellner, but also other influential figures such as Eric Hobsbawm and, most famously in the context of literary studies, Benedict Anderson, the nation does not pre-exist its "imagining" in the modern era; it is, itself, the product of nationalism, an ideology that emerged out of the processes of modernization launched in the wake of the revolutions of the late eighteenth century. The modernist nation materialized as the construct best able to produce the educational and cultural homogeneity required by expanding industrial economies. Smith's ethnosymbolic approach to the nation accepts the modern, constructed emergence of many nations but also insists on the primacy of a historical connection between modern nations and prior, pre-existing ethnic communities or *ethnies*.

The Nation, National Minorities, the State
Anthony Smith's nuanced taxonomy of theories of the nation is particularly illuminating in the present context due to its identification of the subtle link between ethnic cultures and the nation, even the modernist, constructivist nation. As discussed in several chapters in *National Literature in Multinational States*—for example, those dealing with Canada and Nigeria—the place of subnational cultural groups within the nation is a matter of fundamental concern and frequently the primary point of fissure in the national imaginary. Smith emphasizes the *ethnie* as an important historical constituent of the nation. In the rough-and-tumble world of competing visions of the nation illustrated in this volume—where questions of origins and legitimacy gain urgency through their coupling with the exercise of power—the demand for recognition within the nation(-state) and its national literature extends beyond *ethnies* to include numerous other groupings of cultural identity. Thus, it is no longer the *ethnie* or the nation alone that maintains the exclusive privilege of representation, but also national minorities, ethnocultural groups, minority language communities, diasporic populations among various other forms of political and cultural membership. While different in scale, composition, and formal political status, as bearers of collective identity, each may claim the prerogative of recognition within the nation(-state) and the national imaginary. As the respective chapters of *National Literature in Multinational States* illustrate, these are the subnational collectives contesting the claims of cultural uniformity implicit in homogenizing understandings of the nation and, by extension, its national literature.

A further complexity related to comprehending the nation derives from the term's semantic flexibility. The word *nation* famously occupies space in the two conceptually related and yet distinct domains of the socio-anthropological and the political. A nation may designate either a group sharing defining, inherited cultural traits—a people—or a political, territorial group that may or may not share a sense of ethnocultural relatedness—a country. While terms such as *country, state, republic, commonwealth, colony*, or—a Canadian preference—*dominion* are subject to closer definitions, the word *nation* may be applied in reference to the cultural or the political. As a curious illustration of the complexities of the term, Franz Kafka the Jewish, German-language writer could speak of national literature in reference to two *kleine Nationen* within the Austro-Hungarian Empire: the territorialized political entity that would become Czechoslovakia in 1918 and the extraterritorial, diasporic cultural community formed by adherents of the Jewish faith regardless of their place or citizenship (Casanova 287–93).

The overlapping of nation and state, the cultural and the political, reflected in this semantic confusion is no mere coincidence; it is tied to the symbolic and practical importance for any nation of gaining access to political power and the associated potential to shape the national identity, including via recourse to a national literature. In the earliest stages of the nation-state's late eighteenth-, early nineteenth-century history, the prospects for the nation were felt to reside with the capacities of the state. A people's self-identification as a nation was but a prelude to its emergence as a nation-state. In 1817, Georg Wilhelm Friedrich Hegel wrote that a given nation's "substantial purpose is to be a state and to maintain itself as such." For Hegel, without the political and administrative form provided by the machinery of state, the nation had no lasting substance or, in his terms, "no real history" (357).[3] For better or worse, over the past 250 years, the nation-state has emerged as the dominant form of political life around the globe, initially, undoubtedly, because of its success in defeating dynastic and imperial systems and, subsequently, due to its ability to deliver to polities economic, cultural, and political advantages superior to those of other models (Wimmer, "Why" 30). Chief amongst these advantages—and certainly at play at the time of Hegel's writing— was the superior capacity of the nation-state to protect the autonomy of the collective "we," particularly in times of war and occupation. It is no mere coincidence that Johann Gottlieb Fichte's epochal rallying cry, *Reden an die deutsche Nation* (*Addresses to the German Nation*, 1808), was prompted by the outrage of Napoleon's defeat and occupation of Prussia in 1806–1807. More recently, in an age of anti-imperialism and decolonization, aspirations to national sovereignty via the alignment of nation and state have led to the establishment of as many nation-states, if not more, as the exigencies of modernizing industrial economies identified by Gellner (Wimmer and Feinstein 767–70). Indeed, the generative power of historically *post*modern ideologies and cultural developments in fostering nationalisms, nations, and nation-states is implicitly attested to in the very contents of this book. Most of the contradictions and fissures between nations and national literatures referred to in the respective chapters of *National Literature in Multinational States* occur in countries that emerged as political and cultural entities out of the cauldron of empire and colonialism. Nevertheless, whether emergent as modernist or ethnosymbolic nations—to reprise Smith's terminology—a substrata of features related to the political and cultural motivations for positing the nation remains, including the question of the nation's relation to the state and literature.

A nation's assumption of the powers and privileges of the instruments of the state has obvious implications for national literatures. As Paul Gilbert notes, "it is the *state*...which *constructs* a national literature" (200), from whence the anxiety of subnational cultural groups rightly jealous of the state's powers to construct and thereby determine identity. Will Kymlicka and Christine Straehle speak with salutary frankness of the contradictory effects of most, if not all, endeavours at nation-building, which necessarily include a homogenizing drive to uniformity in the creation of a common sense of national identity. Hegemonic articulations of *the* nation—whether presented as legitimized by the long-standing traditions of an originary *ethnie* or as the product of the modernist, constructivist imperative to "imagine" the collective—necessarily entail a threat to pre-existing cultural communities, whether understood as ethnocultural groups or national minorities: "the essence of nationalism is precisely about political movements and public policies that actively attempt to ensure that states are indeed 'nation-states' in which the state and nation coincide...We need to recognize that state nation-building is often connected to minority nation-destroying" (230–31). Aware of this inevitable threat to their sense of national identity, subnational cultural collectives remain acutely attentive to all forms of political and cultural representation, including the composition of the national literature—long an essential tool in nation-building. Another important dimension of "nation-destroying" unremarked upon by Kymlicka and Straehle, but illustrated in several contributions to *National Literature in Multinational States*, is the manner in which national minorities can in themselves destabilize the fixedness of their "national" identity. Here the challenge to the integrity of the national identity comes not from internal minorities seeking inclusion, but via changing understandings of the nation itself. Viewed historically, most nations—whether nation-states or national minorities—demonstrate significant alterations with regard to their self-conception, changes that are illustrated in the very national literature evoked to demonstrate the specificity of the national identity. The "invention" of a community assumes its ongoing "re-invention." The constructivist logic of the inherent malleability of the "imagined" nation-state that renders possible revisionist claims upon the nation-state applies equally well to national minorities themselves, as is attested to in historically evolving understandings of their "national" literatures.

Kymlicka and Straehle identify the implicit threat that homogeneous narratives of origins and belonging pose to cultural groups inadequately contained within the national imaginary. There are still others. For instance, what people form *the* people? What constitutes the national *we* laying claim to sovereignty, and how is this collective configured? What are the criteria and limits of membership? Ernest Renan in his influential lecture "Qu'est-ce qu'une nation?" ("What Is a Nation?") identified the intractable nature of the problem in characterizing as a "chimera" the appeal to such broad, inherited categories of belonging as language, race, religion, and so on—the very elements at the foundation of the ethnonational ideal of the nation. Since then, the pervasive even primordial heterogeneity of social life that Renan recognized in 1882 has grown exponentially, particularly after the Second World War, as liquidity and mobility have become reigning values in an ever-globalizing world. Capital, manufactured goods, and ideas, but also whole populations and even individual senses of identity are increasingly claiming the right to unfettered movement free of impediment, whether political or ideological. That the national fabric is woven of many threads—its compositional warp and weft subject to continual historical change—seems incontestable.

Literature: Writing the Nation, Rewriting the Nation

If the nation is indeed woven of many threads, then one of the greatest of looms is imaginative literature, as evident in its continued evocation as a privileged shaper of the national imaginary. In the earliest expressions of European nationalism, the nation, language, and literature are woven so tightly as to be indistinguishable. For Fichte in the above-referenced *Reden an die deutsche Nation*, for instance, even with the loss of the state to foreign occupation, the nation remains a nation in its language and literature (140). The national vernacular served as a kind of archeological site revealing the earliest traces of the national identity. While language continues to serve as an essential vessel of cultural meaning, the Romantic conception of its powers as expressed by Fichte and many other literary nationalists has proven untenable. It is inadequate not simply in the case of the numerous authors such as Kafka who, through their choice of language, straddle disparate national identities, but also in reference to those countries whose emergence in the nineteenth century as nation-states—such as France, Italy, Germany—entailed the suppression of local languages and dialects. A related inadequacy is to be noted in the case of those nation-states that are multilingual or, further, those with postcolonial national literatures written in the language of the former colonial metropole. Nonetheless, the late eighteenth-century linkage of nation and language has had far-reaching implications for literature and, to the extent that literature continues to be called upon in the building of nations, continues to harbour implicit assumptions concerning the author, the nature of literary representation, and the role of national literary institutions.

An early development of the age of literary nationalism of relevance to the author and language was the advent of the national genius. Writers such as Shakespeare, Voltaire, Goethe, Pushkin, Mickiewicz, Shevchenko, and (even!) Ossian, as well as others, are purported not only to tender metonymic expression of the national character but to demonstrate a given nation's distinctive contribution to humanity (Thiesse 31). The nation-expressing role of the national genius was conceived as intrinsic to the author's very being as a product of the national soil and need not rely on conscious participation in a nationalist project. The tendency to identify authors with the quintessence of national character has greatly diminished, undoubtedly as a part of what Perry Anderson has identified as "the shift from character to identity" in "the discourse of national difference" (n.p.). The identification of national writers nonetheless retains a prominent role not simply in the marketing of a nation's literary institution but in the more focused undertaking of projecting a given understanding of the nation, even in discrete moments of historical time: for example, Michel Houellebecq's consecration as the author of the *gilets jaunes*–era of France (France 24) or Chinua Achebe's importance as an Igbo, Nigerian, and African writer.

While individual authors around the globe continue to play outsized roles in the articulation of a national identity, the "imagining" of the nation is necessarily a collective effort—the result of works accumulated and shaped into a tradition. The complex matter as to *how* individual works of literature achieve representation of the national—by what aesthetic mechanisms salient features of the nation are instantiated in a work of fiction—is rarely discussed in detail. Far more frequently, the theoretical claim that nations are cultural constructs, that they are "imagined communities" written into being in literary texts, is simply asserted in lieu of an explanatory account of the actual aesthetic processes at play in "writing" a given nation or national literary tradition. Reasons for this reticence are plenty. Gilbert is surely correct in observing that "there is no literary taxonomy of national literatures. Each is inescapably *ad hoc*, as each reflects different political requirements" (213). Even in the absence of such a taxonomy, however, a number of frequently recurring elements offer themselves for consideration as the familial resemblance of a taxonomic face. Robert Lecker has identified one source of resemblance in the "realist-nationalist equation" (38). While the realist mode cannot claim exclusive hold on the literary representation of the nation, the advantages of the appeal to the mimetic potential of fiction seem palpable. From the novels of Walter Scott to those of historical metafiction, explicit reference to the nation in the invocation of formative historical events and personages create obvious links. The narrative substantiation of the nation need not be limited to reference to the nation in a literal sense, however. Fredric Jameson, for instance, has suggested that so-called third-world texts ought to be read as "national allegories" that "necessarily project a political dimension" ("Third-World Literature" 69; *Fables of Aggression*).

Jameson's text has been criticized for what has been seen as its grossly generalizing tendencies, and yet the notion of allegory—as a mode both of literary production and of interpretation—offers real, if circumscribed, promise in conceptualizing the link between fiction and nation. Even with those texts that are not allegories in a strict generic sense, the invitation to read allegorically facilitates interpretation of the classic "elements of fiction" in light of their illumination of the sociocultural, socioeconomic, and sociohistorical forces that gave rise to the nation: for example, historical events of relevance to the nation are given fictional treatment; a given protagonist's life traces the fortunes of the nation; a three-generation family structure parallels the historical development of the nation; language choices express the national vernacular; a marriage plot recapitulates the future-oriented choices of the nation, and so on.

Although the representation of the nation is possible in all genres of literary production, including poetry and drama as illustrated in *National Literature in Multinational States*, in the modern era it is the novel that has superseded such earlier genres as epic, folk literature, and drama to claim pride of place. The evident association of nation and novel has been theorized by numerous commentators (Moretti, Parrinder, Craig) in the general spirit of Timothy Brennan's observation that "the rise of European nationalism coincides especially with one form of literature—the novel" (49). Beyond the coincidence of their historical rise, however, the reasons for the novel's affinity with the nation are undoubtedly many—beginning with the "formal realism" (Watt 9–37) of the novel that provides the theoretical foundation for the considerations of both Lecker and Jameson. Inheritor of the epic's concern for the history and destiny of the tribe, the novel is most amenable to the sweep and scope of synecdochal representation of the nation in the particulars of the novel. The novel's heightened capacities to create extended trajectories within narratives is indicative of a still more elemental source of the juncture of literature and nation: narrative. Edward Said's insight that "nations themselves *are* narratives" (xiii) has thus been developed by a number of scholars (Bhabha, Brennan, Whitebrook, Parrinder, Craig) who see in narrative the primary source of the novel's nation-building capacity. It is narrative that, particularly in the form of the novel, most successfully recapitulates the nation's need to assemble the many—characters, languages, symbols, myths—into a single story of collective origins and future development. Importantly, novel and narrative are both almost endlessly malleable and hence also apt media in the ongoing project of not simply "imagining" the nation but in "rewriting" its literary form. What seems certain is that due to its representational power, literature, whether conceived as national or not, will remain at the forefront in both creating the unity of the nation(-state) and in revealing its fissures.

As a means of addressing these and other related topics, *National Literature in Multinational States* offers ten chapters from contributors who discuss a spectrum of representative literary and national contexts in a matter at once synoptic and context specific. The respective contributions fall into two broadly conceived categories of analysis. The first grouping focuses on the complex Canadian situation. Here, the potential contradictions of, and challenges to, a national literature within a multinational state are examined with reference to Canada's dominant national, national minority, and ethnic communities. The second turns to diverse international contexts in Europe, the Caribbean, India, and Africa; disparate in terms of their global range, these latter contributions effectively illustrate the imposing range of differing understandings of the nation (-state) and national literatures in republican, regional, and postcolonial settings.

The Canadian Nation(s), Canadian Literature(s)

For numerous reasons, Canada provides rich terrain for examining the subject of national literature in multinational states. A modernist nation-state formed in the striking absence of a single founding *ethnie*, shared cultural traditions, historic territoriality, or even a unified vision for future development, the Canadian national project has always been more nakedly ideational in the attempt to compose a national narrative out of changing understandings of the past, present, and future of the people(s) who inhabit the country. The national "we" has always been contested, as Canadian literature reveals, even at those times when a given understanding seemed most assured in its hegemonic power. Multiculturalism, the current paradigm of national identity, was launched as a sociopolitical project close to fifty years ago as a means of knitting together the fissures of a potentially fractured polity. Measured from the perspective of social cohesion, multiculturalism has shown significant success, though it, too, is currently under pressure for perceived failures in assuring the same degree of recognition and sociocultural, socioeconomic benefit to all communities within Canada. Unsurprisingly, then, Canadian literature reveals divided, complex responses to issues of the nation. Paul D. Morris, for instance, reads unease in what he identifies as the seeming reticence of recent Governor General's Award–winning authors in either French or English to treat, explicitly, the topic of the nation or even deploy overt markers of the same. This absence is particularly noteworthy in the context of the literary institutions of the country's two "founding nations," both of which were conceived as nationalist enterprises.

Modernist in conception, the Canadian nation-state also famously features both national minorities—the French in their disparate expressions across *la francophonie canadienne*—and peoples, *ethnies*, who may legitimately lay claim to a more perennialist understanding of the nation. Turning from Canada's pan-national identity as a country formed out of two founding nations, Matthew Cormier and Matthew Tétreault examine the aspirations and revindications—literary and national—revealed in the now established institutions of Acadian and Métis writing. Both of these national "minority" traditions exemplify the complications and advantages of identifying and promoting a national imaginary. The complications are most apparent in reference to the implications for the Canadian nation-state as a whole and, as such, exemplify the central premise of *National Literature in Multinational States*. Acadian and Métis literatures, in substantiating a sense of their respective (competing) national identities, perform two functions simultaneously. As a matter of national identity, as Cormier and Tétreault reveal, Acadian and Métis writers and cultural figures have shaped an understanding of their respective nations out of a reading and writing of their collective historical experience. Regardless of the nature of the relation to the colonial past or to *la francophonie canadienne* or even to the pan-Canadian nation-state, through this exercise of cultural agency, they posit the nation as a social and historical presence. While advancing their respective national projects, however, they are also inescapably influencing Canada by contributing to a necessary recalibration of the pan-Canadian national narrative, an undertaking also being advanced by still other—First—nations within the country. It is to be noted, moreover, that a readjustment in national self-understanding of the kind experienced by Canada is also to be observed in these national minority communities themselves. The literary production of both the Acadian and Métis nations reveals not so much the existence of an "eternal" nation, a *Volksgeist*, waiting to be written into history, but the historical evolution of changing manifestations and understandings of each nation. The studies by Cormier and Tétreault also show the particular efficacy of literature in, as Benedict Anderson would have it, "imagining" communities. The Acadian and Métis experience as presented by Cormier and Tétreault also seems at least partially to confirm Gellner's thesis that nationalism creates the nation. Historically denied the nation-building instruments of an independent state, these national minorities have articulated an intensified sense of the nation, particularly since the 1970s, in the wake of an accumulation of nationalist thought and the political, institutional, and literary means of instantiating it from within multicultural, multinational Canada.

The Canadian nation-state is composed of more than founding, and First, nations. The recalibration of the Canadian idea of national self is being prompted not only by the national minorities discussed by Cormier and Tétreault but also by forces emanating from transnationalism and the defining presence of immigrant communities in Canada. The ethnic minorities that influenced the shaping of the national imaginary half a century ago in the adoption of multiculturalism as state policy provide the topic of the collection's two following chapters. Taking Anita Rau Badami's *Can You Hear the Nightbird Call?*, Sabujkoli Bandopadhyay discusses representations of the South Asian communities of Canada focusing on the historically shifting negotiations required by members of these communities as they navigate between changing notions of the nation and nationalism in India and in Canada. The protagonists of Badami's novel—like so many other members of diasporic communities—are compelled by the contradictions of national ideologies to manoeuvre between sometimes conflicting national and ethnic affiliations. Bandopadhyay reads Badami's novel of individuals caught in the ambiguities of divergent models of identity as offering three possible responses to the difficulties of a hybridized national identity, a condition increasingly common to members of mobile communities in Canada and around the world. The multiple national affiliations and identities induced by immigration call forth for adaptations for the individuals themselves but also their national home(s). In the concluding chapter to the section on the Canadian situation, Asma Sayed takes up the perennial nationalist issue of language in its intersections with the nation and institutional power to address the fascinating topic of the Canadian response to literature written in languages other than the country's two official languages. Sayed calls for a national literary institution that expands its representation of the national not merely by accommodating but by actively fostering heritage-language works as a consequential extension of the logic of multiculturalism and the further evolution of the national imaginary. Among the many issues raised in Sayed's chapter is that of the "national" affiliation of diasporic writers, a complex matter that also serves to highlight yet another fissure in the conventional understanding of the culturally homogeneous nation-state. Although illustrated with reference to languages and works from Canada's South Asian diasporic communities, Sayed's contentions apply equally well to the numerous other heritage and Indigenous languages present within Canada.

International Contexts

Canada illustrates well the strains upon both the nation(-state) and the ideal of a unifying national literature that derive from the constructivist logic of the modernist nation. For the Canadian nation-state, transformation is prompted by competing identity-bearing collectives seeking recognition and status—representation—within the national imaginary; for Canada's national minorities, related pressures are being applied by historically evolving conceptions of national identity. Canada's historical experience and social composition thus exemplify a particular constellation of challenges to the nation; there are still others that derive from the very concept of the nation itself, however. Prominent is a fundamental questioning of the legitimacy of the nation as the privileged vehicle of identity and representation. As a matter of sociopolitical organization, various supranational, transnational structures have been theorized as significant alternatives to the nation-state. Within the literary-cultural realm as well, expressions of transnationalism provide an alternative to excessively restrictive ethnic and territorialized notions of the nation with their emphasis on myths of fixed origins. Doris Hambuch's discussion of Dutch-language literary representations of a Caribbean transnational space in "'No Nation Now but the Imagination': No Caribbean Nation without the Dutch Caribbean" offers a particular example of the issue. In an argument reminiscent of Stuart Hall's discussion of Caribbean cultural identity as "not an essence but a *positioning*" (226), Hambuch reveals how the Caribbean cultural realm, while largely a product of colonialism, has the potential to offer the multiple advantages of cultural diversity that are unavailable to the individual nation-states of the region. The Creole languages used throughout the Caribbean tender, in themselves, a kind of metonymic representation of the hybridization of historical memories, cultural practices, and communal collaboration that creates a national whole bigger than the sum of its nation-state parts. The writers and Dutch-language works analyzed by Hambuch reveal how the Dutch Caribbean contributes to the imagining of a transnational Caribbean cultural space.

The title of Hambuch's chapter cites Derek Walcott's implicit identification of an alternative to the nation claim as the privileged source of identity: "no nation now but the imagination." For many writers, it is not the nation that serves as the primary font of identity and affiliation, but other sources, including literature itself understood as a republic of letters. Vladimir Nabokov, for one, famously claimed the right to travel freely between languages, countries, and national literary traditions, asserting that "the writer's art is his real passport" (63). For many, the nation and nationalism conventionally understood are much too constraining, unable to accommodate the system of shifting sources of identity that the philosopher Kwame Anthony Appiah has evoked in the image of "nesting memberships" (20). Jerry White, in his chapter on the French Catalan-language author Joan Daniel Bezsonoff, offers the example of a writer who, in both his life and fictions, depicts the complexities of "nesting memberships" in gestures that complicate the French republican model of national identity. Despite his commitment to facets of his composite identity—most immediately his native language, Catalan, and his partial Russian heritage—Bezsonoff remains a resolutely French author whose primary affiliation rests with France. White demonstrates how Bezsonoff writes against the conventional French republican model of national unity with its historical imposition of standard French, not to weaken it, but to complicate and enrich understanding of what is in effect the reality of a complex multilingual, multicultural state. For Bezsonoff, there is no contradiction in being a *Catalan* French author; his writing can serve republican universalism and a pluricultural France.

The final three chapters of the volume turn from Europe to India and Nigeria, contemporary nation-states whose cultural and political roots long predate the late eighteenth-century rise of the nation. Here, complex issues of past and present mix in a crucible of forces, including European colonization, religious beliefs, economic globalization, minority nationalist aspirations, and the imperatives of national unity within contexts of great ethnosocial diversity and economic disparity. Clara A.B. Joseph's contribution illustrates the frequent crudeness of theoretical configurations of the nation that are often more beholden to the abstractions of ideology than to the subtleties of historical experience. Joseph discusses her experiences translating Geo Thadikkatt's *Mar Joseph Cariattil*—a play from 1983 that treats the struggles of the Thomas Christians of India in the eighteenth century—against an anti-colonial account of Indian nationalism. The prominent view that Indian nationalism arose in Indigenous responses to Western colonialism and their associated discourses is serviceable, though it risks a form of essentialism in remaining insufficiently attentive to cultural influences that complicate the national narrative. Joseph demonstrates how the very act of translating Thadikkatt's play from Malayalam to English—in effect *re*-representing in a different language a depiction of cultural experience—requires tact and sensitivity to alterity that often surpasses the accepted ideological constructions of the nation. The centuries-old (precolonial) history of the Thomas Christians in India, the reception of the play, and Joseph's own experience in translating it reveal the multiple pitfalls of eliding the complexities of historical experience in nationalist attempts to reify the nation. Albert Braz and Uchechukwu Peter Umezurike in their respective analyses of literary works from Nigeria focus on the multifaceted problems associated with the inability of state and society to agree upon the composition of the national *we*. In Nigeria, the ethnic conflicts that have riven the country have been compounded by the legacies of colonialism but also by ethnoterritorial disputes engendered by perceptions of ethnic difference. With the example of Nigeria and the Ogoni author Ken Saro-Wiwa, Braz identifies a flaw too often associated with nationalism: "history suggests that strife is inevitable unless nation-states accommodate the ethnonational diversity within their own borders" (167). This seemingly intractable problem is further aggravated by the often-violent struggle for control of economic and political resources—in Nigeria's case, the country's rich but unjustly distributed oil reserves. Umezurike indicates how the past, supranational scourge of colonialism has evolved to include the predations of transnational capitalism. The failings of the nation(-state) are evinced not merely in the unjust distribution of economic benefits but also in the pollution both of humans in their relations and the environment that sustains them.

NOTES

1. The literature on the theory of the nation—its origins, composition, and relevance—is vast. The ideas presented here have been greatly influence by B. Anderson, Gellner, Greenfeld, Hastings, Hobsbawm, Kohn, Kramer, Renan, Seton-Watson and, above all, A. Smith.
2. "La nation existe avant tout, elle est l'origine de tout. Sa volonté est toujours légale, elle est la loi elle-même...Une nation ne sort jamais de l'état de nature." Authors' translation here and throughout the chapter.
3. "In dem Dasein eines *Volkes* ist der substantielle Zweck, ein Staat zu sein und als solcher sich zu erhalten; ein Volk ohne Staatsbildung (eine *Nation* als solche) hat eigentlich keine Geschichte, wie die Völker vor ihrer Staatsbildung existierten und andere noch jetzt als wilde Nationen existieren. Was einem Volke geschieht und innerhalb desselben vorgeht, hat in der Beziehung auf den Staat seine wesentliche Bedeutung"; ("In the existence of a *people* the substantial aim is to be a state and to maintain itself as such. A people with no state formation (merely a *nation*, as such), actually has no history, like the peoples that existed before the rise of states and others that still exist as savage peoples. What happens to a people, and takes place within it, has its essential significance in relation to the state").

WORKS CITED

Anderson, Benedict. *Imagined Communities: Reflections on the Origin and Spread of Nationalism*. Verso, 1983.

Anderson, Perry. "Nation-States and National Identity." *London Review of Books*, vol. 13, no. 9, 9 May 1991.

Appiah, Kwame Anthony. "The Importance of Elsewhere: In Defense of Cosmopolitanism." *Foreign Affairs*, vol. 99, no. 2, 2019, pp. 20–26.

Bhabha, Homi, ed. *Nation and Narration*. Routledge, 1990.

Brennan, Timothy. "The National Longing for Form." *Nation and Narration*, edited by Homi Bhabha, Routledge, 1990, pp. 44–70.

Casanova, Pascale. *La république mondiale des lettres*. Éditions du Seuil, 2008.

Connor, Walker. "A Nation Is a Nation, Is a State, Is an Ethnic Group, Is a..." *Ethnic and Racial Studies*, vol. 1, no. 4, 1978, pp. 377–400.

Craig, Cairns. *The Modern Scottish Novel: Narrative and the National Imagination*. Edinburgh University Press, 1998.

Fichte, Johann Gottlieb. *Fichtes Reden an die deutsche Nation*. Severus Verlag, 2013, http://www.zeno.org/Lesesaal/N/9781484031254?page=0.

France 24. "'Sérotonine' de Michel Houellebecq, présage du mouvement des Gilets jaunes," 4 Jan. 2019, https://www.france24.com/fr/20190104-france-litterature-serotonine-michel-houellebecq-gilets-jaunes.

Gellner, Ernest. *Nations and Nationalism*. Blackwell, 1983.

Gilbert, Paul. "The Idea of a National Literature." *Literature, Philosophy and Political Theory*, edited by John Horton and Andrea T. Baumeister, Routledge, 1996, pp. 198–217.

Greenfeld, Liah. *Nationalism: Five Roads to Modernity*. Harvard University Press, 1992.

Hall, Stuart. "Cultural Identity and Diaspora." *Identity: Community, Culture, Difference*, edited by Jonathan Rutherford, Lawrence & Wishart, 1990, pp. 222–37.

Hastings, Adrian. *The Construction of Nationhood: Ethnicity, Religion and Nationalism*. Cambridge University Press, 1997.

Hegel, Georg Wilhelm Friedrich. *Enzyklopädie der philosophischen Wissenschaften im Grundrisse*. Holzinger, 2017, http://www.zeno.org/Lesesaal/N/9781484031902?page=357&ps=%21. Accessed 15 June 2020.

Hobsbawm, Eric. *Nations and Nationalism since 1780: Programme, Myth, Reality*. Cambridge University Press, 1990.

Horton, John, and Andrea T. Baumeister, editors. *Literature, Philosophy and Political Theory*. Routledge, 1996.

Jameson, Fredric. *Fables of Aggression: Wyndham Lewis, the Modernist as Fascist*. University of California Press, 1979.

———. "Third-World Literature in the Era of Multinational Capitalism." *Social Text*, no. 15, 1986, pp. 65–88.

Kafka, Franz. *The Diaries of Franz Kafka, 1910–1913*. Edited by Max Brod and translated by Joseph Kresh, Schocken Books, 1948.

Kohn, Hans. *The Idea of Nationalism: A Study in Its Origins and Background*. MacMillan Company, 1944.

Kramer, Lloyd. *Nationalism in Europe and America: Politics, Cultures and Identities since 1775*. University of North Carolina Press, 2011.

Kymlicka, Will. *Finding Our Way. Rethinking Ethnocultural Relations in Canada*. Oxford University Press, 1998.

Kymlicka, Will, and Christine Straehle. "Cosmopolitanism, Nation-States, and Minority Nationalism." *Politics in the Vernacular: Nationalism, Multiculturalism, and Citizenship*, edited by Will Kymlicka, Oxford University Press, 2001.

Lecker, Robert. *Making It Real: The Canonization of English-Canadian Literature*. House of Anansi Press, 1995.

Mathews, Jessica. "Power Shift." *Foreign Affairs*, vol. 76, no. 1, 1997, pp. 50–66.

Moretti, Franco. *Atlas of the European Novel: 1800–1900*. Verso, 1999.

Nabokov, Vladimir. *Strong Opinions*. Vintage, 1990.

Parrinder, Patrick. *Nation and Novel: The English Novel from Its Origin to the Present Day*. Oxford University Press, 2008.

Renan, Ernest. *Qu'est-ce qu'une nation?* [1882], http://classiques.uqac.ca/classiques/renan_ernest/qu_est_ce_une_nation/qu_est_ce_une_nation.html. Accessed 15 June 2020.

Said, Edward. *Culture and Imperialism*. Alfred A. Knopf, 1993.

Seton-Watson, Hugh. *Nations and States: An Enquiry into the Origins of Nations and the Politics of Nationalism*. Methuen, 1977.

Sieyès, Emmanuel Joseph, *Qu'est-ce que le Tiers état?* Éditions de Boucher, 2002, http://www.leboucher.com/pdf/sieyes/tiers.pdf.

Smith, Anthony D. "The Origins of Nations." *Ethnic and Racial Studies*, vol. 12, no. 3, 1989, pp. 340–67.

———. *National Identity*. University of Nevada Press, 1991.

———. "Ethnic Nationalism and the Plight of Minorities." *Journal of Refugee Studies*, vol. 7, no 2/3, 1994, pp. 186–98.

———. *Myths and Memories of the Nation*. Oxford University Press, 1999.

Smith, Rogers M. *Stories of Peoplehood: The Politics and Morals of Political Membership*. Cambridge University Press, 2003.

Szeman, Imre. *Zones of Instability: Literature, Postcolonialism, and the Nation*. Johns Hopkins University Press, 2003.

Thiesse, Anne-Marie. *La fabrique de l'écrivain national: Entre littérature et politique*. Éditions Gallimard, 2019.

Watt, Ian. *The Rise of the Novel: Studies in Defoe, Richardson and Fielding*. 1957. Penguin, 1985.

Whitebrook, Maureen. "Taking the Narrative Turn: What the Novel Has to Offer Political Theory." *Literature, Philosophy and Political Theory*, edited by John Horton and Andrea T. Baumeister, Routledge, 1996, pp. 32–52.

Wimmer, Andreas. *Waves of War: Nationalism, State-Formation, and Ethnic Exclusion in the Modern World*. Cambridge University Press, 2013.

———. "Why Nationalism Works, and Why It Isn't Going Away." *Foreign Affairs*, vol. 99, no. 2, 2019, pp. 27–34.

Wimmer, Andreas, and Yuval Feinstein. "The Rise of the Nation-State across the World, 1816 to 2001." *American Sociological Review*, vol. 75, no. 5, 2010, pp. 764–90.

Reticent Nations
*Governor General's Award–Winning Fiction
and the Representation of Canada*

Paul D. Morris

AVID READERS OF ARTHUR CONAN DOYLE will recall the famous dog that did not bark in "The Adventure of Silver Blaze," a story from 1893 wherein the celebrated Sherlock Holmes is led to the resolution of a murder by a dog's conspicuous silence. In this chapter, I wish to discuss a relative silence of a different kind, a phenomenon that likewise evokes attention due to its unexpected and, upon reflection, even startling absence: the seemingly reticent representation of the nation—whether Canadian or Québécois—in contemporary English- and French-language Canadian fiction. It is important to acknowledge at the outset that while the following comments relate to a purported absence, they presuppose no normative assertions regarding the necessity or nature of literary representations of the national collective(s). Furthermore, as they are based on a very limited sampling of recent writing—five years of Governor General's Award–winning prose fiction in French and English—these observations make no claim to representative status concerning either the nation or its literary depiction. Nonetheless, in the context of a literary institution that has long valourized the nation-building capacities of literature, consideration of the recent laureates of the country's most prestigious literary award—itself established as a gesture of nation-building—offers a potentially promising source of insight into the nature of the contemporary link between fiction and nation in Canada. The following will thus offer no evaluative assessment regarding what I read as the ambivalent treatment of the nation. Rather, a brief, synoptic analysis of ten works of prose fiction will serve as a pretext to reconsider a series of questions related to the nation and the modalities of literary nation-building in Canada. A privileged relationship between literature and nation has long been presumed as a matter of general principle in Canada; evidence of a possible rupture in that relation invites closer consideration of the fictive instantiation of the nation. A collective reading of five years of Governor General's Award–winning works, while focused on a relative silence, will suggest that something is nonetheless being communicated about the current state of the nation in the Canadian and Québécois literary imaginary. The dog that does not bark may nonetheless be revealing something.

Literature has had a long and storied history of influence in shaping the affairs of social and political communities. Plato's revocation of the poet's *droit de cité* in Book X of *The Republic* offers one early, albeit negative, example. If, in this instance, the poet's imitations were thought to excite the passions and thereby undermine the cohesion and proper functioning of the polity, more frequently they have been exalted as privileged expression of the collective character of a people. To adopt Percy Bysshe Shelley's formulation, poets are not only the "unacknowledged legislators of the world" but the first and most eloquent tribunes of the nation. This has been particularly so since the eighteenth-century emergence within Europe of the nation(-state) as the dominant form of social and political organization and the concomitant identification of literature—understood as a national literature—as the preferred means of expressing the insoluble links connecting place, people, and culture. Johann Gottfried von Herder's claim of 1785 that "every people is a people; it has its own national character just as it has a language" (186) offers famous expression to a sentiment influential in the emergent Romantic conceptualization of both the nation(-state) and national literatures.[1] Literature so conceived is uniquely positioned to perform a sociopolitical function in both creating and revealing what is assumed to be the organic relation between place and national character, a role still visible in the divisions of literature into categories of national provenance.

If literature's capacity to reflect and shape the political forms of the social has long been acknowledged—whether Plato's *city*, Shelley's *world*, or Herder's *nation*—the origins, composition, and definition of the nation itself have remained less amenable to easy description. Notwithstanding the lack of definitional clarity, however, there is general if inevitably broad agreement on the key necessary components of the nation, beginning with what Ernest Renan, the great nineteenth-century French theorist, termed *un principe spirituel*. The nation is not an ideal, an *a priori* "essence" that pre-exists its expression in language and literature but a social construct continually negotiated on the basis of memories of past collective experience, a sense of common cause in the present, and the will to shape the future together. Identification of the nation as a project immediately provokes still more fundamental questions regarding the source or origins of the feelings of national attachment identified by Renan: whether in the deep *primordial* roots of shared cultural practices and a sense of collective identity as an ethnic community, what Anthony Smith refers to as an *ethnie* (13), or, alternatively, in the modern ideology of nationalism that since the late eighteenth century has fostered the nation as a cultural artifact charged with responding to the exigencies of industrializing societies (Gellner, Hobsbawm, Anderson). Despite differences regarding the origins of the nation, however, the broadly constructivist cast of Renan's thinking has continued in most, if not all, recent understandings of the nation. Here, literature has been accorded a particular role, theorized as playing an essential role in creating the conditions of what Benedict Anderson famously termed "an imagined political community," a polity based upon a "deep, horizontal comradeship" amongst disparate members of a community who "will never know most of their fellow-members, meet them, or even hear of them, yet in the minds of [whom] lives the image of their communion" (6). If literature was once thought to inevitably reflect the eternal *Geist* of the nation, it is now literature that serves the ideology of nationalism as the medium of its creation.

It is here that discussion may abruptly return to the Canadian context, a country that offers curious illustration of the various elements that animate divergent understandings of the nation and its origins (Kertzer). Canada is home to communities of belonging—Indigenous Peoples—whose claim to shared cultural practices born out of deep identification with the physical environment qualify as (primordial) nations. It also contains two *soi-disant* founding nations, one of which—*les Canadiens*—developed an *ethnie*-like sense of group identity prior to the eighteenth-century emergence of modern forms of nationalism and the nation. Finally, enveloping these and still other configurations of cultural belonging within the country, there is the Canadian nation-state that was legislated into being in 1867 as a modernist national project even in the absence of a single ethnicity, language, religion, or long historical identification with a geographical space. Important differences distinguish these diverse manifestations of the nation in Canada, the perhaps most crucial being differing degrees of access to the instruments of state. As further chapters in this collection demonstrate, other cultural collectives within Canada have found expression in "national" literatures, although it is the (majority anglophone) Canadian nation-state and the francophone national minority that have the most comprehensively utilized literature in the construction of a national identity. As T.D. MacLulich has noted, "nationalism has always been part of the cultural air that Canadian writers and critics have breathed" (19). The force and longevity of this presumptive connection between the nation and literature may be illustrated, if only imperfectly, through reference to two early accounts from each of the country's founding nations. The first, from E.H. Dewart's introduction to his 1864 anthology *Selections from Canadian Poets*, expresses a conception of the nation-building role of literature that would have been serviceable as an account of the importance of literature throughout much of the country's history: "A national literature is an essential element in the formation of national character. It is not merely the record of a country's mental progress: it is the expression of its intellectual life, the bond of national unity, and the guide of national energy. It may be fairly questioned, whether the whole range of history presents the spectacle of a people firmly united politically, without the subtle but powerful cement of a patriotic literature" (ix). The second, from 1874, presents Edmond Lareau's prefatory remarks regarding the nationalist motivation guiding the completion of his history of French-language literature in Canada: "It is apparent to all of the citizens of this country, who are concerned about our future destinies and who consider from close or from afar the role that we are called to play on this land of America, that the national literature must account for much in the accomplishment of that mission" (iii).[2]

Despite these and still other similarly reasoned *plaidoyers* for a sustaining national literature for both founding nations, a nationalist understanding of literature in Canada did not gather impetus until the mid-twentieth century, approximately a century after Confederation. Sarah Corse convincingly argues that it was not a dearth of quality works of fiction in either French or English that hindered the emergence of a canon expressive of the national character and aspirations of the Canadian nation(s). Rather, it was because fiction written in both languages was still identified within the literary traditions of the respective European metropoles: "Canadian writing was not understood as Canadian, was not constructed as an importantly Canadian artefact, until the notion of 'Canada' was meaningful in nationalist terms. As long as English Canadians primarily understood Canada through its incorporation in the British Empire, on the one hand, and the French Canadians understood Quebec as part of the French-speaking world, on the other, the process of national canon formation was largely irrelevant" (37).

The broad lines of Corse's claim seem just. Indeed, Robert Lecker is confident in dating the development of a Canadian national literary canon (in English) to the approximately twenty-year period extending from 1957 to 1978 (*Making It Real* 25–27). Nonetheless, and while the historical dating of Corse's argument may be broadly accepted, it must also be tempered by consideration of individual writers and critics in both French and English who had consciously sought to articulate the sense of an independent nation (with or without the accoutrements of state) prior to the post-war period: from the publication of anthologies like Dewart's and Lareau's, through the establishment of such important national institutions of public culture as the Governor General's Literary Awards in

1936 to the articulation of such nationalist visions as Jules-Paul Tardivel's *Pour la patrie* (1895) and Hugh MacLennan's *Two Solitudes* (1945), to name but two novels.

Regardless as to the weighting accorded these earlier forays into literary nationalism, it seems indisputable that the rapid development of the literary institution in Canada, particularly in the third quarter of the twentieth century, unfolded as a *national* project. In a process that seems to confirm Ernest Gellner's *modernist* thesis of nationalism's promulgation of a nation, the post-war Canadian state in concert with individual writers and critics fostered, as a matter of ideological intent, the establishment of a national literature meant to shore up the idea of a nation around which a continent-wide agglomerate of citizens could identify while distinguishing themselves from older and newer ties to France, England, and the United States. The post-war history of the effort to create a Canadian literary institution that would "imagine" the nation is frequently said to begin with the state-directed Massey Report of 1951, which suggested that a national literature was "the greatest of all forces making for national unity" (Massey Report chp. 15, para. 12, 225). The history of these institutional developments has been well presented in the writings of a number of critics, including MacLulich, Corse, Szeman, and, perhaps especially, Lecker (*Canadian Canons*; *Making It Real*; "Canada Council's Block Grant Program"). It is an account that has centred on the formation of a (changing) Canadian canon and the writing of literary histories—two subjects that provide synoptic purchase on a historically evolving, multidimensional phenomenon (Gerson; Godard). On the matter of canon formation, for instance, Lecker affirms that "it is true that Canadian critics have historically argued in favour of a literature that would identify the nation" (*Making It Real* 37), while McCarthy writes with regard to Canadian literary history that "from its beginnings in the nineteenth century, the writing of Canadian literary history has been organized around the extra-literary concept of the 'nation'" (32), thereby underpinning a later claim by E.D. Blodgett: "not all literary history is explicitly organized around the nation....Somewhere, however, the nation is present, if only implicitly, and in most instances the nation is the dominant" (4). The linkages between literature and the nation within the Québécois literary institution, while following a trajectory specific to the conditions imposed by francophone Canada's multifaceted relationship with anglophone Canada, share tantalizing parallels with that of Canada as a whole in the post-war period, not least in the baptism of a specifically nationalist name—*littérature québécoise*—during the Quiet Revolution of the 1960s (Boivin 66). As recently as 2011, a collection of Québécois educators re-affirmed the nation-building importance of literature by calling for the increased use of Québécois literature in school curricula: "We now have in Québec a rich, expansive literature of our own that has a particular genius of its own and that is a reflection of our reality... The teaching of our literature is based on an ideological (even political) position that is certain to have consequences for the survival of North American French-language culture" (Pilote).[3]

Implicit in the many critical expressions of the mutually enforcing connection between literature and the nation in the Canadian context is the conscious, institutional nature of the process as a project conceived and launched by implementing individuals—whether the faceless functionaries of government policy, the authors of literary histories or the literary elites that, in exercising the levers of institutional power, impose their standards of literary value in the shaping of an (arbitrary?) national canon. Individual authors themselves as well as readers may also exercise a role to the extent that they choose to validate, each in their separate ways, a given vision of the nation. Nonetheless, the relation between nation and literature is generally perceived in terms of institutional *processes* by which the nation is imagined across a broadly conceived collective of texts rather than via consideration of individual works and their specific *writings* of the nation. Moreover, at a still more theoretical level within the literary system, the question remains as to how *individual* texts represent the nation *in the aggregate*, by what specifically aesthetic-literary means are perceptions of the nation reified and communicated artistically. What attributes make one text, or even selection of texts, metonymic of the nation and others not? To adopt the phrasing of Paul Gilbert, what is it that informs the idea of a national literature? For the Romantics, any literary text issuing from a people could no more not "reflect" the culture and character of its national source than a mirror fail to reflect the image in the glass. Understood to form an insoluble organic bond, the nation and the literary text necessarily reflected each other.

More recently, mid-twentieth-century materialist critics from György Lukács's reading of the historical novel to Fredric Jameson's conception of allegory have suggested the potential of fiction in representing the nation (69). In a similar spirit, albeit without the Marxian inspiration, Margaret Atwood's famous handbook of 1972, *Survival*, identified the central traits of a distinctive, pre-existing (anglophone) Canadian nation that was to be discerned through a synoptic reading of its literature. The (epistemologically naïve?) "reflection theory" of the relation holding between literature and nations that underpins such readings is—as in Atwood's case—of undeniable explanatory value in fashioning understandings of the nation. Nonetheless, it is also vulnerable to obvious objections: for one, in any such account important facets of the nation's literary and social experience are inevitably overlooked or ignored, and secondly, not all national writers represent the same image of one and the same nation. A more constructivist understanding emphasizing the wrought, imagined nature of the nation has focused on the progressive emergence of identifiable formal and above all thematic features said to instantiate the nation, hence the mutually reifying role of the national canon and the nation. In the case of Canada, a mimetic, realist form of fiction—what Lecker refers to as the "realist-nationalist equation" (*Making It Real* 38)—has focused on the representation of specific historical and social themes that have come to be read as synonymous with the national character. Whatever the legitimacy of the particular understanding of the nation that has emerged, as a matter of form, Canadian fiction has clearly, perhaps inevitably, valourized a broadly mimetic aesthetic in the imagining of the nation.

Quite apart from the function of language as a marker of shared identity and an enabler of social cohesion within a cultural group, literature seems especially adept at serving in the creation of a sense of common culture. And while the literary institutions of Québec and Canada provide examples of nation-building across a spectrum of genres, it is particularly the novel—the genre of intrinsic "formal realism" (Watt 34–37)—that has predominated in the representation of the nation in Canada as elsewhere. Few would perhaps go as far as Franco Moretti in claiming the novel "as the symbolic form capable of making sense of the nation-state" (20), though many have echoed Aldous Huxley's claim that "nations are to a very large extent invented by their poets and novelists" (50). In recent years, moreover, compelling arguments have been advanced for seeing in the novel the literary pendant of the nation. Both may be said to have risen together as relatively modern institutions dating, in their modern form, from the eighteenth century; both are "democratic" in the ways they are based on the stories told in a popular vernacular as opposed to the myths of gods and monarchs recounted in the forbidding language of high genres; both foreground the development of character, whether in the form of the national character or of a fictional protagonist; the novel, like the nation, is capable of uniting multitudes of discourses, ideologies, and perspectives in a single common "story"—"nations themselves *are* narratives" argues Edward Said (xiii); and lastly in drawing upon its mimetic potential, the novel has been effective in depicting the historical experiences and ideological aspirations of the national collective in narrative form. In adopting the now famous language of Anderson, novels represent communities of individuals, while nations are imagined communities.

Yet, even while acknowledging the formal aptitude of the novel in representing the nation in general and the historical dominance of a mimetic style of representation in the case of the Canadian nation in particular, questions regarding other potential configurations of formal and aesthetic representation remain. Consideration of other stylistic approaches to the nation is relevant not only as a means of allowing a representative function to forms of literature that are not realistic—the parodic, the nonlinear, the fantastical, the narratively discontinuous, the postmodern, and so on—but also as a means of questioning whether texts which otherwise seem to conform to a realist aesthetic but which do not display the conventional tropes of national representation may nonetheless be expressive of the national imaginary. Can a literary text that displays reticence in evoking the nation still instantiate the nation? This latter question in particular is prompted in the example of five years of Governor General's Award–winning fiction, the subject of the following reflection.[4]

Governor General's Award for Fiction (French and English), 2014–2018

	English-language	French-language
2014	Thomas King, *The Back of the Turtle*	Andrée A. Michaud, *Bondrée*
2015	Guy Vanderhaeghe, *Daddy Lenin and Other Stories*	Nicolas Dickner, *Six degrés de liberté*
2016	Madeleine Thien, *Do Not Say We Have Nothing*	Dominique Fortier, *Au péril de la mer*
2017	Joel Thomas Hynes, *We'll All Be Burnt in Our Beds Some Night*	Christian Guay-Poliquin, *Le poids de la neige*
2018	Sarah Henstra, *The Red Word*	Karoline Georges, *De synthès*

Viewed collectively, the ten works of prose fiction here under review offer an impressive array of writing styles and subject matters. Evenly divided between male and female authors, the English-language authors are more broadly dispersed throughout the country's regions, while the authors of the French-language laureates are centred exclusively in Québec; no texts from the Canadian Francophonie *hors du Québec* are represented. In *Prizing Literature: The Celebration and Circulation of National Culture*, Gillian Roberts has described the ideological implications of all awards, including the Governor General's: "they contribute to defining the parameters of the nation and its culture...Prizes dedicated to national literature also reveal a national capital at work. The ideological implications that underpin national cultural celebrations in a Canadian context are essential to understanding the work that national prizes attempt, with varying degrees of success, and the borders of Canadianness that they draw" (17). In the current language of the Governor General's Awards website, the nation-building dimension of the awards is, at most, implicit. The stated goal of the awards is to "recognize Canada's best English-language and French-language books" in the effort to "promote Canadian literature and encourage Canadians to read" (Canada Council for the Arts). In this description, the specific Canadianness or *québécité* of the texts is diffuse, presumably a matter of association with the language of composition. A similar stance is to be noted in the works of literature themselves. Read *au premier degré*, the nation—Canadian or *Québécois*—is only secondarily present. In terms of physical and temporal setting, the events of three of the texts occur almost entirely outside of Canada: the United States in the case of *The Red Word*, China in *Do Not Say We Have Nothing*, and France for *Au péril de la mer*. A fourth, Michaud's *Bondrée*, occupies a diffuse space in the forests between Québec and the American state of Maine. Temporally, the texts tend to be set in the past or framed retrospectively. Those that narrate an unfolding present, such as Hynes's *We'll All Be Burnt in Our Beds Some Night*, do so in a manner that avoids reference to specific historical or social markers of collective, national relevance. Guay-Poliquin's *Le poids de la neige*—a novel that recounts the forced enclosure of two men in the wake of an ill-defined environmental catastrophe—makes no allusion to historical time at all; the assumption that the events of the novel occur in (rural) Québec is gleaned from nothing more than reference to the snow of winter, rural life, a Laurentian-like physical geography, and the French spoken by the protagonists. Those texts that most overtly approach realist specificity in terms of capturing the lived sociohistorical reality of a particular time and space either occur outside of Canada or in the Canadian past: *The Red Word* is set within the particular physical, social, and cultural space of a contemporary American university campus; *Do Not Say We Have Nothing* unfolds across the momentous sweep of twentieth-century China to reveal the tragic workings of communist Chinese history on disparate individuals; *Au péril de la mer* focuses on the historicity of Mont-Saint-Michel in France as a site uniquely evocative of the desires and loss of two protagonists. The stories of Vanderhaeghe's *Daddy Lenin and Other Stories* depict the sociohistorical realia of Canada, but a bygone Canada identified with the meticulously evoked cars, clothing, music, turns of phrase, and, importantly, (male) social mores of an age much regretted for its passing. The formative power of past time is wonderfully rendered in Vanderhaehe's story "Tick Tock" as the protagonist Charley Brewster acknowledges that the physical and existential pain he feels is a result of his anachronistic presence in the contemporary world: "'Me? I guess I'm a rusty time bomb. Either that or an old clock running down. Tick tock, tick tock, tick tock'" (44).

Michaud's *Bondrée* is illustrative of the presence-in-absence of the nation as a political entity; the novel is set in an evocatively liminal border-space between Canada, Québec, and the United States (Maine) in 1967, though this 1967 is a time of the changing social mores represented by such pop songs as "A Whiter Shade of Pale" and "Lucy in the Sky with Diamonds" and not the country's centenary. Hynes's *We'll All Be Burnt in Our Beds Some Night* unfolds in the contemporary present as a modern picaresque novel with overt, narratively important, references to Canadian locations from coast to coast. Nevertheless, the novel's focus on capturing the consciousness of an individual perspective and life lived *in extremis* renders difficult the discernment of implications for a broader social collective. Hynes's protagonist, Johnny Keough, undergoes experiences that reveal certain social and existential truths but which offer little in terms of synecdochal representation of the nation.

An important exception with regard to setting is King's *The Back of the Turtle*. The events of this novel unfold in an undated but recognizably contemporary context (with interspersed references to a parallel chronology of past events that by novel's end lead causally to the narrative present); as a matter of realist historical specificity, however, the novel's few selective references to shared historical time are made, without exception, in the precise designation of ecological disasters, including the fictional catastrophe that precipitates the action of the plot. In a manner similar to the representation of time, the central events of *The Back of the Turtle* occur in a geographic space that is identified as Canada—with pan-Canadian settings in Toronto, Lethbridge, and British Columbia—although the distinguishing features of the novel's Canada derive not from organic links of historical destiny or common communal identity but from embeddedness in a transnational ideology of corporate power and materialist fetishism. Culturally, the Toronto of the novel reinforces the material and psychological depiction of the central character who is closely associated with the city; both are in a certain sense "American," products of a corporatist ideology devoid of organic roots in human community. To the extent that viable, communal life into the future is imagined by *The Back of the Turtle*, it will not be arranged through identification with Canada as it currently exists—or the United States, as both countries are associated with death—but with the establishment of an alternative form of community that is based on a renewed, more Indigenous relationship with the environment. The ideational referent of the nascent, life-sustaining community (nation?) taking shape on the shores of the Pacific Ocean at the end of the novel is Turtle Island, not Canada.

Viewed collectively, the characters of these ten works of fiction are not cast as representative of specifically Canadian or Québécois experience. Though each character could be read to illustrate a facet of one or another quality of the contemporary transnational world, none is perceptibly Canadian either in terms of his or her own self-identification or in terms of externally identifiable Canadian traits. They are Canadian or Québécois politically, usually as a matter of birthright, but not as a function of identification with a people or an *esprit collectif*. All, to varying degrees, are damaged individuals, haunted and harmed both physically and emotionally by diffuse cultural forces beyond their control. Even as a matter of negative depiction, apart from *The Back of the Turtle*, the sociocultural, sociopolitical specificity of neither Canada nor Québec is identified as a particular source of their disquiet. The anxiety felt by all of the protagonists has different sources, though it might collectively be characterized as the *angoisse* of liquid modernity, a troubling sentiment of individual unease resulting from the loss of sustaining forms of economic and social community. The aged protagonist Matthias, a former blacksmith, from Guay-Poliquin's *Le poids de la neige* recounts sociohistorical transformations that could be indicative of the types of changes experienced by Québécois (and pan-Canadian) society, though they are not explicitly identified as such in the novel. Matthias has been traumatized by the loss of all of the identity-giving markers of an entire "époque": a house, a trade with which to sustain himself economically, the natural environment, a church, his native village. The death of his parents and the extinguishment of the flame in the family forge portend the loss of an entire community of belonging and way of being:

> *My parents died young and with them, their era. I took over the house and the past gradually fell silent. There was no longer any flame at the heart of the forge. Newspapers heralded the future and new promises responded in kind. A few kilometres away, the skeletal structure of the city could be seen emerging. Dreams burst forth in plumes of smoke. There was talk of illuminating the streets, digging tunnels,*

raising buildings higher than steeples. My children were born; the fields were entombed in pavement; the church disappeared behind the office towers. The family home melted into the twists and turns of intersections, expressways and billboards. All around, cranes forced themselves onto the horizon; a heavy scent of bitumen weighed on the roofs; in the streets, the city's underbelly was constantly being opened and closed. From my balcony, I could hear the song of the sirens. Sometimes the flashing lights pulsated in passing, sometimes not. They were distant, anonymous distresses. (54–55)[5]

The abiding feeling of alienation produced by Matthias's loss of historical continuity and community is similar to that afflicting many of the protagonists of the novels under review, though for reasons specific to each character. For the adolescent narrator of *Bondrée*, as for Karen of *The Red Word*, it is the dark mystery of human sexuality and the inexplicable violence it seems capable of provoking; for the characters of *The Back of the Turtle* and *Le poids de la neige* it is the threat of environmental and technological disruptions and the danger they pose to human communal relations; for the relatively comfortable and yet alienated characters of *Six degrés de liberté* and *De synthèse* it is a sense of alienation even in the face of technological connectedness. In Thien's epic *Do Not Say We Have Nothing*, it is the impersonal, implacable force of Maoist ideology and the Chinese state. In the stories of Vanderhaeghe's *Daddy Lenin*, it is an incapacity to reconcile previously learned codes of behaviour—particularly those of a white male—with the conflicting demands of the ambient social environment. Johnny Keough, the protagonist of Hynes's *We'll All Be Burnt in Our Beds Some Night*, inhabits a Hobbesian world of violence, crime, and drug addiction where none of society's institutions—from the family to the judicial system—offers anything other than repression and violence. Even the otherwise contented and privileged narrator of *Au péril de la mer* confesses to an indeterminant "floating feeling that never leaves me, even in my sleep" (Fortier 57).[6] Apart from the last character, all of the central characters under discussion are essentially alone and deeply troubled; pain, physical and existential, is a defining element in their lives. None, importantly, is embedded in lasting, stable social networks primarily as a result of the anatomizing influences of the surrounding social, economic, and technological world that they inhabit. For each, history is a source of disruption rather than continuity.

In brief, all of these Governor General's Award–winning texts make lapidary reference to Canada, though in none of them is a specifically Canadian or Québécois sense of collective history or destiny foregrounded, in either approbation or critique. Representation of the nation in these texts is far from Renan's "large collection of men, healthy of spirit and warm at heart" or even Anderson's "deep, horizontal comradeship" across disparate co-nationalists. The texts, while in their own ways exceptionally evocative of social and especially emotional contexts, are largely deterritorialized from either Québec or Canada as a place with an identifiable, historically accrued social and political specificity. Representation has foregone depiction of the nation in its sociocultural particularity as an entity of (even potential) communal sustenance to focus instead on a much larger, more amorphous set of anxieties provoked by impersonal supranational forces: environmental degradation, the Faustian challenges of technology, the difficulties of maintaining sustaining interpersonal relations even within the family, and the breakdown of past norms of human connection and community.

So it is with the Holmesian dog that is not barking of the nation in Canada, at least in this admittedly limited selection of texts. Consideration of the causes for this relative silence or, alternatively, what the silence might portend accrues urgency upon harkening to the frequent, aggressive growlings of *Blut und Boden* nationalism in various contemporary contexts from Brazil to India. Why the silence in French and English Canadian fiction in an age of seemingly resurgent nationalism? Various responses offer themselves, although they remain of necessity tentative.

For one, as Northrop Frye predicted, it could be that Canadian and Québécois literature have outgrown interest in the parochial concerns of the nation to focus on international themes and the more exclusively aesthetic potential of fiction. In this reading, recent writers are pulling "us away from the Canadian context toward the centre of literary experience itself" (Frye 214). Such an eventuality would suggest alignment in the literary realm with the "postnational" situation of the country identified by Prime Minister Justin Trudeau in 2015: "There is no core identity, no mainstream in Canada...There are shared values—openness, respect, compassion, willingness to work hard, to be there for each other, to search for equality and justice. Those qualities are what make us the first postnational state" (Lawson). It is a previously noted irony (Szeman 175–83) that over fifty years ago, Frye should discern in Canadian literature evidence of the advent of a postnational world at the very historical moment of the launching of a self-consciously national literature in Canada: "The writers of the last decade, at least, have begun to write in a world which is post-Canadian, as it is post-American, post-British, and post everything except the world itself. There are no provinces in the empire of aeroplane and television, and no physical separation from the centres of culture, such as they are" (Frye 249). In a second related sense, perhaps the realist aesthetic that sustained the late twentieth-century writing of the nation is fatigued, no longer adequate to depiction of the country's national cultures in the twenty-first century. The cluster of representative formal and thematic elements famously identified by critics such as Corse as the primary markers of Canadian cultural difference could be seen as anachronistic given the current life of the nation or, at least, elite understandings of the life of the nation (63–96). Or again, uncertainty with regard to the representation of the nation could derive from uncertainty concerning what the nation is, what values or events may be used in illustrative, synecdochal depiction of the national collective. For some, acceptance of the notion of the nation as social artifice assumes suspicion regarding the legitimacy of any project which seeks the reification of necessarily partial visions of the nation; not only is such a process associated with the imposition of an elite ideology with its attendant partisan distribution of social and political power but the very notion of a federating nation becomes identified with a hierarchical, totalizing, and essentializing construct that conflicts with the ascendant ideology of diversity and its accommodations of divisions of ethnicity, race, gender, and class. Recent decades of historiographic metafiction have frequently returned to moments of historical event and context—from Rudy Wiebe's *The Scorched-Wood People* through Sky Lee's *Disappearing Moon Cafe* to Louis Hamelin's *La constellation du lynx*—in an effort to recalibrate understanding of the collective past, though rarely in articulation of an affirmative, synoptic vision of the potential of the nation in the manner assumed by Renan. The literary institutions of both French and English Canada know what the past mythologies of the nation have been and seem implicitly to expect of literature a nation-building function, albeit reticently expressed. They evince less confidence, however, in offering a vision for the future. The story of a nation presupposes continuity and coherence as well as the legitimacy that comes with consensus among those who, in Anderson's sense, are imagining it. Continuity, coherence, and legitimacy are difficult in a cultural and political context marked by fissure and contestation.

In such conditions, and in light of the collective impression left by five years of Governor General's Award–winning fiction in French and English, readers might feel encouraged to assume that, as a category of collective identification, the nation has lost its allure in the national imaginary and, as a result, in literature. Such an assumption would be mistaken, as consideration of a final collective dimension of the ten works of fiction would suggest. The nation is largely absent from the works discussed above. Importantly, however, neither is it present as an object of overt rejection or disparagement. Indeed, the reticent presence of the nation itself may be read to have consequences and may even be linked to the precarious existential state of the protagonists who, unbeknownst to themselves, collectively exemplify the intriguing need for, and lasting allure of, collective belonging such as that offered by the nation. Each of the characters lives an existence in exclusion from a stable and just social collective, a viable unity formed in the first-person plural, a "we" in which the individual may develop as a social being. Here again, King's *The Back of the Turtle* may be read as both indicative of the dangers of foregoing community and suggestive of the life-sustaining potential of social collectives. If, as I would suggest, ten works of contemporary fiction are signalling the perils of life devoid of social meaning and collective commitment—a form of suicide in the example of King's novel—then the significance of the nation's absence is indeed being communicated as the dog's missing bark. This invocation-through-absence of the power and necessity of the nation may thus be read as indirect affirmation of a collectivist, communitarian value traditionally present in both Canadian and Québécois literature. Canadian and Québécois literature may not at present be capable of representing the kind of totalizing vision of the nation sought for—imagined—at previous stages in the country's history, but it is revealing the deleterious effects of its absence. Despite its current uncertain presence, the literary representation of the nation in Canadian and Québécois literature is unlikely to disappear as long as the nation itself serves as the most effective means of assuring the political and social life of society. Whether in French or English, Canadian literature is likely to continue to shape understanding of the ever-evolving nation, just as plurinational, multicultural Canada is likely to continue to draw on literature in the attempt to understand and shape the ever-evolving collective. Even the dog that is not barking still has a presence.

NOTES

1. "...jedes Volk ist Volk; es hat seine Nationalbildung wie seine Sprache." Here and elsewhere in this chapter, all translations are by the author.
2. "Il semble à tous les citoyens de ce pays, qui prennent à cœur nos destinées futures et qui examinent de loin ou de près le rôle que nous sommes appelés à remplir sur cette terre d'Amérique, que la littérature nationale doit compter pour beaucoup dans l'accomplissement de cette mission."
3. "Nous avons maintenant au Québec une littérature bien à nous, riche, abondante, qui a son propre génie et qui est le reflet de notre réalité...L'enseignement de notre littérature relève d'un parti pris idéologique (voire politique) qui aura certes des conséquences sur la survie de la culture de langue française d'Amérique."
4. The research and writing of this chapter were completed before the announcement of the Governor General's Awards for French- and English-language fiction in 2019, 2020, and 2021. A cursory reading of the laureates for these subsequent years seems to confirm the broad trajectory of the analysis offered in this chapter.
5. "Mes parents sont morts jeunes en emportant leur époque, j'ai repris la maison et le passé s'est tu peu à peu. Il n'y avait plus aucune flamme au cœur de la forge. Les journaux criaient l'avenir et de nouvelles promesses pressaient le pas. À quelques kilomètres, on voyait poindre la structure osseuse de la ville. Les rêves fusaient de toute part dans les panaches de fumée, on parlait d'éclairer les rues, de creuse des tunnels, de construire des édifices plus hauts que les clochers. Mes enfants sont nés, les champs ont été plombés sous le pavé, l'église a disparu derrière les tours de bureaux. La demeure familiale s'est fondue dans les méandres des intersections, des voies rapides et des panneaux publicitaires. Partout autour des grues s'acharnaient sur l'horizon, un lourd parfum de bitume pesait sur les toits, dans les rues on ouvrait et en refermait sans cesse le ventre de la ville De mon balcon, j'entendais le chant des sirènes. Parfois les gyrophares passer en trombe, parfois pas. C'étaient des détresses lointaines, anonymes."
6. "...sentiment de flottement qui ne me quitte pas, même dans mon sommeil."

WORKS CITED

Anderson, Benedict. *Imagined Communities: Reflections on the Origin and Spread of Nationalism.* Verso, 1983.

Atwood, Margaret. *Survival: A Thematic Guide to Canadian Literature.* Anansi, 1972.

Blodgett, E.D. *Five-Part Invention: A History of Literary History of Canada.* University of Toronto Press, 2003.

Boivin, Aurélien. "Regards sur la littérature québécoise." *La francophonie dans les Amériques,* no. 174, 2015, pp. 65–68.

Canada Council for the Arts. *Governor General's Literary Awards,* https://ggbooks.ca/about. Accessed 13 Mar. 2022.

Corse, Sarah M. *Nationalism and Literature: The Politics of Culture in Canada and the United States.* Cambridge University Press, 1997.

Dewart, Edward Hartley. *Selections from Canadian Poets; with Occasional Critical and Biographical Notes, and an Introductory Essay on Canadian Poetry.* John Lovell, 1864.

Dickner, Nicolas. *Six degrés de liberté.* Les Éditions Alto, 2015.

Fortier, Dominique. *Au péril de la mer.* Les Éditions Alto, 2016.

Frye, Northrop. *The Bush Garden: Essays on the Canadian Imagination.* House of Anansi, 1971.

Gellner, Ernest. *Nations and Nationalism.* Blackwell, 1983.

Georges, Karoline. *De synthèse.* Les Éditions Alto, 2018.

Gerson, Carole. "The Changing Contours of a National Literature." *College English,* vol. 50, no. 8, 1988, pp. 888–95.

Gilbert, Paul. "The Idea of a National Literature." *Literature, Philosophy and Political Theory,* edited by John Horton and Andrea T. Baumeister, Routledge, 1996, pp. 198–217.

Godard, Barbara. "Notes from the Cultural Field: Canadian Literature from Identity to Hybridity." *Essays on Canadian Writing,* vol. 72, 2000, pp. 209–47.

Guay-Poliquin, Christian. *Le poids de la neige.* Les Éditions La Peuplade, 2017.

Harrington, Lyn, *Syllables of Recorded Time: The Story of the Canadian Authors Association 1921–1981.* Dundurn, 1981.

Henstra, Sarah. *The Red Word.* ECW Press, 2018.

Herder, Johann Gottfried. *Ideen zur Philosophie der Geschichte der Menscheit,* 2 bände, band 1, Aufbau, 1965, http://www.zeno.org/Lesesaal/N/9781482559736?page=0. Accessed 20 Sept. 2019.

Hobsbawm, Eric. *Nations and Nationalism since 1780: Programme, Myth, Reality.* Cambridge University Press, 1990.

Huxley, Aldous. *Texts and Pretexts.* Chatto & Windus, 1959.

Hynes, Joel Thomas. *We'll All Be Burnt in Our Beds Some Night.* HarperCollins, 2017.

Jameson, Fredric. "Third-World Literature in the Era of Multinational Capitalism." *Social Text,* no. 15, 1986, pp. 65–88.

Kertzer, Jonathan. *Worrying the Nation: Imagining a National Literature in English Canada.* University of Toronto Press, 1998.

King, Thomas. *The Back of the Turtle.* HarperCollins, 2014.

Lareau, Edmond. *Histoire de la littérature canadienne*. John Lovell, 1874, http://numerique.banq.qc.ca/patrimoine/details/52327/2022431. Accessed 20 Sept. 2019.

Lawson, Guy. "Trudeau's Canada, Again." *New York Times*, 8 Dec. 2015, https://www.nytimes.com/2015/12/13/magazine/trudeaus-canada-again.html.

Lecker, Robert. "The Canada Council's Block Grant Program and the Construction of Canadian Literature." *English Studies in Canada*, vol. 25, no. 3/4, 1999, pp. 439-69.

———. *Making It Real: The Canonization of English-Canadian Literature*. House of Anansi Press, 1995.

———, editor. *Canadian Canons: Essays in Literary Value*. University of Toronto Press, 1991.

MacLulich, T.D. "Thematic Criticism, Literary Nationalism, and the Critic's New Clothes." *Essays on Canadian Writing*, vol. 35, 1987, pp. 17–36.

Massey Report [Royal Commission on National Development in the Arts, Letters and Sciences: 1949–1951], https://www.collectionscanada.gc.ca/massey/h5-430-e.html. Accessed 20 Sept. 2019.

McCarthy, Dermot. "Early Canadian Literary Histories and the Function of a Canon." *Canadian Canons: Essays in Literary Value*, edited by Robert Lecker, University of Toronto Press, 1991, pp. 30–45.

Michaud, Andrée A. *Bondrée*. Nomades, 2015.

Moretti, Franco. *Atlas of the European Novel: 1800–1900*. Verso, 1999.

Pilote, Arlette. "La littérature québécoise souffre d'indifférence." *Le Devoir*, 21 Nov. 2011, https://www.ledevoir.com/opinion/idees/336544/education-la-litterature-quebecoise-souffre-d-indifference.

Renan, Ernest. *Qu'est-ce qu'une nation?* [1882], http://classiques.uqac.ca/classiques/renan_ernest/qu_est_ce_une_nation/qu_est_ce_une_nation.html. Accessed 20 Sept. 2019.

Roberts, Gillian. *Prizing Literature: The Celebration and Circulation of National Culture*. University of Toronto Press, 2011.

Said, Edward. *Culture and Imperialism*. Alfred A. Knopf, 1993.

Smith, Anthony D. *Myths and Memories of the Nation*. Oxford University Press, 1999.

Szeman, Imre. *Zones of Instability: Literature, Postcolonialism, and the Nation*. Johns Hopkins University Press, 2003.

Thien, Madeleine. *Do Not Say We Have Nothing*. Vintage Canada, 2016.

Vanderhaeghe, Guy. *Daddy Lenin and Other Stories*. McClelland & Stewart, 2015.

Watt, Ian. *The Rise of the Novel: Studies in Defoe, Richardson and Fielding*. 1957. Penguin, 1985.

2

Cultural Memory, National Identity
The Changing Paradigms of Acadian Literature

MATTHEW CORMIER

WHILE ACADIE IS NOT UNIQUE by virtue of its contested status as a nation—a fate shared by many peoples across the globe—it certainly holds a distinctive place in Canada's sociopolitical and cultural history. Both colonizer and colonized, the Acadian people, who inhabit a geographical space within parts of Canada's Maritime provinces that can claim neither defined borders nor official national recognition, have long attempted to define themselves as a francophone nation. From a historical perspective, most critics have understood Acadie's nationalism from recorded events: the Deportation of 1755, the national Acadian conventions, and the election of Acadie's first provincial premier in Louis J. Robichaud (1960–1970). Although none of these events has resulted in the unambiguous conferral upon Acadie of the status of an official nation within Canada, as David Creelman has argued with respect to their literature, "Acadians of both the first and second Renaissance were more aware than any cultural producers outside Quebec that their attempts to define themselves against hegemonies were a matter of cultural life and death. With their distinct language, historical narrative, ethnic identity, collective memory, and common folkloric heritage, the Acadians were the Maritime community most successful in achieving the cohesive homogeneity necessary to forge a national identity" (158). Hence, the most apt point of entry into understanding Acadie's national position remains through its literature because its writings work through *cultural memory* to construct identity.

With respect to cultural narratives, and particularly regarding questions of nationalism within "multinational" states, memory does different work than history as a *"mode of remembering,"* concerning itself with not only *what* is remembered but *how* it is remembered (Erll 7, emphasis added). Max Saunders explains further that "memory...is necessarily a transformation of the remembered event or experience" (323).[1] This labour of memory as a kind of mediation of history can take on the forms of tradition, myth, and commemoration, among others (Erll 3), but it also summarizes precisely the work of the Acadian literary imaginary as it represents an arguably "national" identity. Literature has always been the prominent cultural and collective vehicle in Acadie, from its traditional and pastoral curation by the Church to its modern, urban expressions. This chapter borrows from the works of Acadian writers from different periods—including Napoléon Landry, Raymond Guy LeBlanc, Guy Arsenault, Antonine Maillet, and France Daigle—to examine the ways in which, as Acadie's cultural memory has grown, so have the forms of its national identity as revealed in literary representation, from its burgeoning roots in Landry's poetry to its international presence in Daigle's fiction.

Acadian Nationalism: A Tale of Two Renaissances

Acadie, where French colonists established several settlements in the early seventeenth century, has a complex colonial history. After exchanging ownership with France on several occasions in the wake of a number of wars, Great Britain claimed Acadie permanently in 1713 and, from 1755 to 1763, shipped off the Acadian people, primarily to the United States, in an event that would come to be known as the Deportation or *Grand Dérangement*. The Deportation, a moment of cultural trauma, has since become a key chapter in Acadian history, culture, and, chiefly, literature.[2]

According to Jeffrey C. Alexander, "cultural trauma occurs when members of a collectivity feel they have been subjected to a horrendous event that leaves indelible marks upon their group consciousness, marking their memories forever and changing their future identity in fundamental and irrevocable ways" (1). For Acadians, the Deportation of 1755 has been that lasting, scarring event; it has marked their collective identity and shaped their aesthetic productions. Hitherto, Acadie has figured most often in literature as a disenfranchised minority among an occupying majority. While the Deportation continues to be engaged through literary representation in Acadie, much criticism on Acadian writing over the past few decades has been undertaken through variations of and expansions on Gilles Deleuze and Félix Guattari's conceptualization of a minor literature, which is defined by "the deterritorialization of language, the connection of the individual to a political immediacy, and the collective assemblage of enunciation" (18). Deleuze and Guattari's work on minor literatures has had a significant impact on Franco-Canadian criticism in general, and particularly on scholars such as François Paré, Raoul Boudreau, Lucie Hotte, and Andrea Cabajsky, among others, who have written extensively on Acadian literature and thus contributed to understandings of its status as a national literature.

In *Les littératures de l'exiguïté*, Paré specifically identifies four types of "small literatures": "insular literatures," "small national literatures," "colonial literatures," and "minor literatures" (17).[3] Paré certainly acknowledges that his types are not mutually exclusive, yet he directly names Acadian literature as an example of an insular literature because of its simultaneous self-reliance and isolation, comparing the literature to an island (30). This distinction of "insular" seems to undermine Boudreau's claim that Acadie is bound to the francophone majorities of Québec and Paris ("La littérature acadienne" 8) since, according to Paré, it is isolated and self-reliant. Yet, if Acadian literature is isolated and self-reliant, it is not closed off from the rest of the literary world. In fact, while Paré makes a case for Acadian literature as insular, it could also fall under any of the three other types that he establishes, and Paré admits this multiplicity himself. First, given Acadie's national conventions, flag, anthem, and holiday, Acadian literature could be seen as a small national literature, especially when considering the nationalism that defined the poetry of the first and second Acadian renaissances. Second, Acadian literature is definitively a colonial literature—at its very core, it wrestles with unresolved issues stemming from the Deportation and beyond, and this struggle is a direct repercussion of the conflicting French and British colonial enterprises. The questions of language and the reason for the untranslatability of the Chiac dialect in particular are due to the singular relationship between an archaic French, which was retained in Chiac because of the isolation that came with Acadie being a linguistically French colony, and because of Chiac's cultural and linguistic evolution, which occurred alongside and in submission to the linguistic and administrative dominance of English. Third and last, Acadian literature also falls under the rubric of Paré's fourth category, minor literatures. Critics like Boudreau have commented on Acadie's minority status in relation to Québec and France, but the area also remains a minority in its own geographical space, both surrounded and infiltrated by the majority anglophone population on the East Coast. This anglophone influence has chiefly pervaded French in Acadie, as the present dialect of Chiac in urban areas suggests. Paré's work on small literatures is thus foundational and highly insightful, yet even he realizes that literatures such as that of Acadie can be difficult to situate in relation to others, particularly because of their complicated pasts.[4]

Two major renaissances are generally recognized in Acadian literature and culture, the first occurring around the mid-nineteenth century and the second shortly after the mid-twentieth century. Both waves of writers during these transitional periods shared the desire to promote an Acadian nationalism, yet championed distinct values and ideals to their respective movements. The first wave of Acadian nationalism was born alongside the publication of Henry Wadsworth Longfellow's influential poem *Evangeline: A Tale of Acadie* (1847). During the period spanning the first renaissance (c. 1864–1890) to the late 1950s, Acadie inaugurated and cultivated its various institutions, namely St. Joseph College (1864) and the newspaper *Le Moniteur Acadien* (1867).[5] The development of these institutions gave rise to an Acadian nationalist movement that culminated in a series of national Acadian conventions at which Acadians decided upon cultural and political matters, such as their national holiday, August 15 (1881), and their national flag (1884).[6] This movement ensured a unified patriotism that dominated Acadian literature up until the late 1950s.

The second Acadian renaissance was the result of several political movements converging into a militant literary voice, or, as poet Raymond Guy LeBlanc calls it, a *"cri de terre."* As mentioned, a significant aspect of the eventual Acadian neonationalist renaissance was the rise to power of Louis J. Robichaud as premier of New Brunswick. Under Robichaud, New Brunswick became officially bilingual, a move which gave more power to the French-speaking Acadians, namely students at the Université de Moncton. In 1968, these students protested against various expressions of anglophone domination in Moncton, demanding equal rights for francophones. Joel Belliveau contextualizes the student protests in *Le "Moment 68" et la réinvention de l'Acadie*: "The wave of protests is the result of the exasperation felt by the younger generation of Acadians at the traditions of their forefathers, especially at what is perceived to be their submission to anglophone domination. It thus speaks to a generational gap tied in particular to the minority position of Acadians, but also to a disagreement with the previous generation's nationalist strategy" (18–19).[7] Several factors thus contributed to the student protests at the Université de Moncton and the subsequent publications of militant literature: a general dissatisfaction with traditional representations of Acadie, a rebellion against anglophone cultural domination, and a disagreement with respect to the nationalistic strategy of Acadie. Most Acadian writers of the second wave, such as Raymond Guy LeBlanc, Guy Arsenault, and Herménégilde Chiasson attempted to redefine Acadie in relation to its traditional depiction at this time, while simultaneously reclaiming it from anglophone oppression. Alongside the political turmoil caused by the Quiet Revolution in Québec and the student strikes at the Université de Moncton, the poetics of these writers at the time were militant, breaking from tradition and ushering in a modern style of cultural resistance that was reflected in its style and tone. Furthermore, these writers made space for the feminist Acadian poets of the 1980s—namely Hélène Harbec, Rose Després, and Dyane Léger—who, to a certain extent, heralded the work of France Daigle in their radicalized style that focused more on the personal act of writing itself than on politics.

These movements mostly involve poetry, as prose fiction did not hold such an important place in the history of Acadian literature until fairly recently, as often occurs in the early stages of minor literatures. Still, prose fiction did not become popular in Acadie until Antonine Maillet emerged onto the literary scene during the late 1950s. Over the next few decades, Maillet would gain local, national, and international renown, winning a Governor General's Award for *Don l'Orignal* (1972) and France's prestigious Prix Goncourt for *Pélagie-la-Charrette* (1979), becoming the first ever non-European to receive the award. *Pélagie* is a revealing novel in terms of Maillet's tendency to romanticize and even mythologize Acadie: it tells the epic story of Pélagie and her ten-year journey to return her family and other Acadians picked up along the way to Acadie after the Deportation. The tale is recounted by a storyteller who is a descendant of one of Pélagie's companions on this odyssey. Maillet is still active as a writer, with her latest novel, *L'Albatros*, appearing in 2011; however, in the fifty years since the publication of her first novel, *Pointe-aux-Coques* in 1958, Acadian fiction has developed at a slower pace than that of Québec, its closest majority francophone counterpart in terms of geopolitics, and, as Boudreau points out, few writers of fiction from the area have produced significantly outside of Maillet and Daigle, with poetry remaining Acadie's preferred genre ("Le roman acadien" 29–30). The delayed rise of the novel in Acadie, considering the genre's storied ties to nationalism, adds another layer of complexity to Acadie's ties to the idea of nationhood, and thus another reason to look closely at its cultural memory rather than history.

Acadian Cultural Memory and Its Implications for the Nation
Literary scholars have ceaselessly and comprehensively pondered questions of identity, both in generic and thematic terms—how does one define identity and what are its components?—and in its *methodological* implications: How is it constructed, represented, *written*? Despite the attention extended to it according to these sweeping yet central questions, the concept of identity remains persistently fluid, with its significance shifting depending on the critical gaze imposed on it, whether cultural, national, or postcolonial, among others. Furthermore, even in the past century, scholars witnessed the evolution of philosophical views on identity from the modernist propensity to contemplate one's place in the universe to the postmodernist proclivity to look inward and

self-reflect. Questions of identity continue to be of great significance to literary critics and theorists, especially with respect to minor literatures as they study various means of validating the work done by authors from marginalized cultures. The literatures from these cultures are particularly potent for scholarship with regard to questions of identity precisely because they often have cultural, national, and postcolonial stakes while their writers, caught between the influence of the majorities surrounding them and their own perception of themselves, struggle to understand their respective identities. Due to its innate complexity, researchers increasingly inspect identity through the nuanced scope of memory studies to understand its myriad representations in minor literatures.

As previously mentioned, memory functions at an intersection with history because it takes into account perceptions, emotions, and affects related to recorded events; in other words, memory mediates history. The concept of a cultural memory is, therefore, appealing for studies on identity because it offers greater agency—or at least a central presence—to the culture in question. Various but comparable definitions of cultural memory are prominent in current memory studies: Astrid Erll claims that cultural memory is the "interplay of the present and past in sociocultural contexts" (2), insofar as culture is a three-dimensional concept consisting of "social (people, social relations, institutions), material (artifacts and media), and mental aspects (cultural defined ways of thinking, mentalities)" (4). Likewise, Jan Assmann describes cultural memory as "a kind of institution. It is exteriorised, objectified, and stored away in symbolic forms that...are stable and situation-transcendent: They may be transferred from one situation to another and transmitted from one generation to another" (110–11). Some scholars, such as Michael Rothberg, posit memory—and by extension, cultural memory—more explicitly "as *multidirectional*: as subject to ongoing negotiation, cross-referencing, and borrowing; as productive and not privative" (3). In any case, cultural memory is necessarily the backdrop to a cultural identity since the former prefigures any conscious, self-reflexive constructions and representations of this identity.

The idea of an Acadian cultural memory can be defined and related to the notions of history and even culture by referring to examples. For example, history tells of the "equal opportunities" resulting from

Robichaud's implementation of the Language Rights Act in 1969. Acadie's cultural memory, however, remembers this past event from its own perspective: as an increase in freedoms, rights, and opportunities, certainly, but all the while recognizing that Acadians are still a minority in New Brunswick; this tension, incidentally, drove the revolutionary Acadian poetry of the 1970s rising against anglophone oppression in the province, namely in Moncton.[8] A collective sense of cultural identity is thus always evolving along with cultural memory. Acadian culture was much different before the addition of discrete institutional developments that expanded its repertoire, then it changed when French received its official status in New Brunswick, then again when Maillet folklorized Acadie's origins, and once more, I would argue, when Daigle's and other writers' urban representations became a part of the nation's cultural memory. The culture of a collectivity evolves as the memory of its people expands, and so do its representations of identity. *Pour sûr* could be taken superficially as a snapshot of Acadian culture, of the present; yet Daigle's work also represents a longer lineage, taking into account the labour of memory: her attention in the novel to the evolution of Chiac, the importance of family and tradition in the text, as well as Daigle's many references to her other works all speak to her project of labouring through memory to represent an identity that is in flux, always changing.

Cultural memory, even with its anticipatory nature, is not *strictly* a pre-conscious process of identity construction; the construction of identity also requires personal agency. Linked to this idea of the personal, Erll asserts that "identities have to be constructed and reconstructed by acts of memory, by remembering who one was and by setting this past self in relation to the present self [because] ways of making sense of the past which are intentional and performed through narrative, go hand in hand with the construction of identities" (2). The mention of the "personal self" in this case and "narrative" as a method to work through memory and construct identity is highly significant for several reasons. If identity is in constant flux between the personal and the cultural collective, as Assmann argues (109), with each depending upon the other, then tensions persist between personal and cultural memory, building upon each other to construct identity. Moreover, if, as José van Dijk suggests while engaging Andreas Huyssen's work, "all memory, whether preserved in image, word, or sound, is grounded in representation" (268), then readers can begin to understand fully how narrative representations of memory enact a personal construction of identity because, as Saunders explains, "our memories are always already textualized. They are by definition 'after the event,' but also, as representations or mediations or narrativations of the event, they have always begun to turn the event into something else" (323). A prime form of textual, narrative representation of memory—and consequently identity—is thus literary fiction. In discussing fiction as a textual, narrative representation of memory and the process of writing fiction as a personal means of working through cultural memory, the postmodernist movement comes to mind. Postmodern fiction, for instance, due to its self-reflexive nature, does compelling work with respect to working through memory to construct a representation of identity; like memory, postmodernist representations are often fragmented and intertextual in ways that are not always immediately evident and that are intrinsically tied to language.

Acadie's Early Nationalist Poetry

The contrast between Acadie's history and its cultural memory, especially in terms of both its colonial and postcolonial pasts, is quite evident in some of its earliest, most celebrated literary works, such as Landry's collection of poetry, *Poèmes de mon pays* (1949). As the title implies, Landry's volume concerns itself chiefly with Acadie's colonial, nation-building endeavour; the author, a member of the clergy, even dedicates the collection to "the French Survival" (n.p.).[9] In a number of ways, Landry sets up the nationalist paradigm of Acadian literature for future generations: on the one hand, a colonial, religious view of Acadie as a promised land; on the other hand, a postcolonial ideology of exile and victimization as a result of British colonialism. For instance, in "Our Acadie" (12), Landry describes France's colonialist enterprise as a peaceful settlement on promised, bountiful land:

A small people from France,
carved out a place, near the ocean,
in a land of abundance (1–3)[10]

He goes on to claim that "Our Acadie!" (8) basks in a new light—"the purest in the universes" (11)—and that "Every soul is exalted in Acadie" (20).[11] By contrast, however, in "Exile" (17), Landry describes the British colonials as tyrannical figures; in doing so, he effectively creates a sense of pathos for the Acadian people:

A tyrant came to the country.
See! His steps leave footprints
Of blood!—He takes all: scythes, guns,
Houses! He burns the churches!
Red soldiers, under the trees,
Pass, wave torches
In the air. All is full of dread! (2–8)[12]

Even though Landry claims that his poetry is born from "the land, the history, and the 'Acadian Faith'" (2), his literary manipulation of these elements shapes Acadian cultural memory and identity, namely in terms of suffering at the hands of the British during the Deportation.[13] In so doing, he proposes a strong sense of nationalism to his readers with his poetic disposition, propagating an ideology of the collective martyrdom of the Acadians—in their cultural memory, their own colonial practices dissolve to be replaced by a nationalist mythology based on exile and victimization.

Landry builds on this nationalist ideology of martyrdom in his next book, *Poèmes acadiens* (1955). With this work, the poetry is not only identified as being from his country, but as being born from the martyrdom of the Acadian nation: "The Acadian people, having plucked the palm of martyrdom in dark days, rises today triumphantly, in the glory of a resurrection that moves the whole world" (7).[14] The collection features a continuation of Landry's nationalist—and in retrospect quasi-propagandist, considering its colonial overtures—poetry, including titles such as "Our Acadie" (13), "The Acadian Land" (13), and "The Voice of the Acadian Land" (15).[15] Moreover, Landry develops several long poems as nationalist epics of Acadie's trials in becoming a country; in a section titled "By Rereading Our Acadian History" (42), these poems work to rewrite Acadian history in an artistic medium and shape Acadie's cultural memory.[16] Namely, "Idelka: Indian Heroine of Grand-Sault" (43), situates the Acadian, "civilized" colonial perspective on an Indigenous legend, that of Idelka, a virgin Maliseet woman who sacrifices herself to kill an entire army of enemy Mohawk warriors.[17] The fact that Idelka, who is at the heart of the warring "savages," as Landry calls these Indigenous Peoples, is the "muse of [his] country, on a new rhythm" (43) demonstrates the settler disposition of the author and his nationalist writing, not only in its civilizational voyeurism, but also in its co-opting of Idelka's story to draw comparisons to Acadie's own suffering as well as to build on it to promote Acadie's nationalist project.[18] In retelling Idelka's story in the form of a long poem, Landry on the one hand minimizes the cultural memory of Acadie's role as a colonizing force, while on the other hand furthers Acadie's nationalism, which is based on martyrdom. This colonial, nationalist ideology persisted in Acadie as its cultural memory evolved in the coming decades.

Mythologizing a Colonial Past into a Postcolonial Present
Later literary works, also built on Acadian cultural memory, continued to shape a sense of national identity as well, in particular with the rise of fiction and novelists such as Antonine Maillet. As I mentioned, Maillet put Acadie, both literally and figuratively, on the map by winning France's coveted Prix Goncourt in 1979 for *Pélagie-la-Charrette*, which was later translated by Philip Stratford as *Pélagie: The Return to Acadie*, cited here. The impact that Maillet's *Pélagie* had on Acadians over two centuries after the actual Deportation speaks to the colonial background of Acadian literature and, to a greater extent, Acadian identity. As Maillet's novel repeatedly reminds readers, memory, particularly colonial memory, is central to the solidification of Acadian cultural and literary identity: "For Acadia, tossed from one royal master to another, had managed to slip between the two and fool them both, going about its own business right under the old-country noses of Louis and George still sniffing the wind for spices. And without breathing a word, the little Atlantic colony had let the kings of France and England send back and forth their revised and corrected maps of Acadian and Nova Scotia, and had happily gone cultivating its garden" (7). This passage demonstrates the intricacies at the core of Acadie as the colonial enterprise of two countries

that fought wars over its bountiful, promised land, while the colonists themselves over time gained an independence that would become nationalistic after the post-Deportation return of Acadians. In any case, the fact that Acadian literature appears to be colonial *as well as* postcolonial allows for intriguing dynamics. Maillet's storytelling shapes Acadie's cultural memory and identity by folklorizing its colonialism as a virtuous endeavour for which the Acadian people suffered at the hands of British colonialism, exiled and victimized, before persevering to return to a "promised" land in a postcolonial context: "Like the wheel of a cart, the helm of a building, the new Acadia had launched to the four corners of the country the rays of its compass rose, without a doubt. She had played Blind Man's Bluff with destiny and had ended up labouring all her fields and replanted her seeds all over" (314).[19] In a concluding statement to the novel, then, and in a fashion similar to Landry's poetry, Maillet washes away Acadie's colonial past from its cultural memory while simultaneously painting a picture of a people's triumphant return to its promised land, "replanting its roots," and constructing its identity. In doing so, Maillet effectively mythologizes Acadie's colonial past into a postcolonial present.

As other critics have pointed out, Pélagie's epic account has biblical resonances, with her tale of exodus closely resembling that of Moses; however, Maillet also borrows from creationist traditions to mythologize Acadie. For instance, one of her earliest novels, *On a mangé la dune* (1962)—part of a trilogy that also contained the later works *Le chemin Saint-Jacques* (1996) and *Le temps me dure* (2003)—features young, Acadian heroine, Radi, a precursor to Pélagie who is compelled to rally her people to create a new world for themselves. Perhaps her most well-known creation is that of the "Île-aux-Puces," first appearing in Maillet's Governor General's Award–winning *Don l'Orignal*: the characters from this island, risen from the sea, include Citrouille, Noume, Don l'Orignal, la Sainte, and, of course, la Sagouine, her most renowned character. In these early works, Maillet sets the scene for much of her oeuvre, which pits a disenfranchised cast of carnivalesque Acadian characters—born from destiny on a seemingly promised land to be defended—against invaders from what is assumed to be the European continent, the colonizers. In *The Tale of Don l'Orignal*, Barbara Godard's translation of the original, the island is described as having "there [arisen] one fine morning in the middle of the ocean a sort of yellow blob that looked just like a golden whale" (7). Maillet effectively mythologizes this island and its inhabitants as defenders against the colonizers who wish to exploit or destroy it:

> *To anyone who has never set his mind to such a task, the destruction of an island might seem like child's play, just a matter of sending it back to where it came from—in this case to the bottom of the sea. Since it had already grown too big for a single kick or blow to sink it, the barber proposed to cut it first into little pieces, then give each district of the town its slice of island to set upon and finish off. The milliner found this method shameful and pernicious and suggested instead a powerful insecticide, capable of reducing the very roots of life to cinders, drying up the island so it would float away over foreign seas and run aground some day at the other end of the world. The merchant expressed the opinion that they should sell it to a neighbouring country and, to this end, at once began to proclaim the discovery of a new world. (8–9)*

Maillet's lengthy and metaphorical narration demonstrates the colonial threats faced by the islanders from the privileged villagers from the mainland: the dividing of the island into territories by the mainland villagers, these villagers committing genocide upon the islanders and deporting survivors, or the villagers selling the island as a commodity of a new world. While these examples stand in for the British colonists' treatment of Acadians as postcolonial victims, Maillet's mythologizing of these events also serves to erase Acadie's own colonial past from its cultural memory.

The "Other" Quiet Revolution

The 1970s, however, also represent a literary divergence in Acadie's cultural memory and identity: while writers such as Maillet would further folklorize Acadie, poets like Raymond Guy LeBlanc and Guy Arsenault stood to legitimize Acadie's claim to nationhood in a contemporary Canadian context alongside Québec's Quiet Revolution. In particular, and in the context of New Brunswick's bilingual, yet still majority anglophone status, Acadians began using art to criticize the province's educational and administrative institutions. Arsenault's *Acadie Rock* (1973), a kind of poetic manifesto, is possibly the most recognizable Acadian work that questioned authority during these revolutionary times. The first poem in the collection, "New School Policy," attacks the education system and sets the tone for the condemnation of other institutions; the speaker claims that "school is a factory / the student is the product" (8). This Marxist and satirical rhetoric continues in "Acadie Rock" (21), in which Arsenault condemns Irving, a major company operating in the province, by comparing the mass-produced houses built along the highway by the company to a garden:

> *A garden of*
> *Kent Homes*
> *Beside the Highway*
> *cultivated by:*
> *Irving Plus. (8–12)*[20]

Given that Irving's primary sectors include forestry and energy, Arsenault ties the company to the environment, signalling its control of natural as well as youth resources. In addition to the critiques of these institutions, Arsenault dissects the workings and influence of the Catholic Church in Acadie in nationalist poems like "My Country" (60). In doing so, the poet sets up a strong link between political revolution and nationalism for Acadie during the early 1970s.

Raymond Guy LeBlanc was another young, politically charged writer at the time. Building on the poetics of Acadian modernist poet Ronald Després (Cormier, "Modernity"), LeBlanc's *Cri de terre* advocates for a joint, nationalist project with Québec in "Plan for a Country (Acadie-Québec)" (qtd. in LeBlanc 75):

> *Now is the hour of enlightened men*
> *With their memory contained in the detailed plan*
> *Now begins the march toward the future (1–3)*

His attempts to unite these causes are somewhat circumstantial in trying to follow Québec's Quiet Revolution, yet LeBlanc's iconic poetry did mobilize a particular political ideology in Acadie; LeBlanc's work is grounded in a frustrated, immediate political reality, one that promulgates the unsatisfied present moment, linguistically and geographically, as the final poem in his collection makes clear (qtd. in LeBlanc 82):

> *I swear in English all my* goddam *bastards*
> *And often* fuck its *rise in my throat*
> *With* Jesus Christs *hurled against the windshield*
> *Bleeding* medium rare... //
> *I am Acadian*
> *Which means*
> *Fucked dispersed plural bought alienated sold*
> *Man torn toward the future (1–4; 19–22)*

LeBlanc's poetry underscores a time of political unrest, certainly; however, the immediacy of his work demonstrates an alternative ideology from that of Maillet, one that has moved beyond issues of colonialism to centre itself with conviction as a victim of postcolonialism with respect to the cultural dominance anglophone majority. Often, as the works of other writers at the time such as Guy Arsenault and Herménégilde Chiasson also show, to be a nationalist Acadian, and poet especially, was to produce works that took "domestic risks" in presenting themselves as disenfranchised citizens—a kind of pride in being exiled, which has since come to be perceived as an irreconcilable problem, particularly in Acadian poetry.

Globalizing Acadie

If Acadian poetry has since the 1970s often had difficulty in defining Acadie's nationalism in terms that extend beyond this problematic sentiment of pride in disenfranchisement and exile, the rise of novelist France Daigle allowed for yet another understanding of Acadian nationalism, one that seemed to recognize that Acadie had to move beyond its localist concerns to be noticed by readers outside of Acadie. Maillet won the Goncourt in France for her mythologizing work in *Pélagie*, but Daigle constructed an Acadie with her novels that was attractive in an international context. From the outset of her Moncton Quartet, which comprises the novels *Pas pire* (1998), *Un fin passage* (2001), *Petites difficultés d'existence* (2002), and *Pour sûr* (2011), Daigle ties Acadie to the rest of the world in terms of the responsibilities of Acadian writers in the face of globalization. She does so by fictionalizing herself in *Pas pire*'s narrative as an agoraphobic author, "France Daigle," who has been invited to speak on a talk show in France, Bernard Pivot's *Bouillon de culture*. The metafictional representation of the author and her agoraphobia—which can be defined as a fear of leaving one's home for vast or crowded spaces—speaks to the general tendency of Acadians to refrain from considering themselves and, consequently, their nationalism, on an international or global scale; instead, as mentioned previously, Acadian writers historically preferred to deal with questions of nationalism on exclusively "domestic" terms. Her travel companion, Camil, summarizes this ideology when he tells her in Paris that "Acadians, we have a hard time when we distinguish ourselves. It's like we're afraid to shine" (158).[21] Of course, the novel concludes with Daigle's fictional avatar leaving the safety of her home and travelling to France with a new friend in order to discuss her work on a global stage, crossing a long-standing boundary for Acadian writers. Going even further, Daigle's avatar—and her fiction more generally—does not simply leave Acadie, but also returns with new experiences.

With *Pas pire*, Daigle cleverly inverts the Acadian narrative of an "exiled" people attempting to return home, to one that—though not without reluctance—opens up to, and thrusts Acadie into, the world. This work continues over the course of her Moncton Quartet: for instance, she introduces internationally renowned visual artist Étienne Zablonski, who eventually settles in Moncton with this wife. Daigle also creates new institutions in her fictionalized Moncton, such as Zed's project to construct a building of lofts that also hosts a bar and a library. This community attracts individuals from all over the world, setting up Moncton as a cultural and artistic hub on a global scale. Furthermore, Daigle explores and pushes the boundaries of Chiac, working to give the dialect standard spelling rules, grammar, and syntax, and in doing so further legitimizes her Acadie with a recognizable, distinctive status all its own. She achieves this distinction in part, too, because of her insightful self-reflection and provocative fragmentation, particularly in the final instalment of this quartet, *Pour sûr*. The novel culminates Daigle's literary work of adding to Acadie's cultural memory the inclusion of a global perspective and, in doing so, contributes to a changing of ideas of nationalism in Acadie to include ones that could be qualified as postnationalist. These understandings reflect thoughts such as Édouard Glissant's of "a world system of interlocking small worlds" (qtd. in Apter 411) or even, more recently, Emily Apter's work on the idea of "phantom inter-nations," though Apter's concept still implies a kind of "competitive nationalism" (411) that sets itself apart through difference. The cultural collective that Daigle creates in her literary works perhaps falls best under what Homi K. Bhabha, recalling Benedict Anderson's term of "imagined community," has called a "locality of culture": "This locality is more *around* temporality than *about* historicity; a form of living that is more complex than 'community'; more symbolic than 'society'; more connotative than 'country'; less patriotic than *patrie*, more rhetorical than the reason of state; more mythological than ideology; less homogenous than hegemony; less centred than the citizen; more collective than 'the subject'; more psychic than civility, more hybrid in the articulation of cultural differences and identifications" (292). Due to the historically fluid and precarious status of Acadie, Bhabha's nuanced and contemporized idea of a "locality of culture" seems better suited to define the universe of *Pour sûr* than others, and especially with respect to the manner in which this intricate and at times contradictory universe has established an alternative to nationalism in Acadie's cultural memory. In other words, Bhabha implies the potential for a robust cultural collectivity without a state that befits Acadie and, in its literary representation, Daigle's work.

Pour sûr, translated to the English *For Sure* by Robert Majzels and cited here, is particularly intriguing because of its postmodernist aesthetics, which allow Daigle to be self-reflexive about the Acadian cultural memory to date while also attempting to distance herself from certain traditions. In one such moment, she states that Acadie's chief endeavour has been "protecting one's heritage, saving one's heritage: an essential preoccupation of Acadians. From the beginning of time, defending one's village, cattle, lands, church, and ultimately one's language. From the beginning of time, and most likely until the end" (705). The author shows in this instance an awareness of Acadie's sense of cultural self-understanding, its defensive nature with respect to its postcolonial history; however, she seems to want to escape it. She demonstrates this desire by using irony and wit to address the pillars of this postcolonial, Acadian cultural memory when, among other moments, she uses an unidentified speaker to exclaim, "Anudder film on The Deportation? Ferget the popcorn, it's chocolate we'll be needin'" (456). In this instance, she takes a jab at the Acadian cultural memory and its relationship to the Deportation, implying it to be a kind of love affair, an unhealthy romanticization allowed by the passage of time. She furthers this distanciation in cultural memory—of a preoccupation with an event in the Deportation that, seemingly according to her, should no longer define Acadians—through a conversation between two young boys, Étienne and Chico:

> "Wot does ee tink about?"
> ...
> "Eh? Wot's ee tinkin' about?"
> "The Deportation."
> "Wot's dat?"
> ...
> "Eh? Wot's dat?" (643)

In this passage, the two young boys are contemplating an event so far removed from them that they do not understand why Terry, Étienne's father, would be so pensive about it. To them—who represent, quite literally, the next generation of Acadians—the Deportation means nothing. In this short scene, Daigle thus suggests that a future Acadie must relinquish haunting elements of its cultural memory in order to move forward and meet the world.

Conclusion

In looking at some of the ideas that inform several of its key literary texts, then, one can see clearly that Acadie's cultural memory and, consequently, Acadians' understanding of collective identity as a nation, has evolved over the past century. From colonial centricities through postcolonial victimization to globalist aims, writers such as Landry, Maillet,

LeBlanc, and Daigle have continuously built upon and reframed Acadie's cultural memory to promote new representations of its collective sense of self, both culturally and nationally. For Acadie, understanding the region in terms of a "nation" within a "multinational state" is difficult because of its complex colonial history and the ways in which Acadian writers' interpretations of this history stray from recorded events; however, in studying Acadie's literary contributions towards constructing its cultural memory, scholars can begin to trace compelling patterns and witness movements in Acadie that speak to the multiple and developing ways in which it sees itself and in relation to others. With Daigle's most recent works, at least, Acadie appears ready to reconceptualize its cultural identity according to the exigencies of the global age, perhaps having finally transcended the status of being one of Canada's "other" minor francophone collectives outside of Québec.

NOTES

1. Memory studies and its credited founder, French theorist Maurice Halbwachs, owe much of their understanding of history to historiography, the extensive tradition of studying the ways in which historians have understood or approached the notion of history.
2. For a detailed account of Acadie's history and the Deportation, see Landry and Lang, and Viau.
3. "petites littératures," "les littératures insulaires," "les petites littératures nationales," "les littératures coloniales," and "les littératures minoritaires" (17). All translations are mine.
4. A variation of this summarization of Paré's work alongside the case of Acadian literature appears in my article, "Complicating World Literature in the 'Minor' Context: Translation and the Acadian Literary Ecosphere," in *Studies in Canadian Literature*, vol. 45, no. 1, 2020.
5. The duration of the first Acadian renaissance varies among critics, with some opting to lengthen the period to 1847, the publication date of *Evangeline*. See Belliveau.
6. See Bourque et al. for a detailed summary of the conventions.
7. "La vague de manifestations est présentée comme le résultat d'un ras-le-bol chez la jeunesse acadienne des traditions de ses pères et, surtout, de ce qui est perçu comme leur soumission à la domination anglophone. Il s'agirait donc d'un choc entre les générations, mais d'un choc bien particulier, lié avant tout à la situation minoritaire des Acadiens et d'un désaccord sur le type de stratégie nationaliste à favoriser" (18–19).
8. See Lonergan for a full account of the history and factors that led to the 1970s revolution in Acadie.
9. "la Survivance Française" (n.p.)

10. "Notre Acadie" (12); "Un petit people, issue de France, / Se tailla, près de l'Océan, / Dans une terre d'abondance" (1–3).
11. "Notre Acadie!" (8); "La plus pure de l'univers" (11); "Toute âme exalte en Acadie" (20).
12. : "L'Exil" (17); "Un tyran vint dans le pays. / Vois! Ses pas ne font qu'une empreinte // De sang!—Il prend tout: faux, fusils, / Maisons! Il brûle les églises! / Des soldats rouges, sous les bois, / Passent, agitent dans la brise / Des flambeaux. Tout est plein d'effroi!" (2–8).
13. "la terre, de l'histoire, et 'la croyance acadienne'" (2).
14. "Le peuple acadien, après avoir cueilli la palme du martyre, en des jours bien sombres, se lève aujourd'hui triomphant, dans la gloire d'une résurrection qui émeut le monde entier" (7).
15. "Notre Acadie" (13); "La Terre acadienne" (13); "La Voix de la terre Acadienne" (15).
16. "En relisant notre histoire acadienne" (42).
17. "Idelka: Heroïne indienne du Grand-Sault" (43).
18. "muse de [son] pays, sur un rhythme nouveau" (43).
19. "Comme une roue de charrette, comme le timon d'un bâtiment, l'Acadie nouvelle avait lancé aux quatre coins du pays les rayons de sa rose des vents, sans s'en douter. Elle avait joué à colin-maillard avec le destin et avait fini par labourer tous ses champs et replanter ses racines partout" (314).
20. "nouvelle politique d'école"; "l'école est une manufacture / l'écolier est le produit" (8); "Acadie Rock" (21); "Un jardin de / Kent Homes / au côté d'la Highway / cultivay par: / Irving Plus." (8–12).
21. "les Acadiens, on a ben de la misère quand on se distingue. C'est comme si qu'on avait peur de briller" (158).

WORKS CITED

Alexander, Jeffrey C. "Toward a Theory of Cultural Trauma." *Cultural Trauma and Collective Identity*, edited by Jeffrey C. Alexander et al., University of California Press, 2004, pp. 1–30.

Anderson, Benedict. *Imagined Communities: Reflections on the Origins and Spread of Nationalism*. Verso, 1983.

Apter, Emily. "A New Comparative Literature." 2006. *The Princeton Sourcebook in Comparative Literature: From the European Enlightenment to the Global Present*, edited by David Damrosch et al., Princeton University Press, 2009, pp. 409–19.

Arsenault, Guy. *Acadie Rock*. Éditions d'Acadie, 1973.

Assmann, Jan. "Communicative and Cultural Memory." *A Companion to Cultural Memory Studies: An International and Interdisciplinary Handbook*, edited by Sara B. Young et al., 2008, pp. 109–18.

Belliveau, Joel. *Le "Moment 68" et la réinvention de l'Acadie*. Presses de l'Université d'Ottawa, 2014.

Bhabha, Homi K. "DissemiNation: Time, Narrative, and the Margins of the Modern Nation." *Nation and Narration*, edited by Homi K. Bhabha, Routledge, 1990, pp. 291–392.

Boudreau, Raoul. "La littérature acadienne face au Québec et à la France: Une double relation centre/périphérie." *Regards croisés sur l'histoire et la littérature acadiennes*, edited by Madeleine Frédéric and Serge Jaumain, Peter Lang, 2006, pp. 33–46.

———. "Le roman acadien depuis 1990." *Nuit blanche*, no. 115, 2009, pp. 26–30.

Bourque, Denis et al. *Les conventions nationales acadiennes*. Institut d'études acadiennes, 2013.

Cormier, Matthew. "Complicating World Literature in the 'Minor' Context: Translation and the Acadian Literary Ecosphere." *Studies in Canadian Literature*, vol. 45, no. 1, 2020.

———. "Modernity in Acadian Poetry: The Case of Ronald Després." *Canadian Poetry: Studies, Documents, Reviews*, vol. 78, 2016, pp. 28–44.

Creelman, David. "Congruence and Recurrence in the Literatures of New Brunswick." *New Brunswick at the Crossroads: Literary Ferment and Social Change in the East*, edited by Tony Tremblay, Wilfrid Laurier University Press, 2017, pp. 155–66.

Daigle, France. *For Sure*. Translated by Robert Majzels, House of Anansi Press, 2013.

———. *Pas pire*. Éditions d'Acadie, 1998.

Deleuze, Gilles, and Félix Guattari. *Kafka: Toward a Minor Literature*. 1975. Translated by Dana Polan, University of Minnesota Press, 2003.

Erll, Astrid. "Cultural Memory Studies: An Introduction." *A Companion to Cultural Memory Studies: An International and Interdisciplinary Handbook*, edited by Sara B. Young, Ansgar Nunning, and Erll Astrid, De Gruyter, 2008, pp. 1–15.

Halbwachs, Maurice. *La mémoire collective*. Les presses universitaires de France, 1950.

Landry, Napoléon. *Poèmes acadiens*. Éditions Fides, 1955.

———. *Poèmes de mon pays*. École Industrielle des Sourds-Muets, 1949.

Landry, Nicolas, and Nicole Lang. *Histoire de l'Acadie*. Éditions du Septentrion, 2001.

LeBlanc, Catriona. *Cri de terre: A Translation of Raymond Guy LeBlanc's Cri de terre*. 1998. Dalhousie University, Master's thesis. *Bibliothèques et Archives Canada*.

Lonergan, David. *Acadie 1972: Naissance de la modernité acadienne*. Prise de parole, 2013.

Maillet, Antonine. *Pélagie: The Return to Acadie*. Translated by Philip Stratford, Goose Lane Editions, 2004.

———. *The Tale of Don l'Orignal*. Translated by Barbara Godard, Goose Lane Editions, 2004.

Paré, François. *Les littératures de l'exiguïté*. 1992. Les éditions du Nordir, 2001.

Rothberg, Michael. *Multidirectional Memory*. Stanford University Press, 2009.

Saunders, Max. "Life-Writing, Cultural Memory, and Literary Studies." *A Companion to Cultural Memory Studies: An International and Interdisciplinary Handbook*, edited by Sara B. Young et al., De Gruyter, 2009, pp. 321–31.

van Dijk, José. "Mediated Memories: Personal Cultural Memory as Object of Cultural Analysis." *Continuum: Journal of Media & Cultural Studies*, vol. 18, no. 2, June 2004, pp. 261–77.

Viau, Robert. *Les Grands Dérangements: La déportation des Acadiens en littératures acadienne, québécoise et française*. MNH, 1997.

Literary Resistance
Situating a Métis National Literature

MATTHEW TÉTREAULT

IN RECENT YEARS, increasing numbers of Métis poets and novelists have published works that directly address the political struggles and the armed resistances of the Métis Nation in the nineteenth century. While this turn toward the national is not new, as seen in the works of Pierre Falcon and Louis Riel, volumes of poetry and fiction by writers such as Gregory Scofield, Marilyn Dumont, and Katherena Vermette exemplify an imaginative, even "combative," turn toward historical narratives of Métis struggles. Scofield's *Louis: The Heretic Poems* (2011), Dumont's *The Pemmican Eaters* (2015), and Vermette's young-adult graphic novel series *A Girl Called Echo—The Pemmican Wars* (2017), *Red River Resistance* (2018), *Northwest Resistance* (2020), and *Road Allowance Era* (2021)— epitomize a historically informed, meta-fictive turn in Métis literature. In many ways, these texts also complicate classical definitions of nationhood. That is, in producing narratives less strictly *of* or *about* armed Métis resistances—the Red River and North-West Resistances—than ones that *move through* and *resonate with* these histories, as well as through their evocation of distinctly Indigenous ethnocultural symbols and traditions, these texts re-story Métis history in ways that contest pervasive settler-written accounts of the armed resistances and contribute to the reshaping of a Métis national identity.

Weaving a critical and interpretive framework with which to locate a Métis national literature, I borrow from the French literary theorist Pascale Casanova's concept of "combative literatures" to situate a body of writing increasingly concerned with the national and to probe some of the ways in which Métis literature has been shaped by its relationship with settler-Canadian literatures. "The notion of 'combative literatures,'" writes Casanova, "suggests the idea of a collective movement [as] these literary spaces are engaged...in struggles for recognition which are both political and literary" (133). Drawing out key elements of Casanova's "structural hypothesis" (123) allows for a broader consideration of Métis literature as an emerging national literature in a multinational settler-state. Casanova points to four elements that distinguish the "combativeness" of a small national literature: (1) the apprehension and articulation of a collective heritage of culture and memories that signal "a stake in the symbolic rivalries between nations" (125); (2) the articulation of national identity in relation to other nations, and how national literatures become in part shaped by "direct literary rivalry" (128); (3) the structural inequality, or how the size or scale of a national space can affect the intensity of literary articulations of national identity; "'[s]mall' literatures," writes Casanova, "have generally had a very strong link with anything that touches on national definition, history or honour" (129); (4) and lastly, what Casanova names as culture and imperialism reveals how a "direct link can be established between literature and politics" (132), which, in Indigenous contexts, we might refer to as settler-colonialism.

While Casanova's concept provides a means of apprehending the broad "structural" elements of small national literatures in multinational states, I also heed Métis interdisciplinary scholar Jennifer Adese's call to read Métis literature as an "extension of...Métis peoplehood" (51), or more precisely, to read through those "tenets...[which bring] the Métis together as a collective people...kinship and relatedness, mobility, and geography" ("The New People" 61). Applying Casanova's "combative literatures," alongside Adese's interpretation of "peoplehood," to trace this literary return to history, I demonstrate how in reclaiming and narrating a sense of their national history—that is, in wresting authority over the narrative of Métis resistances and other events from settler-colonial histories—contemporary Métis writers are carving out space amid a constellation of national literatures, while both asserting a sense of national identity and contributing to a renewed understanding of the Métis Nation.

Situating Métis National Literature: A Brief History

Resistance in "many forms," as Métis literary scholar Emma LaRocque notes, has long marked Métis history and literature (129). As a post-contact Indigenous people of the northern plains of North America, the Métis emerged in the late eighteenth and early nineteenth centuries from the myriad encounters between First Nations and Europeans during the fur trade. Arising from a complex web of kinship networks, cultural practices, and economic activities across the North-West, but centred on specific places of settlement such as Fort Edmonton and most importantly, Red River, the Métis developed their own language (Michif), laws (of the prairie), and customs. Métis sociologist Chris Andersen largely positions "Métis nationhood or peoplehood as a form of [Benedict] Anderson's imagined communities" (91), albeit with some differing respects, namely, their prior existence to settler-states, relational political designations, and "'pre-state' origins and associated historical power... [which] clashed with European, state-based understandings of nationalism, particularly in relation to kinship" (92). Andersen argues that the struggles which punctuate Métis history—such as the Battle of Seven Oaks in 1816, the Sayer Trial in 1849, and the Battle of Grand Coteau in 1851—"cemented the Métis hunters' sense of 'horizontal comradeship' characteristic of affiliations of nationhood" (113). The events of the Red River Resistance in 1869–1870, and the North-West Resistance in 1885, which occurred in an "increasingly colonial landscape" (113), were sharply national in character. However, out of these points of national struggle, often against incipient settler-colonialism, Métis wordsmiths produced contrasting expressions of nationalism. We can see shifting approaches in the literary depiction of Métis nationalism between, for instance, Falcon's famous song "La Chanson de la Grenouillère" and Riel's later poetry. Written in the wake of the Battle of Seven Oaks, Falcon's song celebrates "the victory that we have won" (12) against those "here to pillage our country" (11), and gives expression to nascent forms of "horizontal comradeship" that resonate with Anderson's imagined communities;[1] some half a century later, Louis Riel's poetry would begin to show a more explicit ethnonationalism. Although he wrote proudly in his poem "La Métisse" of belonging "to this nation" (4: 88),[2] asserting Métis nationalism in general opposition to an English Canadian colonialism, Riel would later increasingly turn to ethnonational symbols in his writing. His famous ode "Le peuple Métis-Canadien-français," for instance, emphasized kinship with French Canadians and their shared adherence to Catholicism.

In the years after the military defeat at Batoche and Canada's execution of Riel in 1885, Métis nationalism was stifled and repressed. The Métis did not vanish, but as Métis historian Fred Shore notes, "their days of national activity were over" (106). What followed were the "forgotten years" when, defrauded and dispossessed of land, largely ignored, and consigned, as a blurb on the back cover of Maria Campbell's *Halfbreed* aptly describes it, to "a little-known world that coexists alongside Canadian society," the nation fractured under the pervasive weight of settler-colonialism into smaller, disparate communities. While some Métis in Alberta obtained land in the late 1930s and formed what is today the Alberta Métis Settlements, many in other provinces were relegated to road allowances.[3] "Family was pretty much all the Métis had," writes Shore (109). Some "shied away from the identity," Jean Teillet argues, "because of the prejudice they experienced" (432). Only after the Second World War did a broad political reorganization gain traction and national activity gradually resume; Métis national identity would be reimagined and expanded to include not only French-speaking Métis, but also English-speaking "Half-breeds." After decades of political struggle, the Métis National Council was created in the 1980s (Teillet 437–58). Contemporary articulations of Métis nationhood—by political leaders, scholars, writers, and others—largely position the Métis as an Indigenous nation, and increasingly anchor national claims in respects that resonate with ethnonationalist logics such as kinship, links to specific territory, and evidence of genealogical descent from nineteenth-century Red River Métis. Questions remain regarding how much of this turn toward ethnonational formulations reflects an ethnonationalist impulse within the nation itself, as a sort of reactionary and exclusionary stance prompted by centuries of settler-colonialism, not to mention appropriations by recent non-Métis groups and communities of Métis identity and symbols, or to what extent it may represent an ethnosymbolic turn within the cultural nationalism of imagined communities.[4]

This trajectory of national decline and subsequent reawakening is mirrored in the history of Métis literature, where production became restricted for a significant portion of the early twentieth century. Riel's execution undoubtedly marked the silencing of an important political voice, but the posthumous publication of a selection of his poetry, *Poésies religieuses et politiques* in 1886, signalled an ongoing, literary form of resistance. Métis literary production did not disappear; rather, it was relegated to small, regional publications, such as newspapers and periodicals across the Prairies. Although circulation was limited, Métis writers such as Louis Schmidt, Alexandre de Laronde, and members of L'Union nationale métisse St-Joseph du Manitoba, a society formed by relatives and associates of the leaders of the Resistances, continued to produce works into the twentieth century: Schmidt's memoirs appeared in *Le patriote de l'Ouest*, in Duck Lake, Saskatchewan, in 1911–1912; Laronde penned poems in French and other writings in Saulteaux (Léveillé 244); L'Union nationale "formed a Historical Committee to fight, restore history, and seize every opportunity to respond to those that attacked the Métis, and in a word to impose respect for the truth" (Comité Historique 17),[5] by "respond[ing] to all slights...in the newspapers of the day" (Ens and Sawchuk 115). In asserting a sense of territoriality and ensuring the survival of the historical memory of the Resistances, these writers helped sustain a vision of the nation that would be developed and reshaped by subsequent generations of authors.

The nation would also gradually diminish, and even disappear, from focus for some writers. Marie Rose Delorme Smith, writing in Alberta during the Depression, would come to portray it negatively. In her autobiographical "Eighty-Years on the Plains," which appeared in nine instalments in the ranch-focused periodical *Canadian Cattlemen* in 1948 and 1949, Smith traces her journey from Saint François-Xavier, Manitoba, to her eventual settlement and ranching life in Pincher Creek, Alberta, by the early 1880s. However, "despite the abundance of oral testimony that she had access to" (MacKinnon 20), Smith's accounts of the Resistances of 1869–1870 and 1885 are reduced to two brief anecdotes—Thomas Scott's execution in 1870, and Riel's return to Canada in 1884. What is more, Smith allows her brother-in-law, "George Ness...an Englishman by birth" (Smith 212), to largely convey and frame the Resistances as the Métis "ignorantly [taking] up arms against the government" (212). The silences, the abundance of connections and relationships that she does not disclose are striking, and yet these silences are not surprising, given that, as Diane Payment explains, "'*Le grand silence*' was the legacy of 1885" (269). Payment locates this reticence in the "strong legacy of fear among the veterans of 1885" and consequently how "they rarely spoke of the resistance outside their ranks" (270). Doris Jeanne MacKinnon touches upon this "fear" as well, but in noting how Smith's "cautious approach to reporting her own identity in her historical accounts" was likely "justified given the increasingly rigid social boundaries of Alberta in the 1930s" (7), she shows how such fear and silence extended across the prairies.

In contrast, around the celebrations of Canada's and Manitoba's Centennials, Franco-Manitoban Métis writer Marie-Thérèse Goulet-Courchaine would cast a very different look back on the Red River Resistance. Whereas Smith wrote of Riel as "a clever half-breed" who "made a grave mistake" (212), Goulet-Courchaine extolled the national struggle and memorialized "the struggle against enemies of the first hour" (qtd. in Juéry 33).[6] Writing in English and French for small newspapers in Manitoba and Saskatchewan, but predominantly for the French-language paper in Saint-Boniface, *La Liberté*, Goulet-Courchaine worked in the tradition of L'Union nationale toward the rehabilitation of Riel (Juéry 11). Goulet-Courchaine's words "[it is time to] honour our own as they deserve" (34),[7] leave no doubt that she takes, and displays, a more open pride in her heritage.[8]

The watershed moment in contemporary Métis literature came in 1973 with the publication of Maria Campbell's ground-breaking memoir, *Halfbreed*. Campbell "didn't just open the door for us," declares Métis writer Joe Welsh, "she kicked the damn thing down" (5). Notably, opening her initial chapter with a brief account of the Métis Resistances and "Ottawa's broken promises" (5), Campbell traces a history of discrimination, violent racism, and the dispossession of the Métis back to the

Resistance of 1885. In contrast to earlier writers, Campbell would also decouple Métis national identity from more exclusive associations with the French language and Catholicism and instead emphasize Indigenous cultural knowledge and symbols. LaRocque contends that Campbell's memoir forever "changed the course of Aboriginal writing...in Canada," as she "inspired younger generations of Indigenous authors to re-inscribe the Canadian narrative," and challenge "dominant interpretations of Canadian history" (135). With Campbell at the forefront, a new wave of Métis writers emerged in the 1970s and 1980s to contest settler narratives by deploying strategies of "discursive resistance," and (re)collecting the "scattered parts" (134) of personal, community, and national histories. Grappling with both historical and contemporary identities, what LaRocque describes as "[the acceptance] of Metis culture and heritage" became a "consistent" (136) theme in the works of early contemporary Métis writers.[9]

Alongside questions of "racial shame" (LaRocque 135), and following critical declines in the use of French, French Michif, and Cree Michif in view of the imposition and the dominance of English throughout the twentieth century, language emerged as another area of resistance and recovery. In an article examining "the resurgence of Michif...in literary texts" (95), Pamela Sing argues that the use, reference, and allusion to French Michif "contributes to the fashioning of a textual space within which the subject can negotiate a continual, self-defined trajectory" (103); in other words, "[Cree] Michif and Michif French" (111) disrupt otherwise unilingual textual spaces of Canadian English or French in ways which "[have] the potential to reinscribe a space that, to the Métis, feels like a *home*land" (112). In studying the presence of Cree and Cree Michif in English-language texts by Cree and Cree Métis writers, Susan Gingell similarly concludes that code-switching and other such uses of language represents "a moving toward self-government of the tongue," as well as a "way of coming home and claiming kin, territory, space, and place in contemporary Canada" (56). That said, contemporary Métis texts are produced almost entirely in English, and language survival remains a critical concern.

In the context of her observations on over three decades of Indigenous literatures in Canada, LaRocque has suggested that, in the proliferation of

Indigenous writers, a shift occurred between "endurance," or the imperative to represent the fact of continued being, to the sense that Indigenous writers "have had about enough of [just] enduring" (qtd. in McKegney 409). Building upon LaRocque's claims, Sam McKegney considers the question of what comes next, that is, what lies "beyond continuance" (409). However, in contemplating this "beyond," there remains if not an explicit focus on continuance an implicit recognition of its intimate link with what comes next. The recognition that Indigenous futurities stem from present relationships to the past underscores and further impels the question as to how the future might be envisioned through the recovery and reaffirmation of traditions.

In terms of Métis literature, nationalism, and narrative authority over representations of Métis history, the dynamic of what lies beyond continuance occurs through the shifting articulations of literary nationalism. In imaginatively reclaiming authority over historical narratives, Métis writers contribute toward rebuilding the nation by strengthening cultural roots and envisioning what the nation might be. Métis legal scholar Paul Chartrand touches upon this idea when he writes about the "resurrection of Falcon's anthem" and wonders "if Métis nationalism is not so much about the memory of what we have been, or even the reality of what we are today, but the vision of what, thinking, acting and singing together, we can become" (4). For Chartrand, the act of envisioning a future would seem to imply that the Métis Nation is an "imagined community" as opposed to a strictly ethnonational one. Rather, the focus on "acting and singing together" (4) evokes a sort of cultural nationalism. Examining multinational federalism in Canada and building on John Hutchinson's work that understands nations as internal zones of conflict, Eric Woods notes that Hutchinson's argument "provides...insights to go beyond primordialism and modernism [or ethno- and imagined conceptions of nationhood]," and more specifically, in the ways that "nationalists' cultural 'repertoires' are limited by an already existing pool of myths and symbols" (279). Summarizing Hutchinson's argument, Woods writes that the "constant evocation and re-evocation of different myths and traditions sustains and reifies the nation over time, even as its trajectory and definition is transformed" (279). The Métis Nation seems to provide an intriguing, complex case of such transformation: the shift away from

French and the growing emphasis on Indigenous cultural traditions might be understood less as an ethnonational turn than an ethnosymbolic re-evocation that reshapes the Métis Nation. However, despite an internal agency, the possibility of envisioning "what...we can become" (Chartrand 4) is also inextricably linked, as Casanova alludes, to how "literary spaces are engaged...in struggles for recognition which are both political and literary" (133). Re-envisioning is shaped in relation to pervasive settler-colonial narratives.

Samples of Settler (Political) Narratives

What does it mean to "struggle for recognition...both political and literary" (Casanova 133) and what does it mean to wrest authority over historical Métis narratives? As narrative is one of the areas in which literature and politics intersect, I illustrate below how struggles over Métis narratives are not simply literary. On February 18, 2019, or Louis Riel Day, a statutory holiday in Manitoba, then-leader of the Conservative Party of Canada, Andrew Scheer, posted a statement on Twitter celebrating the famed Métis leader's contributions to Manitoba in which he described Riel as a "Canadian politician of Métis background," and the "driving force behind the creation of Manitoba as a new Canadian province." Although reference to the creation of Manitoba without an attendant reference to the Resistance of 1869–1870 demonstrated a lack of nuance and context, the characterization of Riel as a "Canadian politician of Métis background" seemed particularly egregious. In foregrounding Riel as "Canadian" and relegating his Indigeneity to "background," Scheer discursively undermined Métis nationhood by appropriating Riel as a Canadian hero.

Some six months later, in the wake of a polarizing federal election, on November 7, 2019, then-Manitoba Premier Brian Pallister, opining in *The Globe and Mail* on how Manitoba was a unifying force in Confederation, completely reversed the narrative of the Red River Resistance: "It's worth remembering," Pallister wrote, "that Manitobans actually staged a rebellion to join Canada." Aside from the astonishing and anachronistic claim that *Manitobans* rebelled (against whom, Pallister does not elaborate) to *join* Canada, it is worth noting how Pallister's historical inaccuracies and generalizations wholly elided the Métis and other Indigenous nations from the narrative, subsuming them into a settler-state identity.

In promulgating this narrative reversal only months ahead of Manitoba's sesquicentennial in 2020, Pallister exposed sites of "struggle." To the extent that his comments elided the complexities of Métis stories, histories, symbols, and representations in a narrative of Canadian nation-building, Pallister's comments not only showed ongoing colonial impulses (theft and erasure) but underscored the need for Métis narratives at the intersections of politics and literature.

Strategies of Discursive Resistance in Contemporary Métis Literature
As my brief account of Métis literature shows, there is a long history of "struggle...both political and literary" in Métis letters, and Métis literature has undoubtedly been shaped by its literary and political relationships with settlers. I do not suggest that the texts below are more "combative" than those mentioned earlier, nor is the selection exhaustive;[10] rather, what this section considers is how through the peeling of onion layers of historical narrative, utilizing strategies of discursive resistance, some recent Métis texts ironically push "beyond continuance." In other words, in asserting narrative authority over historic(al) Métis resistances, writers such as Scofield, Dumont, Vermette, and others,[11] are actively re-envisioning what Métis nationhood might become.

In contrast to albeit increasingly sympathetic English Canadian literary representations of Riel published since the 1990s, such as Chester Brown's *Louis Riel: A Comic-Strip Biography*, Scofield's collection of poetry *Louis: The Heretic Poems* is not simply another "Canadian text" on Riel. It is a critical rejoinder, a decidedly Indigenous renarrativization of an Indigenous story. Often focalized through its eponymous subject, Scofield's collection attempts to provide an intimate, humane, portrait of the historic Métis leader, to chronicle the dispossession of the Métis, and to meditate on settler-colonialism and historical Métis Resistances by locating Riel within broader Indigenous contexts. From the opening poem, which is written in the voice of Riel's paternal, great-grandmother, and purportedly "translated from Chipewyan to English" (13), Scofield situates Riel in the North-West. With poems portraying a young Riel reconciling his embodied desires with a deep and austere Catholicism, and suggesting how he experienced racism in Montreal, "Maybe I am too wild for afflictions / Sauvage! Sauvage!" (25), to imagining an angry Riel back in Red River, hurling expletives at John A. Macdonald, and weaving Cree into the Lord's Prayer, Scofield's text works to position Riel within Indigenous worldviews grounded in the traditions of the northern plains. In foregrounding such contexts by means of code-switching, and juxtaposing Métis and Cree leaders against Macdonald's looming, overarching antagonism and colonialism, Scofield largely de-emphasizes Riel's distinct French-Canadian-Métis nationalism and linguistic affinities, especially in comparison to the historical figure's own writings. The use of English and Cree in the Lord's Prayer appears at odds with the historical Riel's mostly French-language writings and seems to be an unlikely characterization. As Scofield limits the presence of French or French Michif to section titles and the occasional word throughout the collection, this choice resonates with the claim that Riel has been largely transformed into an "English-speaking [hero]" (Braz 198), although this resonance is tempered by the use of Cree. Nevertheless, this tends to de-emphasize or recentre the historical diversity and cultural heterogeneity at Red River, and across the homeland, away from francophone cultural contexts, and produces dissonance between Scofield's Riel and the historical Riel.[12] We may also apprehend in this dissonance the unfolding effects of settler-colonialism on the Métis—it is a contemporary representation of Riel mediated through a history of territorial dispossession, linguistic assimilation, and national ruptures. These cultural and linguistic elisions may serve as evidence of Métis losses over generations, as well as gesture to some of the ways contemporary Métis writers are reshaping historical and national narratives through the evocation of different myths and traditions than those articulated by historical Métis writers.

Reweaving a representation of Riel through allusion to complex and expansive kinships, Scofield recentres articulations of Métis belonging upon place and connection; "For the land is our Kingdom," he pens in his parody of the Lord's Prayer, "and the power of our children" (34). It is in the matter of land, rather than in language and religion, that Scofield's text resonates most closely with the historical Riel. "We are not birds," declared Riel in his address to the court in Regina, as if anticipating the large-scale dispossessions and fraud that would plague the Métis Scrip system, "We have to walk on the ground" (3: 547). Placed against Scheer's and Pallister's (politically) appropriative gestures, Scofield's text functions not only as an important counter tug in the symbolic struggle over Riel's narrative, but as an act of nationalist literary resistance, and it reminds readers that despite all that the Métis have lost—land, language, and so on—they still belong to specific cultural and territorial spaces.

Marilyn Dumont's *The Pemmican Eaters* performs similar work, but in a different way. Subtending historical events, people, and stories with the contemporary Métis Nation, her poems largely eschew narrativizing military engagements or political machinations as they touch upon the broader narratives of the North-West Resistance. The battles—at Duck Lake, Fish Creek, and Batoche—remain peripheral as Dumont contextualizes the resistance by culturally, linguistically, and geographically situating the Métis as a post-contact Indigenous people. Her collection embodies and presents "tenets [of Métis peoplehood]" with poems that invoke "kinship and relatedness, mobility, and geography" (Adese, "The New People" 61). In a suite of poems dwelling on "the brothers that fed and clothed us / and gave us reason to dance" (15), for instance, Dumont gestures to the economic, cultural, and spiritual significance of the bison, or "Li Bufloo" (11) in Michif. Employing evocative images of bison "pulling the universe in their sway" (10), cradling "buffalo rocks" (11), and describing "How to Make Pemmican" (12), Dumont illustrates shared significance among Plains Indigenous cultures such as the Pawnee, Blackfoot, and Métis, among others. In "These Are Wintering Words," a poem envisioning the birth of Michif, "la lawng of double genetic origin" (16), Dumont traces the emergence of the Métis's language through their winters of sharing "different tongues buffalo, a / delicacy source language right from the cow's mouth" (16), and suggests how bison nourished the Métis not only physically but culturally and linguistically. This all-encompassing significance strengthens the affective power of Dumont's lament over the bison's near-extinction, "gone, and now the prairie is mute" (15). While these poems gesture toward expansive kinship networks and relationships between human and non-human kin, it is in her suite of poems about beading that Dumont most explicitly collapses the borders and distinctions between the human and non-human. There, in the quiet, meditative practice of bead-work, a bead becomes a seed becomes a berry becomes a prayer. Juxtaposing meditative resonances of prayer and bead-working, "each bead-berry clasped / to the next in prayer / Miyo Saint Anne—" (33), with the act of creation, where "her sisters, the flowers / her brothers, the berries / emerge from the beadwork" (39), Dumont draws attention to the multiple resonances of beads (from the spirituality of rosaries, to the pregnant, life-giving roundness of Saskatoon berries), and underscores the centrality of women in Métis culture. Touching upon a wide range of subjects from bison, beadworking, material culture, jigging, and fiddling, these poems become a rhizomatic exploration of Métis history and culture that follows not a single narrative thread but instead weaves together multiple perspectives to broadly represent the breadth and diversity of the Métis Nation as it chronicles its emergence, "neither Cree, Salteaux nor French exactly, but something else / not less not half not lacking" (16). That is, Dumont's focus on cultural representation resonates with an ethnosymbolic re-evocation of the myths and traditions of nineteenth-century Métis, fleshing out that which has been frequently overlooked or forgotten in older (and mostly settler-colonial) retellings of the resistances.

Poems recounting Gabriel Dumont's flight south to the United States after the military defeat at Batoche (23–26, 50), reflecting on Métis dispossession in the Edmonton area (43–45), as well as addressing a long-dead Macdonald (9), also increase the geographic and temporal scope of the collection. Much like how Scofield's text serves as an assertion of presence and gestures toward ongoing struggles, Dumont's text unequivocally declares:

Dear John: I'm still here
and halfbreed,
after all these years (9)

Recalling Casanova's notion of "direct literary rivalry," we might also argue that Dumont's text demonstrates how Métis literature comes to be shaped by its relationship with settler literatures. The form and content of the poem "To a Fair Country" (52–53), for instance, alludes to, as well as rebuts, Canadian novelist and public thinker John Ralston Saul's *A Fair Country* (2008). In his book, Saul uses the concept of "métissage" to theorize and recast Canada as a "métis" nation, but to do so, elides the actual Métis Nation. In its implicit rationalization of the dispossession and dissolution of Métis nationhood, Saul's book reveals a link between "literature and politics" (Casanova 132) as it perpetuates Indigenous erasures. In Dumont's poetic and ironic response, Canada is not shown to be a fair country at all, but rather is unmasked, through a stark litany of its "fraud and forgery" (53), as a settler-colonial power that by way of scrip fraud dispossessed the Métis of land: "Less than one percent," writes Dumont, "hold property from that scrip today" (53).

Katherena Vermette's young-adult graphic novel series *A Girl Called Echo* delivers yet another approach. Through sparse prose, Vermette's work offers a brief glimpse of key events in Métis history. In this series, the protagonist, Echo, a young present-day Métis woman, navigating her way through high school and the dynamics of her fractured family, is cast back in time to witness these events. In the first volume, *Pemmican Wars*, Echo comes across a group of Métis bison hunters on the plains near the Qu'Appelle Valley as they contend with the growing conflict between the North-West and Hudson's Bay companies. Befriending a young woman named Marie, Echo participates in the camp life of Métis bison hunters (20–29), before the broader conflict culminates in the Battle of Seven Oaks, in 1816 (33–36), when Métis hunters largely aligned or employed by the North-West Company confronted a group of Selkirk settlers and Hudson's Bay Company clerks, just north of present-day downtown Winnipeg. As discussed earlier, this confrontation marked a key point in a then-emerging Métis nationalism.

Vermette's second and third volumes, *Red River Resistance* and *Northwest Resistance*, respectively explore the events of 1869–1870, when the Métis of Red River formed a provisional government to negotiate the terms of Manitoba's entry into Confederation following Canada's purchase of the North-West, and the events of 1885, when driven by Canada's deaf ear to their repeated petitions, and under Riel's visionary leadership, the Métis of the Batoche area took up arms to defend their land. In the second volume, Echo is once again cast back in time, befriends a young man, Benjamin, in Red River, and witnesses the activities of the Métis-led provisional government, the trial and execution of Thomas Scott, as well as the arrival of Canadian troops under General Garnet Wolseley and their incipient reign of terror, all in between moments of her life as a contemporary high-schooler. In the third volume, Echo is drawn to Batoche and meets a now older Benjamin, befriends his teenaged daughter, Josephine, and again witnesses important moments in Métis national history: Echo weeps over the bodies of Métis dead after the Battle of Duck Lake (23); learns, in her high school history class, about Cree chiefs Big Bear and Poundmaker, and Cree participation in the broader resistance (25–29); returns to Batoche, and takes part in its defence even as Canadian soldiers overwhelm the Métis in their final assault (36–38); and lastly glimpses the Métis's utter dispossession. "Where do we go now?" Josephine asks her father, Benjamin, "We have no home, we have no land, no treaty" (41). This great sense of loss and even national dissolution is made visible in a series of three panels in which the town of Batoche literally dissolves and vanishes around a weeping Echo (42). In the fourth volume, *Road Allowance Era*, Vermette does not narrativize the nineteenth-century armed resistances as much as illustrate their consequences on twentieth-century Métis communities by tracing effects like territorial dispossession from 1885 onward. Vermette dwells on the dissolution of particular communities, such as Ste. Madeleine (Manitoba) and Rooster Town (edge of Winnipeg).

Whether or not Echo is physically transported back in time, dreams, reimagines the events, or has visions of the actual past—perhaps alluding to Riel's visions and prophecies—is not clear; regardless of how these shifts occur, Echo becomes not only a witness to history, but as her name suggests, a testimony to its occurrence. Vermette renders this witnessing of history personal and explicit with a subplot of kinship mending as Echo visits her seemingly estranged mother and begins to tentatively speak about their heritage. In the third volume, Echo's mother offers Echo their "genealogy chart" (43), revealing ancestors eight generations back, including the familiar names of Marie, Benjamin, and Josephine. Through her growing and complex knowledge of Métis history, Echo demonstrates how the repercussions of historical struggles, dispossession, and settler-colonialism continue to affect the Métis, but further demonstrates how these repercussions are also personal and familial—the story of the Métis Nation is rooted in the kinship of its people. The mirroring of her growing historical knowledge, and the reweaving of family histories, within the arc of her emotional development suggests an emergent confidence and empowerment—a coalescing sense of being, place, and belonging—that allegorically represents the nation itself. This sense of belonging evokes a sentiment similar to that expressed in Riel's "La Métisse," which opens with the declaration "I am Métis and I am proud / To belong to this Nation" (4: 88).[13] Echo's sense of pride, amour propre, or self-respect comes—through the strengthening of kinship, culture, and historical awareness—to re-establish the foundation upon which both the self and the nation might flourish.

The "Combativeness" of Métis National Literature

This collective renarrativization of Métis history and culture resonates profoundly with Casanova's concept of "combative literatures." Scofield's re-storying of Riel's life as well as his resituating of Riel within Indigenous contexts, Dumont's recontextualization of the North-West Resistance and attention to women's centrality in Métis culture, and Vermette's account of Métis resistances through the multigenerational experiences of one family not only reveal a collective heritage of culture and memories but assert and demand "recognition of a collective existence" (Casanova 126). Although Dumont's poetic response to Saul seems to evidence "direct literary rivalry" between Métis literary works and English Canadian settler-texts, it more importantly suggests a deeper discursive resistance as Métis writers reclaim their stories. Rephrasing Ernest Renan's claim of the centrality of forgetting in nation-building, in light of settler-colonialism's long history of Eurocentrism and forced assimilation, might we ask what must be remembered to rebuild a nation? "Rivalry is structural" (129), Casanova reminds us, and these texts provide a small glimpse of the immense structural inequalities between Métis and settler literatures: such as the differences of scale separating these literary spaces in terms of production, publication, dissemination, and so on, as well as with respect to settler-colonial control of broader discourses and assimilative structures. Thus, what is remembered, what is emphasized, even what is forgotten, in this reclamation of narrative authority are shaped by these structural inequalities. While some aspects of Métis history are elided or de-emphasized in Métis texts, such as conflict with other Indigenous nations, or linguistic and religious tensions within communities, what are emphasized are historical and cultural aspects that root the Métis in the North-West. That is,

Métis literary nationalism sheds light on processes of cultural recovery as well as national reconstruction, but it is a cultural recovery shaped in its response by more than a century of Eurocentrism and settler-colonialism that sought to erase the Métis and their indigeneity.

What these brief readings of Métis texts reveal perhaps above all is that reclaiming narrative authority over Métis histories is not only a matter of national identity or definition but using Casanova's term again, a matter of "national existence" (129). Métis literature's combative gestures are about reclaiming narrative authority, asserting contemporary Métis presence, and as previously suggested, envisioning what Métis nationhood might become; and it is in the myriad ways that Métis writers re-story the past that they rebuild and reshape the nation. One such way foregrounds Métis-specific epistemologies. Marilyn Dumont demonstrates this by interweaving the Cree Métis concept of *wahkohtowin* in *The Pemmican Eaters*. *Wahkohtowin* is, as Métis historian Brenda Macdougall defines it, a "sense of relatedness with all beings, human and non-human, living and dead, physical and spiritual" (3); it situates individuals in a complex web of relations and kin, and "conveys an idea about the virtues that an individual should personify...such as reciprocity, mutual support, decency, and order" (8). Tracing and underscoring this concept's significance through an examination of select Métis life narratives, Adese contends that such knowledges "call us home to remember that our relationships to our ecosystems must be at the core of contemporary expressions of Métis nationhood" ("Spirit Gifting" 51). In Dumont's text, *wahkohtowin* links historical nationalist narratives with people and places, with human and non-human kin. The evocation of kinship between Gabriel Dumont and the bison in the poem "Notre Frères" (10), for example, and the blurring of borders between the human and non-human in the beads poems, where "through tiny seed beads / she is linked / to lineage" (40), illustrate vibrant recognitions of expansive kinships. For Adese, *wahkohtowin* allows Métis literature to be reclaimed as a "vital expression of Métis peoplehood" (64). The renarrativization of Métis history alongside *wahkohtowin* presents not only an opportunity to assert continued presence and affirm "national existence" through traditional ways of knowing, but to reweave a national tapestry, that web of relations that has been frayed, torn, broken, or otherwise damaged.

Ultimately, this chapter echoes calls by Métis scholars such as LaRocque to consider and include "meanings of nationalism" (143), and Adese to "take [the] tenets of Métis peoplehood into account" ("The New People" 59) in the study of Métis literature. It is through such historically informed methods that we better apprehend how contemporary writers are immersed in collective "struggles for recognition" (Casanova 133), in discursive resistance, and in the re-storying of personal, community, and national histories that revisions a national literary space. Moreover, it is by such methods that we might better discern similarities and divergences from historical Métis literature, ponder shifting articulations of national identity, from ethnosymbolic re-evocations of different myths and traditions, to shifts in linguistic identity and expression and reaffirmations of Indigenous relations, and better contemplate how such "struggles" affect, and perhaps even reshape other national (Indigenous and settler) literatures and imaginaries in Canada. While Métis national literature may complicate classical definitions of nationhood and nationalism, blurring lines between "imagined" and "ethnic" communities, its rearticulations of Métis narratives also challenge historically dominant settler narratives. This not only destabilizes the narratives and myths upon which Canada is founded but serves to illuminate present cultural, political, and material considerations related to constitutional recognitions, legal decisions, issues of land, sovereignty, and possible restitutions between the Canadian state and the Métis Nation. With respect to literary relations, a renewed attention to Métis national narratives could lead to increased space for Métis authors and more nuanced considerations of the past and present by non-Métis writers. Borrowing Casanova's framework to trace Métis literature's "combative" gestures, this chapter has demonstrated how, in wresting authority over narratives of historical events, contemporary Métis writers are forging a national literature and helping reinvigorate a national Métis space.

NOTES

1. "[L]a Victoire que nous avons gagnée" (Falcon 10); "Qui sont ici pour piller notre Pays" (10). Unless otherwise noted, all translations are mine.
2. "[À] cette nation" (Riel 4: 88).

3. A road allowance is land "set aside for roads...[and] not normally used for any other purpose" (Shore 107).
4. See Gaudry and Leroux for examples of settler self-Indigenization, and its implications for the Métis Nation.
5. "Un Comité Historique fut formé pour lutter, rétablir l'histoire, saisir toutes les occasions de répondre à ceux qui attaquaient les Métis, et en un mot pour imposer le respect de la vérité" (Comité Historique 17).
6. "[L]a lutte contre les ennemis de la première heure" (Courchaine-Goulet qtd. in Juéry 33).
7. "[H]onorons les nôtres comme ils le méritent" (Courchaine-Goulet qtd. in Juéry 34).
8. Goulet-Courchaine's grandfather, Élzéar Goulet, was murdered in September 1870 by members of the Red River Expeditionary Force, when volunteer soldiers from Canada hurled stones at him as he tried to swim across the Red River, from Winnipeg to Saint-Boniface. Goulet drowned after being struck by the stones (Teillet 245).
9. Questions of race and belonging recur in the works of Métis writers from the late twentieth to early twenty-first centuries. See LaRocque's "Contemporary Metis Literature" (2016) for a brief survey of Métis literary production in the 1990s and early 2000s. LaRocque does not look much beyond 2010 but recognizes that "much remains to be explored" (143).
10. The recent growth of Métis poetry, fiction, and non-fiction presents a wealth of texts; I focus on texts that directly take up narratives of nineteenth-century Métis national Resistances.
11. Rita Bouvier's collection of poems *papîyâhtak* (2004) juxtaposes contemporary experiences with brief reflections on Gabriel Dumont and the North-West Resistance; Maia Caron's novel, *Song of Batoche* (2017), explores women's experiences through the resistance, and its narrative arc culminates with the Battle of Batoche.
12. See my article "Reading Scofield through Riel: *Louis: The Heretic Poems* as Dissonance" for a deeper consideration of the cultural and linguistic dissonances produced by Scofield's representation of Riel.
13. "Je suis métisse et je suis orgueilleuse / D'appartenir à cette nation" (Riel 4: 88).

WORKS CITED

Adese, Jennifer. "The New People: Reading for Peoplehood in Métis Literatures." *Studies in American Indian Literatures*, vol. 28, no. 4, 2016, pp. 53–79. Project MUSE, http://muse.jhu.edu/article/649878.

———. "Spirit Gifting: Ecological Knowing in Métis Life Narratives." *Decolonization: Indigeneity, Education & Society*, vol. 3, no. 3, 2014, pp. 48–66, https://jps.library.utoronto.ca/index.php/des/article/view/22191/18005.

Andersen, Chris. *"Métis": Race, Recognition, and the Struggle for Indigenous Peoplehood*. UBC Press, 2014.

Bouvier, Rita. *papîyâhtak*. Thistledown Press, 2004.

Braz, Albert. *The False Traitor: Louis Riel in Canadian Culture*. University of Toronto Press, 2003.

Campbell, Maria. *Halfbreed*. Goodreads Biographies, 1973.

Caron, Maia. *Song of Batoche*. Ronsdale Press, 2017.

Casanova, Pascale. "Combative Literatures." *New Left Review*, no. 72, 2011, pp. 123–34, https://newleftreview.org/issues/II72/articles/pascale-casanova-combative-literatures.

Chartrand, Paul. *Pierriche Falcon, the Michif Rhymester: Our Métis National Anthem: The Michif Version*. Gabriel Dumont Institute, 2009.

Comité Historique. Avertissement. *Histoire de la nation métisse dans l'Ouest canadien*, by A.-H. de Trémaudan. Éditions Albert Lévesque, 1935, pp. 15–28.

Dumont, Marilyn. *The Pemmican Eaters*. ECW Press, 2015.

Ens, Gerhard, and Joe Sawchuk. *From New Peoples to New Nations: Aspects of Métis History and Identity from the Eighteenth to the Twenty-First Centuries*. University of Toronto Press, 2016.

Falcon, Pierre. "La Chanson de la Grenouillère." *Pierriche Falcon, the Michif Rhymester: Our Métis National Anthem: The Michif Version*, edited by Paul Chartrand, Gabriel Dumont Institute, 2009, pp. 10–12.

Gaudry, Adam, and Darryl Leroux. "White Settler Revisionism and Making Métis Everywhere: The Evocation of Métissage in Quebec and Nova Scotia." *Critical Ethnic Studies*, vol. 3, no. 1, 2017, pp. 116–42. JSTOR, http://www.jstor.org/stable/10.5749/jcritethnstud.3.1.0116.

Gingell, Susan. "Lips' Inking: Cree and Cree-Métis Authors' Writings of the Oral and What They Might Tell Educators." *Canadian Journal of Native Education*, vol. 32, 2010, pp. 35–61, https://www.academia.edu/392468/Lips_Inking_Cree_and_Cree_Metis_Authors_Writing_of_the_Oral_and_What_They_Might_Tell_Educators.

Goulet-Courchaine, Marie-Thérèse. "Un centenaire, c'est quoi?" *Manie Tobie: Femme du Manitoba*, edited by René Juéry, Les Éditions des Plaines, 1979, pp. 33–34.

Juéry, René. *Manie Tobie: Femme du Manitoba*. Les Éditions des Plaines, 1979.

LaRocque, Emma. "Contemporary Metis Literature: Resistance, Roots, Innovation." *The Oxford Handbook of Canadian Literature*, edited by Cynthia Sugars, Oxford University Press, 2016, pp. 129–49.

Léveillé, J.R., ed. *Anthologie de la poésie franco-manitobaine*. Les Éditions du Blé, 1990.

Macdougall, Brenda. *One of the Family: Metis Culture in Nineteenth-Century Northwestern Saskatchewan*. UBC Press, 2010.

MacKinnon, Doris Jeanne. *The Identities of Marie Rose Delorme Smith: Portrait of a Métis Woman, 1861–1960*. Canadian Plains Research Center Press, 2012.

McKegney, Sam. "Beyond Continuance: Criticisms of Indigenous Literatures in Canada." *The Oxford Handbook of Indigenous American Literature*, edited by James H. Cox and Daniel Heath Justice, Oxford University Press, 2014, pp. 409–26.

Pallister, Brian. "Some Friendly Advice from Manitoba on Fixing Western Discontent and Healing Canada's Divisions." *The Globe and Mail*, 7 Nov. 2019, www.theglobeandmail.com/business/commentary/article-some-friendly-advice-from-manitoba-on-fixing-western-discontent-and/.

Payment, Diane. *The Free People / Li Gens Libres: A History of the Métis Community of Batoche, Saskatchewan*. University of Calgary Press, 2009.

Riel, Louis. *The Collected Writings of Louis Riel / Les écrits complets de Louis Riel*, vol. 1–4. Edited by George F.G. Stanley et al., University of Alberta Press, 1985.

Saul, John Ralston. *A Fair Country: Telling Truths about Canada*. Viking, 2008.

Scheer, Andrew. "Happy Louis Riel Day! As a Canadian politician of Métis background, Louis Riel was the driving force behind the creation of Manitoba as a new Canadian province. Today, Manitobans will honour his life's work and pause to reflect on the province's proud history." *Twitter*, 18 Feb. 2019, 7:15 a.m., http://twitter.com/andrewscheer/status/1097499728219172865.

Scofield, Gregory. *Louis: The Heretic Poems*. Nightwood Editions, in collaboration with Gabriel Dumont Institute, 2011.

Shore, Fred J. *Threads in the Sash: The Story of the Métis People*. Pemmican Publications, 2017.

Sing, Pamela. "Intersections of Memory, Ancestral Language, and Imagination or the Textual Production of Michif Voices as Cultural Weaponry." *For the Love of Words: Aboriginal Writers of Canada*, special issue of *Studies in Canadian Literature / Études en littérature canadienne*, vol. 31, no. 1, 2006, pp. 95–115, http://journals.lib.unb.ca/index.php/SCL/article/view/10202/10553.

Smith, Marie Rose. "Eight Years on the Plains: Part 4." *Canadian Cattlemen*, vol. 12, no. 1, 1949, pp. 212–25, www.canadiancattlemen.ca/history/eighty-years-on-the-plains-part-4/.

Teillet, Jean. *The North-West Is Our Mother: The Story of Louis Riel's People, The Métis Nation*. Harper Collins Publishers, 2019.

Tétreault, Matthew. "Reading Scofield through Riel: *Louis: The Heretic Poems* as Dissonance." *Studies in Canadian Literature / Études en littérature canadienne*, vol. 45, no. 1, 2020.

Vermette, Katherena. *Pemmican Wars: A Girl Called Echo*, vol. 1. Illustrated by Scott B. Henderson. Coloured by Donovan Yaciuk. Highwater Press, 2017.

——. *Red River Resistance: A Girl Called Echo*, vol. 2. Illustrated by Scott B. Henderson. Coloured by Donovan Yaciuk. Highwater Press, 2018.

——. *Northwest Resistance: A Girl Called Echo*, vol. 3. Illustrated by Scott B. Henderson. Coloured by Donovan Yaciuk. Highwater Press, 2020.

——. *Road Allowance Era: A Girl Called Echo*, vol. 4. Illustrated by Scott B. Henderson. Coloured by Donovan Yaciuk. Highwater Press, 2021.

Welsh, Joe. *Jackrabbit Street*. Thistledown Press, 2003.

Woods, Eric. "Beyond Multination Federalism: Reflections on Nations and Nationalism in Canada." *Ethnicities*, vol. 13, no. 3, 2012, pp. 270–92. *JSTOR*, https://www.jstor.org/stable/43572650.

Intersections of Nationhood, Multiculturalism, and Globalization in South Asian Canadian Fiction

A Study of Anita Rau Badami's Can You Hear the Nightbird Call?

SaBUJKOLI BanDOPaDHYaY

THE TWENTIETH CENTURY witnessed successive waves of human migration prompted by military conflict, globalizing economies, and ecological transformations. Among other effects, these transfers of human populations have led to a reassessment of traditional theories of citizenship and to the development of new models of identity that include transnational and postnational frameworks of national belonging (Bloemraad 389). The concept of the postnational has often been affiliated with the "global civil society" or a form of "multinational corporate constitution" that operates beyond the national boundaries. In the context of the European Union, postnationalism has been related to the idea of "an end of the nation state," which brings the "great universalist project of modernity to a fitting conclusion" (Balibar 13). Throughout this chapter, the term *postnationalism* is used as an autonomous and counter-hegemonic form of collective belonging and existence. As Nivedita Menon

65

has pointed out, postnational politics and identity operate in both explicit and subversive ways to find alternatives to nationalism and politics of exclusion.

The mass scale transfer and displacement of population groups, especially those from non-European provenances to the countries of the Global North, influenced the host nations to adopt policies for managing the demographic changes occasioned by the inclusion of diverse bodies of immigrants. In the same process, migrants themselves have seen their collective senses of belonging and national affiliation altered as they transition from their "home" countries to arrival in their "host" countries. In the second half of the twentieth century, various postcolonial countries developed variants of multiculturalist policies in an effort to manage diversity while integrating minority populations by allowing multiple national cultures to coexist within the pre-existing cultural framework of the new host country. Many new immigrants in multinational nation-states "wish to cling to their civil-political identity without shedding or tampering their specific cultural identity and the notions of ancestral 'homeland'" (Nanda 25). By the 1960s, most multinational postcolonial states had begun "to shift their self-definitions from 'ethnic' to 'civic' criterion" (Kauffmann 1). Debates on the efficacy of multiculturalism policies continue to be relevant in current discourses of citizenship; prominent multiculturalism theorist Will Kymlicka argues that "in the context of multination states, these new citizenship agendas must promote a distinctly multinational conception of citizenship if they are to be fair and effective" (282).

The efficacy of multiculturalism and the multinational concept of citizenship has been probed and highlighted in South Asian Canadian literature since its establishment as an academic field of inquiry in the 1980s. Early examples of systemic engagement with South Asian Canadian literature primarily involved anthologies and surveys that established the "South Asian Canadian" subject, what Miriam Pirbhai has referred to as "a productive marker of socio-religious and ethnocultural affinities." Pirbhai has also indicated how this construct may also be viewed as "a multiculturalist invention, shaped for the experience of a nation attempting to accommodate a vast and unruly influx of new immigrants connected to an equally vast and unruly place, the Indian subcontinent" (9). As a result of this confluence of population transfer and of its conceptualization as a sociological category, the questions of migration and national belonging have become intertwined elements of South Asian Canadian literature. This chapter draws attention to the lived experience of the conception of "multinational citizenship" by focusing on Anita Rau Badami's *Can You Hear the Nightbird Call?*, a South Asian Canadian novel that illustrates how national affiliations and citizenship identities are constructed under conditions of displacement, globalization, and multiculturalism.

Badami, who immigrated to Canada from India to pursue an MA in English at the University of Calgary, is part of the "new" Indian diaspora that arrived in Canada during the mid- to late twentieth century as a group of immigrants (the "new" Indian diaspora) marked by the "overriding characteristic...of mobility" (Mishra, "Diasporic Imaginary" 422). Badami's MA thesis, which was published in 1996 as *Tamarind Mem*, was her first published work in Canada. She subsequently published *The Hero's Walk*, which was awarded the Regional Commonwealth Prize in 2001. Badami's novels continue to engage with the social and psychological constructs of home within regional, national, and transnational contexts. Her third novel, published in 2006, *Can You Hear the Nightbird Call?* asks its readers to reflect on colonial history and postcolonial politics in an effort to understand the hyphenated cultures and politics of the South Asian Canadian communities. Tracing the regional displacement and transnational migrations of South Asians during the British Empire and the postcolonial era, Badami's novel urges its readers to develop a sense of critical engagement with the social and cultural history of migration to address its effects in the lives of immigrants in such pluricultural democracies as Canada and India. The fictional text frames the connection between India and Canada through two major historical events involving the transportation of people from South Asia to Canada: the first is the 1914 journey of the Japanese passenger ship *Komagata Maru*, which carried subcontinental men across the Pacific but which was refused landing and disembarkation in Vancouver, while the second is that of Air India flight 182, which was blown up in mid-air over the Atlantic in 1985, resulting in 328 deaths. In between the two catastrophes, the narrative witnesses the independence and partition of India in 1947, the resulting communal violence, Operation Blue Star in 1984, the assassination of the Indian Prime Minister Indira Gandhi, also in 1984, and the subsequent anti-Sikh riots; in contrast to the attention accorded to historical events of the Indian subcontinent, the narrative maintains a curious distance and estrangement from Canadian politics and mainstream culture. This unwillingness of the diasporic community to engage with the civil and political lives of mainstream Canada can be attributed to the pre-existing dynamics of asymmetric power relations between the formerly colonized and their perception of mainstream Canada as an extension of their former colonizers. The historical antagonism of the colonizer-colonized relationship (perceived through a racial axis) is further accentuated by everyday experiences of systemic racism in the settler nation, which contributes to the segregation between the dominant Anglo-European settler populations and the immigrant communities of colour.

The turbulent relationship, both material and affective, between the citizen-subject and their nationhood offers the forward momentum in Badami's novel. While *Can You Hear the Nightbird Call?* can be compared to works like Salman Rushdie's *Midnight's Children* in reflecting on the relationship between the postcolonial subject and their national identity, Badami's novel is distinct in emphasizing the materiality of relationships that connect the citizen-subject with the nation as well as with their fellow citizens. This study focuses on the concrete movements of peoples, products, and information in the novel to demonstrate how a sense of postcolonial citizen-subjectivity and national identity are informed by the movements initiated and controlled by globalization and multiculturalism. Due to the scope and construction of *Can You Hear the Nightbird Call?*, with its appeal to historical events of national importance, its deployment of a multigeneration trajectory of family and social development and its cast of socially and ethnically representative characters, Badami's novel might seem apposite for the type of allegorical reading of the nation famously suggested by Fredric Jameson. Jameson's efforts to "allegorize" and "reduce" all third-world cultural productions "into a mimetic epistemology that throws into flattering relief the sophisticated and nuanced deprecation" (Dayal 117) have not been without controversy. Rather than follow this approach, however, this chapter focuses on how Badami contributes to an understanding of the postcolonial condition in relation to the citizen-subject for her twenty-first-century audience. This historicist and materialist reading situates *Can You Hear the Nightbird Call?* within a trajectory of globalization that shapes the citizen-subjectivities of South Asian women in the twenty-first century. As will be suggested, Badami's novel is not directed toward the representation of a specific nation and homogeneous national identity in the sense suggested by Jameson, but in the problematization of the very concept of national identity.

Can You Hear the Nightbird Call? revolves around the intersecting lives of the three female protagonists—Sharanjeet Kaur, Leela Bhat, and Nirmaljeet Kaur—whose narratives are refracted through the violence of Indian partition and the anti-Sikh riots of 1984, and who ultimately disperse in different directions in the aftermath of the flight bombing of 1985. Through each of these protagonists' life journey, the novel explores how South Asian women and their diasporic counterparts in Canada participate in a process of negotiation between multiple competing ethnic and/or national identities. This chapter documents how the internal and transnational migration of people from the imperial to the global era has contributed to hybridized and heterogenous cultures for the subcontinental communities whose national identities have been simultaneously fragmented through dislocations and multiplied through hyphenations. The novel depicts the identities and actions of individuals experiencing multiple nationhood in globalized democracies by presenting three possible outcomes of belonging: affiliation to two or more national-cultural spaces; belonging to or prioritizing one national cultural identity over multiple contenders; and finally, loosing access to any available national cultural identity. Badami's novel explores the struggle of the hyphenated and hybridized identities of the characters using the metaphors of the frog and Trishanku (a mythic Hindu king suspended in a liminal space between heaven and earth). While the amphibian metaphor shows how individuals and communities can survive in two or more national and cultural environments, through metaphoric reference to Trishanku, the novel also represents a state of existence for hybridized identities where an individual is stuck perpetually in a world of in-betweenness, thus belonging to neither environment. Vijay Mishra writes, "Diasporas refer to people who do not feel comfortable with their non-hyphenated identities as indicated on their passport" (*Literature of the Indian Diaspora* 1), and Badami's fictional characters constantly yearn to exist as an amphibian expressed through the frog metaphor while struggling in an in-between space like that of the King Trishanku. It is worth mentioning here that the term *diaspora*, derived from Greek etymology, had a positive connotation in its earliest renderings in Hellenic traditions (Cohen 507), though the term subsequently acquired a negative implication as diaspora came to represent a state of victimhood through its association with the Judaic tradition and history.

The historical shadow of the ill-fated *Komagata Maru* passengers looms over the novel's fictional space and offers the backstory for the central protagonist, Sharanjeet Kaur, who inherits her father's dreams of starting a new life in Canada. A narrative connection between Punjab and Vancouver is traced through Harjot Singh, Sharanjeet's father. Harjot was born in colonial Punjab and his life was shaped by the British colonial policies in Punjab and the empire's racist laws abroad. The British government collected revenue from Punjab within a Mahalwari system where entire bodies of villagers were jointly and separately responsible for the revenue extraction of the entire village (Hussain and Sarwar 19). British Punjab was transformed into an agrarian heaven and British interest in cash crops, including wheat, tobacco, sugarcane, and cotton, for their profitability in the global market replaced the traditional crops (Talbot 5). As the prices and wages became dependent on the global market, smallholders and landless peasants, who relied on labour-intensive means of cultivation, were most negatively affected. Although per capita crop production increased by 45 per cent between 1891 and 1921 (Talbot 5), smallholders were forced to incur exceeding amounts of debts. As the British government and its policies discouraged investing in industrializing Punjab, the debt-ridden farmers had very limited access to alternative occupations. Out of desperation and economic insecurities, which were by-products of the British colonial policies, Punjab provided a steady supply of men for the British military despite the racism and poor wages. The province also witnessed an emigration of labour destined for other British colonies during this period, and the earliest settlements of Sikh immigrants in Canada were an outcome of these British economic policies.

Debt-ridden and desperate to find economic security, Harjot departs for Hong Kong to work as a security guard and subsequently boards the *Komagata Maru* to sail to Vancouver in search of new opportunities. Despite their status as British subjects, subcontinental individuals seeking economic opportunities lacked free mobility, being controlled and denied entry into Canada through the "continuous journey addendum" of the Canadian Immigration Act in 1908. As there were no continuous routes for arrival at a Canadian port from India, the policy was effective in denying these migrants access to the land, resources, and infrastructure of the far shores of the British Empire, which had relied on the subcontinental colony for much of its wealth. Furthermore, all subcontinental immigrants were required to produce two hundred dollars upon arrival in Canada, which worked as a further deterrent. As the modern nation-state of Canada was settled by largely European migrants, institutionalized discrimination against immigration from regions of Asia was prevalent and was administered through Canada's immigration policies. Despite knowledge of the challenges and discouraging prospects, Harjot, a fictional passenger, boarded the *Komagata Maru*, which embarked on a voyage to reach Vancouver. Historical documents indicate that the ship started with 150 passengers in Hong Kong and subsequently recruited more passengers, ultimately boarding 376 people as the voyage progressed via the ports of Shanghai, Moji, and Yokohama. In reality, the ship itself was never allowed to dock in Vancouver, while only 20 returnees were allowed to land in Vancouver; ultimately, after a month-long standoff, the case was presented to the court, and the judge ruled in favour of the government's decision to deny entry to the travellers. With their dreams crushed, the passengers embarked on their return journey, only to experience another altercation, this time with British colonial officials, when their ship arrived in the port city of Kolkata, in eastern India. The passengers were ordered to board a special train destined for Punjab and denied permission to stay in the city of Kolkata. The British officials shot and killed twenty passengers and jailed many for attempting to resist the instructions and to escape (Johnston n.p.). Within the narrative space, Harjot never recovered from the trauma resulting from the *Komagata Maru* incident. Unable to operate within the economy and culture of imperialism, Harjot retreats into his psychological world upon his return to India; he confines himself to the string cot and eventually disappears, carrying the burden of the abject rejection of his being. As economic opportunities and mobility were denied to the subcontinental subjects in the historical period under consideration, the narrative cannot allow Harjot to exist in an in-between place as a diasporic individual whose identity and culture float across territories and borders between India and Canada. His disappearance indicates the denial of the possibility of dual or multinational identities for subcontinental subjects in the early decades of the twentieth century.

The repressive economic policies of the British in Punjab and the racist immigration policies of Canada determined the conditions under which Harjot's daughter, Sharanjeet, experiences her childhood. As producers of cash crops for the global market, Sharanjeet and her family are dependent upon imperialist globalization, and the debt-ridden family's economic struggle is an outcome of a happy marriage between the imperial economy and global markets. Though the consumer products were circulated across the globe through improved ocean transport, the mobility of the racialized people of the colonies was tightly controlled to ensure optimum opportunities for Anglo-European settlers (Thomas and Thompson 146). The timeline of Harjot's struggles and failed attempt to achieve opportunities through globalization's induced mobility coincides with the era of high imperialism, which was founded on the labour and resources of the colonies and lasted from late nineteenth century to the Second World War. During this time, the British Empire expanded its territorial horizons, which can be traced as the first phase of modern globalization.

The subsequent or second phase of modern globalization coincides with the end of the Second World War and the communal violence that preceded and followed the birth of the modern South Asian nations of India and Pakistan, which is depicted within the narrative space through the mobility of Sharanjeet. After the disappearance of Harjot, Sharanjeet and her elder sister, Kanwar, are brought up by their mother and eventually both sisters are married off; Sharanjeet's beauty allowed her to steal the groom who had already settled in Canada and who was originally arranged for Kanwar. Sharanjeet had to stay back in India to await her immigration to be processed while her husband returned to Canada. On the other hand, Kanwar, who is married off to a widower farmer with two young children, has a happy marriage and gives birth to a daughter, Nirmaljeet, or Nimmo. Sharanjeet maintains a close relationship with her sister and her new family until she moves away to prepare for her relocation to Vancouver to join her husband, Kushawant Singh. After years of delay caused by the war, Sharanjeet is finally reunited with her husband in 1946, which marks a new trend in the era of globalization after the Second World War that allowed for new opportunities for racialized immigrants whose mobility was previously denied. This period of postcolonial globalization in the narrative space represents the emergence of a nascent South Asian Canadian sense of dual nationhood, which would ultimately dissolve into an exclusive Sikh nationalism for Sharanjeet. Upon her arrival and settlement in Vancouver, Sharanjeet discovers a white settler society within which a distinct subculture of homeland has been carved out by members of the Indian diaspora. Her husband, Kushawant's early encounter with white Canadian society influences him to develop an antagonistic nationalist affiliation with the mainstream; as a result, he cultivates a racialized identity within the ethos of heroic, patriotic, Sikh narratives from the homeland. Kushawant falls within the category of the "old" diaspora that grappled with the new questions of belonging in the aftermath of the Indian independence that initiated a process of rebranding individuals like him as members of newly formed nations of India and Pakistan, which were erstwhile parts of the British Empire (Chatterji 311). The Sikh religion, Indian colonial history, and their Canadian passports provide three different aspects of their national consciousness, a postnational identity that functions well until the appearance of Dr. Raghubir Randhawa, the ideologue of the Khalistan movement.

The second phase of modern globalization, which allowed Sharanjeet to move to Canada, coincided with the mass displacement of people in the aftermath of Indian independence in 1947. The idea of modern nationalism in the subcontinental context is intertwined with the experience of European colonialism. In a paradoxical way, the ideology was appropriated and utilized by the colonized to achieve political autonomy, self-determination, and eventual independence from British rule in 1947. But the very birth of the nations of India and Pakistan was ridden with the unprecedented violence of the religious nationalism that claimed the lives of approximately half a million people in the border state of Punjab (Aiyar 13), the geopolitical epicentre of Badami's narrative. The partition of 1947 leaves Nirmaljeet, Sharanjeet's niece, orphaned as her pregnant mother commits suicide after being raped; her two elder brothers and their father are presumed to have been killed in the violence (Badami 154–56). The correspondence between Sharanjeet and her sister Kanwar provides glimpses of anxiety and confusion about the impending partition that the border provinces were caught in. The narrative does not provide a detailed eyewitness account of the lived experience of the violence. Rather, Nirmaljeet's childhood trauma is depicted in the form of fragmentary sketches that recount a five-year-old orphan's memories of a journey with a caravan of dislocated people whose lives were caught between the imperial policies and the national borders. Nirmaljeet, the five-year-old girl, is ultimately cared for by another family with two children, and after days of walking along with the caravan, they finally settle in the refugee camps in the outskirts of the Indian capital of Delhi. A postcard sent from Canada that Nirmaljeet had found tucked inside her clothing becomes her only material connection to her family and past while she is haunted by "the memory of a pair of feet dangling above a dusty floor, their clean pink soles smelling delicately of lavender soap" (159). At eighteen, Nimmo is married to Satpal and subsequently has a family with three children, Jasbeer, Pappu, and Kamal. The course of Nirmaljeet's life is determined by the ethnopolitics of the subcontinent, first in 1947 and subsequently in 1984.

Parallel to the threads of Sharanjeet's and Nirmaljeet's narratives, the novel presents the story of Leela Bhat, who was born in 1938 to a German mother, Rosa Schweers, and an Indian father, Hari Shastri, who had met in London while the latter was a law student at the centre of the empire. Leela's mother, Rosa, accompanied her father back to his ancestral home in the outskirts of Bangalore, India, where Leela was born. Though the Shastri family was an upper-caste Hindu household with financial security and high social standing, Rosa could never get accustomed to the traditional ways of the Indian lifestyle. Their marriage decayed, and eventually Rosa drowned in 1946, leaving an eight-year-old

Leela, "a half-and-half hovering on the outskirts of their family's circle of love" to navigate the complex life of a biracial identity (Badami 74). Leela, who would navigate an in-between space trying to find the locus of her heritage and culture, was a consequence of British imperialism that created opportunities of transcultural mobility and allowed Hari and Rosa to conceive a mixed-race child. However, the decay and death of Leela's mother illustrate the contradictions and tensions caused by the unjust laws, patriarchal-Brahminical customs, and racialized presumptions of Anglo-European superiority enforced within the colonial world. In such conditions, the harmonious coexistence of races and cultures was rendered exceptional with tragic consequences for some, such as Rosa. The inequality of globalization, which exacerbates pre-existing inequalities, is highlighted when Hari Shastri's social and professional opportunities are compared with Harjot Singh's misfortune. Narrative representations of Harjot and Rosa are shortened as the structure of imperial and colonial conditions could not easily accommodate their presence as both characters trespassed the boundaries of imperial-capitalism and heteropatriarchy. Their sudden disappearance and accidental deaths demonstrate that multinational and transnational identities and cultures were monitored or forbidden to ensure the reproduction of racial-colonial hierarchies on the one hand and traditional patriarchy on the other.

In Vancouver, Sharanjeet learns about the partition of India only through letters from her sister, which stop after 1947; following the communal riots, she visits many of the refugee camps in search of her sister's family, her only blood relative, but is unable to locate them. In this process, the gurudwaras emerge as sites of networking and communication and thereby confirm their historic role as Sikh places of worship that, throughout the world, provide community support while connecting the Sikh diaspora to the "homeland" of Punjab. In contrast to the narrative of Sharanjeet, who settles in Canada, and Nirmaljeet, who grows up in a refugee camp, in the other thread of the novel, Leela struggles to claim and cultivate an upper-caste, upper-class Hindu Indian (Kannada) identity for herself, as her grey eyes and wheat complexion remain a constant reminder of her Eurasian ancestry. Leela attends university and subsequently marries Balachandra Bhat, a chemistry professor, and settles into a wealthy, aristocratic family with two children, Arjun and Preetha.

Eventually, Leela moves to Vancouver in 1967 to join her husband, who had previously accepted a position as an instructor at the Vancouver Community College, and meets Sharanjeet, her landlady.

While the border states of India lived through the trauma of religious nationalism and violence, Leela's family in Bangalore, in the southern Indian province of Karnataka, did not experience Indian independence with such loss. The novel captures the different ways that the collective experience of national historical events were experienced; it also illustrates how different linguistic, ethnic, and cultural identities have contributed to the formation of the heterogeneous state of India. Founded upon anti-colonial sentiments and created through the violence of imperial policies and sectarian religious beliefs, the subcontinental nationalism espoused by the diverse groups has contributed to the continued internal fragmentation of the Indian nation. This fragmentation is initially ignored in the diasporic lives of racialized immigrants. As advice to the newly arrived Leela about how to settle in Vancouver, Sharanjeet encourages her to become comfortable as "an *in*visible minority" and accept her location on the precarious "Minority Boat" alongside "the Chinese, the Japanese, the Italians, that barber Majid" (Badami 137). This conversation illustrates the social reality of a heterogeneous nation composed of diasporic Canadians whose cultural and historical backgrounds are diverse. Leela initially clings to her Hindu Indian national identity, which leads her to dislike Chinese descendants, owing to the Sino-Indian War and border conflict of 1962, and she also distances herself from the Anglo-Europeans as a result of her own personal history and anti-colonial sentiments. However, by 1971, Leela transitions into a phase of postnationalism where her citizenship identity does not require her to participate in a politics of othering that is based on historical events associated with the culture of her origins and that serves as a prerequisite to acceptance within the prevailing understanding of the nation; instead, she considers her colleague Erin of Anglo-European descent to be "like One of Us" (227) and bonds with Linda Lu, a fellow immigrant parent of Chinese descent, over their mutual frustration with the school curriculum for their children (228–29).

Leela's narrative also connects Sharanjeet's life with Nirmaljeet's. Satpal, the taxi driver who drives Leela and her children to the airport in Delhi, asks Leela to inquire about a "Sharanjeet" in Canada; Satpal, Nirmaljeet's husband, had presented the same request to numerous passengers through the years but it was Leela who would finally connect Sharanjeet with her long-lost niece Nirmaljeet. As a consequence of this connection, Nirmaljeet and Satpal were convinced to send their eldest child, eight-year-old Jasbeer, to Canada to live with Sharanjeet, who was childless, for a better education and opportunities. Separated from his family and community, young Jasbeer struggles emotionally and socially in Canada, while Nirmaljeet, Satpal, and their two other children navigate through a time of high nationalism followed by the rise of ethnonationalism and separatist politics in India.

Though the racialized immigrant communities cultivate a sense of heterogeneous nationhood that transcends ethnic, racial, and historical-cultural boundaries, Badami's characters still construct themselves as an "other" to the dominant Anglo-European national culture and identity. The imperial-racial policies of the British Empire lingered in Canadian social policies as the pre-existing patterns of inequality were reproduced through hierarchical social structures, which enabled the marginalization of the ethnic populations in Canada (Ghosh 18). When Sharanjeet adopts her niece Nirmaljeet's eldest son, Jasbeer, from India and brings him to Vancouver in 1968, the young boy struggles to find a locus of identity. His cultural othering within the school system becomes evident during a meeting in 1971 when the principal, Mr. Longbottom, comments, "I understand in your part of the world it is okay to carry swords" (210). When Sharanjeet responds that nobody on Vancouver's Main Street carries swords, the principal corrects her stating, "I don't mean Main Street...[but] *Poonjab*...I realize it is part of the Sikh religion to carry swords...and grow long hair and...a steel bracelet and underwear" (210–11). Jasbeer, who was a maladjusted and withdrawn child, was bullied by one of his "white" peers because of his long hair, and in response, had dressed up as a Sikh martyr to teach his classmate a lesson. While the principal frames him as "Poonjabi," rather than a Vancouverite, and his action as a cultural expression of an inferior society, his guardian and Grand Uncle, Khushawant, praises his behaviour (outside the school) and calls him a "Punjabi lion" for teaching the bully a lesson and frames the action as an extension of chivalric anti-colonial resistance. Both framings create a sense of othering, and fuel the growing sense of non-belonging in the eleven-year-old Jasbeer. The meeting also highlights how the Sikh community of Vancouver was perceived as an outsider by mainstream Canadian social institutions; on the other hand, the diasporic community interpreted this othering as an extension of the colonial experience of the subcontinent. Moreover, the novel also captures how the South Asian Canadian community of the 1960s abstained from participating in Canadian national cultural practices by normalizing the absence of celebrations like the 1967 Centennial. Thus, the nascent postnationalism of the immigrant communities remains limited in scope as they continue to be constructed as and construct themselves as others to Canadian national culture, identity, and interests.

Jasbeer's experience in Vancouver is contrasted with that of Leela's two children Arjun and Preetha, who belonged to the same age group and immigrated within the same time frame. Preetha, the youngest of the three, adjusts well and integrates herself within her peer group in both her community and school; however, Arjun struggles to establish new social connections and instead finds refuge in the academic and imaginative worlds. The novel emphasizes the ability of immigrant women to facilitate new social networks and co-ordinates of belonging based on their positionalities in the new environments, while many of the male characters fail to recreate new social and political identities as they focus on re-establishing past positionalities and historical experiences. Social interactions within private circles and domestic spaces often offer immigrant women the opportunity to cultivate this sense of a postnational collective.

The novel portrays how Leela, Arjun, Preetha, Sharanjeet, and Jasbeer attempt to find their national and collective affiliations in a Canada that was beginning its shift to a paradigm of national identity based on Pierre Elliott Trudeau's multiculturalism; on the other hand, the narrative of Nirmaljeet depicts how ethnoreligious identities and regional nationalisms impose themselves on the lives of the citizens of a postcolonial India. Historically, the Indo-Pakistan War of 1971 and the eventual liberation of Bangladesh were responsible for the arrival of approximately ten million refugees fleeing rape, genocide, and brutal oppression by the Pakistani military; these refugees were sheltered in the city of Calcutta. The Indian government officially hosted the refugees for a temporary time period—"only until such time as they were able to go back to their country of permanent residence with dignity" (Mukherji 399). However, anti-refugee sentiments became apparent throughout the country, which is represented in Satpal's (Nirmaljeet's husband) comment, "Indira Gandhi should keep her head down, stay out of this matter, send those Pakistani refugees back where they came from. As if India did not have enough people! As if they did not have urgent needs" (Badami 239). Satpal's lack of empathy and his rejection of the refugees can be compared to the sentiments of the Anglo-European settlers' sentiment in Canada.

Earlier in the novel, Gandhi is introduced as a character in absentia, who serves as role model and cultural icon of women's emancipation in independent India. Nirmaljeet would attend Gandhi's political rallies, secretly wishing that someday her own daughter could also assume a prominent leadership role in the country. However, throughout the 1970s the political spectrum of India witnessed growing opposition towards Gandhi's policies, which provided the background for the Khalistan movement, and historical events such as Operation Blue Star, the assassination of Gandhi and the anti-Sikh riots of 1984, as well as the Air India bombing in 1985. This corresponding conflict of ethnicity and nationalism, which created new co-ordinates of belonging and otherness, disrupts Nirmaljeet and her family's lives as they become non-consenting participants in the political turmoil of India during the 1970s and subsequently perish during the anti-Sikh violence of the 1980s.

The government's plans for the redistribution of regional resources had caused collective political discontent in the Punjab region, and the separatist Khalistan movement was formalized in London in 1970 (Fair 135). The pre-existing ethnonationalism of the region was exacerbated when inhabitants of the prosperous region were forced to share the products of their labour with the rest of the country and their political dissonance was met with violent reprisal from the nation's armed forces. Young Sikh men like Pappu (Nirmaljeet and Satpal's second child) and his cousin Sunny welcome the possibility of an exclusive Sikh nation; in contrast, Nirmaljeet, who had once lost everything to the politics of nationalism, retains her position as a citizen of a multi-ethnic postcolonial nation and addresses the failures of the national policies in maintaining its integrity.

The material-historical events of the signified world of Badami's novel include the events of June 1984, when Indira Gandhi ordered her military to march into the Golden Temple, the holiest site of worship for the Sikh community, to tackle the armed militants who had taken refuge within. The military operation known as Operation Blue Star claimed the lives of innocent tourists. In the fictional space, Sharanjeet's husband, Kushawant, who had gone to visit the holy site along with his wife on a religious pilgrimage, died during this operation. The incident caused a ripple effect, igniting extreme anti-government sentiments that translated into increased popular support for the Sikh separatist movement. The novel focuses on the emotional response of the Vancouver-based Sikh diaspora, which had provided steady support for the separatist Khalistan movement. While the diasporic community was already hosting ideological heroes such as Dr. Raghubir Randhawa, in the aftermath of Operation Blue Star, the dedication and support for the movement intensified in both material and emotional sense. In desperation for a locus of identity, the diasporic community grasped onto an imagined conception of a homeland. Some critics have suggested that this response was motivated by "a genuine sympathy for the domestic struggles of their overseas kin. Sometimes these communities may also feel a sense of guilt because they are safe while their kin are involved in a brutal and bloody struggle" (Byman et al. 55). According to Gabriel Sheffer, diasporic communities can "support irredentist, secessionist or national liberation movements" and offer "resources such as fighters, weapons, military intelligence and money," as well as planning and executing "attacks in their host countries" (64–65). In Badami's narrative, Jasbeer becomes the embodied example of the ways in which the Sikh diaspora had participated and facilitated the Khalistan movement. In the aftermath of Operation Blue Star, the fictional narrative also finds a radicalized Sharanjeet, who distances herself from all non-Sikh members of the Indian diaspora. She had earlier conceived of herself as a minority Canadian of Indian origin, now she can only perceive herself as a Sikh, with no further sense of kinship with the diverse ethnic nationalities that she had once perceived as a part of her diasporic and postnational identity.

Historically, Prime Minister Gandhi was assassinated in October of 1984 by her Sikh bodyguards, as a retaliation for the desecration of the Golden Temple; subsequently, anti-Sikh riots, organized by the ruling party, broke out throughout Delhi and its outskirts. Badami's fiction represents the chaos and turmoil of the time by focusing on Nirmaljeet, who finds herself alienated from her neighbours in the immediate aftermath of the public announcement of the prime minister's death. Her long-time neighbour Asha's husband, who has lived in the fringes of the family and society through the years, emerges as a patriotic Hindu nationalist avenging the death of Indira Gandhi; he leads a mob to Nirmaljeet's house, which is set on fire, resulting in the death of her youngest child, Kamal, who was burnt alive with the house. Nirmaljeet and Satpal's second child, Pappu, is hunted and dragged out of the house of his father's business partner and burnt alive on the street. Satpal meets a similar fate as he tries to get back to their home in Delhi from Modinagar, where he had travelled earlier to buy parts for his autobody shop; a mob sets him on fire after insulting him. Sikh nationalism was already brewing as a collective ideology and was met with resistance for threatening India's sense of national sovereignty but in the aftermath of the assassination of the prime minister, Sikh communities living in different parts of India were targeted as enemies of the state in a process that was reciprocated throughout the decade.

India was founded upon the ideals of a multi-ethnic, secular, and anti-colonial form of nationalism. Nonetheless, the eruption of the violent ethnonationalisms of the 1980s repeated the history of India's birth as a nation-state in the violent outburst of religious nationalism at the time of partition. The South Asian diaspora in Canada initially transcends its inherited nationalist politics of exclusion and inclusion and contributes to a postnational consciousness of nationalism. Most members of this community identify themselves as transitional subjects who consciously resist assimilation and thus force the national imagination to embrace its pluralities and fragmentations. However, without a firm locus of collective belonging within the Canadian national cultural imaginary, a selective group of the Sikh diaspora of Badami's novel opts to embrace Sikh nationalism instead of their previous postnational stance when introduced to an exclusive understanding of the Sikh nation-state through the Khalistan movement. Though the daily interaction amongst people of diverse cultural, ethnic, linguistic, racial backgrounds, facilitated multi-ethnic nationalism in India and postnational diasporic nationalisms in Canada, historical events like the Operation Blue Star, as well as the assassination of Indira Gandhi, provoke the ethnic populations of the subcontinent and their counterparts in the diaspora to re-evaluate their nationalist affiliations.

Badami's novel ends with the catastrophe of the Air India bombing of 1985, which claimed the life of a fictional passenger, Leela, along with another 328 real human beings; a part of the Sikh diaspora in Vancouver actively participated in the planning and execution of this bombing as a retaliation while Sharanjeet remained a silent observer. She did not feel the need to warn Leela about the impending disaster as she no longer shared a collective affiliation with her former tenant. Sharanjeet's new exclusionary nationalism does not allow her to subscribe to either a pan-South Asian collective identity or a Canadian diasporic, postnational identity as she becomes an embodiment of the metaphor of Trishaku, destined to exist in isolation in an exclusive space. On the other hand, Leela, who struggled all through her life to accept her biracial identity but managed to connect with multiple nationalities in her diasporic life, perished in the plane crash in 1985, in mid-air, alluding to the in-between space of Trishanku, where she was placed through her birth.

The bombing of the Air India flight also alludes to the alienated status of the South Asian diaspora in Canada, who exist like a Trishanku in an in-between space. The incident received little attention within the dominant discourses of citizenship and identity in Canada until Clark Blaise and Bharati Mukherjee excavated the narratives of the victims and framed them within a broader debate over citizenship rights and racialization of South Asians descendants in Canada. Subsequently, Chandrima Chakraborty's work directed further academic attention to the incident and pointed out that the Canadian government's official response to the incident represented "the state's and its majority citizens' belated acceptance of racialized minorities as citizens with rights and protections guaranteed by the state" (112). Furthermore, the initial framing of the bombing as an Indian problem with its domestic Sikh population ignored the long history of racial tension between Anglo-European Canada and its South Asian minority communities, and failed to acknowledge the bombing as a Canadian tragedy. Badami's novel asks twenty-first-century readers to reflect on this history to understand how minority identities and citizenship rights are framed within the national cultural imaginaries of countries like Canada; further, it alludes to the possibility of a harmonious and collaborative existence for citizens from diverse ethnic, religious, linguistic, and national backgrounds through the process of conscious critical engagement with history.

By framing the fictional narrative within the two historical events/catastrophes, the *Komagata Maru* incident of 1914 and the bombing of Air India Flight 182 on June 23, 1985, *Can You Hear the Nightbird Call?* shows how the narratives of people and communities shaped by historical events cannot be represented or comprehended without their historical backgrounds. The narrative also indicates how the global migration of people has played a pivotal role in the construction of multicultural democracies and multinational states. In other words, the novel traces the origins of multicultural nationalisms within pre-existing structures of globalization. Focusing on women's role in navigating national identities in situations of multiple and completing ethnicities, *Can You Hear the Nightbird Call?* demonstrates how kinship ties, nurtured in the private spaces of households, influence political identities of communities that play out in the public sphere. Sharanjeet plays an important role in the Khalistan movement as her household provides a place of networking for the proponents of the idea. She also plays an important role in planting the idea of a postnational consciousness in Leela's mind when the latter first arrives in Canada. The everyday actions of the community members in the private spaces and their interactions with the majoritarian society in the public spaces contribute together to assigning national-collective identities to the diasporic members. Similarly, Leela's positionality as a mixed-race immigrant of Indian origin allows her to theorize the possibility of a postnational and transcultural consciousness. On the other hand, Nirmaljeet continues to participate in a multi-ethnic national consciousness by continuing the affective relationships with her fellow citizens, especially with her Hindu neighbour Kaushalya. Ultimately, the novel presents a quest to find a home or a space of material and psychological belonging for the characters whose lives are shaped by globalization-induced mobility and new nation formations. For Sharanjeet, Nirmaljeet, and Leela, home is represented as "the competition between two movements: a homing, life-giving instinct and an unhoming, deathly impulse" through the "imagery of transportation" (Ryan 157).

In contrast, the afterlives of anti-colonial and ethnoreligious nationalisms are embodied in the narratives of the three children, Preetha, Arjun, and Jasbeer, all of whom were born in India and arrived in Canada in late 1960s. Despite the continued othering by the majoritarian cultures of the two nations, at the end, these South Asian Canadian children attempt to find a new national consciousness that transcends affiliation to one specific nation, ethnicity, or culture. Separated from his family against his wishes, Jasbeer is lost between citizenships and cultures, as he is rejected by the mainstream Anglo-European Canadian culture and is unable to reclaim his Indian identity. Jasbeer's trajectory explores "why the members of an ethnic group settled in overseas countries may continue to attach themselves to their country or region of origin or their 'homeland'" (Tatla 2), as the novel demonstrates how the different stages and degrees of alienation shaped young Jasbeer, who found a sense of belonging only in an imaginary homeland. He finds an opportunity for a locus of identity in the imagining of a Sikh state based on his ethnoreligious identity and eventually becomes indoctrinated by Dr. Randhawa, who visits the Vancouver-based Sikh diaspora in 1971 for the first time to mobilize sympathy and support for the notion of an independent Sikh state. In a letter written to Preetha from an Indian prison, Jasbeer acknowledges his involvement in the militant activities as he describes his role in coercing financial support from non-partisan Punjabis in supporting the Khalistani movement. At the end of the novel, Jasbeer traces his route back to his mother's house in 1986, indicating the beginning of a search for a new identity within a multi-ethnic, postcolonial democracy.

Leela's children, Arjun and Preetha, who immigrated to Canada around the same time as Jasbeer, adjusted well in their Canadian environment, excelled in education, and established themselves as professional middle-class citizens. By the end of the novel, Arjun is engaged to Fern, a Canadian of Anglo-European descent, repeating the cycle of transnational, biracial relationship that was embraced by Leela's parents. Almost forty years after Rosa's death, her grandson Arjun is able to establish and maintain a biracial, bicultural relationship in Canada. While British India could not and did not encourage and support racial intermixing, 1980s Canada allows for mixed-race and hyphenated identities to blossom and thrive. Though the novel does not expand onto the lives of Arjun and Fern, their relationship alludes to the possibility for individuals to cultivate multiple cultural, racial, and national affiliations expressed through the amphibian (frog) metaphor.

The complexity of establishing and maintaining the new forms of collective belonging within multinational states calls for an examination of the associated ideas of nationalism and patriotism. According to Niraja Jayal, "Contemporary concerns about patriotism and nationalism inhabit two levels simultaneously: the first is about identifying a principle of political affiliation that can create the conditions for citizenship in diverse societies; while the second is about creating citizens for a world beyond national boundaries" (4515). In Badami's novel, Jasbeer, Preetha, and Arjun are left to navigate this two-step process of identifying their respective political affiliations and citizenship responsibilities beyond specific national boundaries. Inserting the question of ethnoreligious nationalism within the context of multinational states and their multicultural policies, the novel also asks "whether, how, and to what extent can religion be included within commitments to multiculturalism" (Sikka and Beaman 3). Badami's novel presents the external conditions that manipulate the characters to choose and negotiate amongst multiple co-ordinates of their pluralistic diasporic identities, which cannot be "simply understood in immigrant/host society dichotomy and its dynamics" but also need to address the "internal dynamics of the community" (Judge 1727).

Can You Hear the Nightbird Call? is simultaneously reflective and speculative as it urges readers to engage with history to imagine a possible postnational world. The promise of a collective identity that can transcend past understandings of nationalism is deliberately left as an equivocal future. From the era of high imperialism to the advent of postcolonialism, the movement of commodities, capital, and people around the British Empire has complicated the perception of a unified national consciousness for countries with diverse and heterogeneous populations. In contrast to the settler-colonial societies where the cultural identity of the empire was preserved and reproduced, the newly independent racialized colonies were faced with carving out a national identity that extended beyond their anti-colonial history to bring together multiple ethnicities within the purview of a unified national consciousness. The settler colonies, as well as the centre of the British Empire, transformed into multinational states because of the mobility offered to members of the privileged classes in the colonies while limiting access to economic and educational opportunities to the struggling classes. The novel alludes to the possibility of hybridized, transnational, and intersectional identities as functional units of this postnational paradigm. However, it also points out that a conscious excavation of history is essential for the multicultural and multi-ethnic countries of Canada and India to embark on this journey towards postnationalism.

WORKS CITED

Aiyar, Swarna. "'August Anarchy': The Partition Massacres in Punjab, 1947." *South Asia: Journal of South Asian Studies*, vol. 18, no. 1, 1995, pp. 13–36.

Badami, Anita Rau. *Can You Hear the Nightbird Call?* Alfred Knopf Canada, 2006.

Balibar, Étienne. *We the People of Europe?* Princeton University Press, 2004.

Blaise, Clark, and Mukherjee, Bharati. *The Sorrow and the Terror: The Haunting Legacy of the Air India Tragedy*. Viking, 1987.

Bloemraad, Irene. "Who Claims Dual Citizenship? The Limits of Postnationalism, the Possibilities of Transnationalism, and the Persistence of Traditional Citizenship 1." *International Migration Review*, vol. 38, no. 2, 2004, pp. 389–426.

Byman, Daniel, Peter Chalk, Bruce Hoffman, William Rosenau, and David Brannan. "Diaspora Support for Insurgencies." *Trends in Outside Support for Insurgent Movements*, RAND Corporation, 2001, pp. 41–60. JSTOR, https://www.jstor.org/stable/10.7249/mr1405oti.11.

Chakraborty, Chandrima. "Official Apology, Creative Remembrances, and Management of the Air India Tragedy." *Studies in Canadian Literature*, vol. 40, no. 1, 2015, https://journals.lib.unb.ca/index.php/SCL/article/view/24283.

Chatterji, Joya. "Partition Studies: Prospects and Pitfalls." *The Journal of Asian Studies*, vol. 73, no. 2, 2014, pp. 309–12.

Cohen, Robin. "Diasporas and the Nation-State: From Victims to Challengers." *International Affairs*, vol. 72, no. 3, 1996, pp. 507–20. JSTOR, https://www.jstor.org/stable/2625554. Accessed 11 Feb. 2020.

Dayal, Samir. "Postcolonialism's Possibilities: Subcontinental Diasporic Intervention." *Cultural Critique*, no. 33, 1996, pp. 113–49.

Fair, C. Christine. "Diaspora Involvement in Insurgencies: Insights from the Khalistan and Tamil Eelam Movements." *Nationalism and Ethnic Politics*, vol. 11, no. 1, 2005, pp. 125–56.

Ghosh, Ratna. "Multiculturalism in a Comparative Perspective: Australia, Canada and India." *Canadian Ethnic Studies*, vol. 50 no. 1, 2018, p. 15–36. Project MUSE, doi:10.1353/ces.2018.0002.

Hussain, Hamid Md., and Sarwar, Firoz High. "A Comparative Study of Zamindari, Raiyatwari, and Mahalwari Land Revenue Settlements: The Colonial Mechanisms of Surplus Extraction in the 19th century British India." *Journal of Humanities and Social Sciences*, vol. 4, no. 2, 2012, pp. 16–26.

Jameson, Fredric. "Third-World Literature in the Era of Multinational Capitalism." *Social Text*, no. 15, 1986, pp. 65–88.

Jayal, Niraja Gopal. "Revisiting Nationalism." *Economic and Political Weekly*, vol. 41, no. 42, 2006, pp. 4513–15.

Johnston, Hugh. "Komagata Maru." *The Canadian Encyclopedia*, 7 Feb. 2006, https://www.thecanadianencyclopedia.ca/en/article/komagata-maru.

Judge, Paramjit. "Social Construction of Identity in a Multicultural State: Sikhs in Canada." *Economic and Political Weekly*, vol. 38, no. 17, 2003, pp. 1725–31.

Kaufmann, Eric P. *Rethinking Ethnicity: Majority Groups and Dominant Minorities*. Routledge, 2004.

Kymlicka, Will. "Multicultural Citizenship within Multination States." *Ethnicities*, vol. 11, no. 3, 2011, pp. 281–302.

Menon, Nivedita. "Thinking through the Postnation." *Economic and Political Weekly*, vol. 44, no. 10, 2009, pp. 70–77.

Mishra, Vijay. "The Diasporic Imaginary: Theorizing the Indian Diaspora." *Textual Practice*, vol. 10, no. 3, 1996, pp. 421–47.

———. *The Literature of the Indian Diaspora: Theorizing the Diasporic Imaginary*. Routledge, 2007.

Mukherji, Partha. "The Great Migration of 1971: II: Reception." *Economic and Political Weekly*, vol. 9, no. 10, 1974, pp. 399–408.

Nanda, Subrat K. "Cultural Nationalism in a Multi-national Context: The Case of India." *Sociological Bulletin*, vol. 55, no. 1, 2006, pp. 24–44.

Pirbhai, Miriam. "Introduction South Asian Canadian Literature: A Centennial Journey." *Studies in Canadian Literature*, vol. 40, no. 1, June 2015, https://journals.lib.unb.ca/index.php/SCL/article/view/24278.

Ryan, Laurel. "Constructing 'Home': Eros, Thanatos, and Migration in the Novels of Anita Rau Badami." *South Asian Review: Perspectives on South Asian Women's Writing*, vol. 29, no. 1, 2008, pp. 156–74.

Sheffer, Gabriel. "Ethno-national Diasporas and Security." *Survival*, vol. 36, no. 1, 1994, pp. 60–79, http://www.doi.org/10.1080/00396339408442724.

Sikka, Sonia, and Lori G. Beaman, editors. *Multiculturalism and Religious Identity: Canada and India*. McGill-Queen's University Press, 2014. *JSTOR*, https://www.jstor.org/stable/j.ctt7zsz9c.

Talbot, Ian A. "The Punjab under Colonialism: Order and Transformation in British India." *Journal of Punjab Studies*, vol. 14, no. 1, 2012, pp. 3–10.

Tatla, Darsham Singh. *The Sikh Diaspora: The Search for Statehood*. Taylor and Francis, 2013.

Thomas, Martin, and Andrew Thompson. "Empire and Globalisation: from 'High Imperialism' to Decolonisation." *The International History Review*, vol. 36, no. 1, 2014, pp. 142–70.

5

Canadian Literature in Heritage Languages and the Politics of Canon Formation

ASMA SAYED

What is Canadian literature? What is a Canadian novel? I am not going to be so foolhardy as to attempt to define these terms; many have wandered into this wilderness—and returned, what else but bewildered if they were honest, or with simplistic or outdated notions if they were naive; this is hardly surprising—the country is changing around us even as we speak, stirring up a host of conflicting ideas and interests, and to look for an essence, a core, a central notion within that whirlwind is surely an illusion. To define this country or its literature seems like putting a finger on Zeno's arrow: no sooner do you think you have done it than it has moved on.
—M.G. VASSANJI, "Am I a Canadian Writer?"

GIVEN THE TWENTY-FIRST-CENTURY FOCUS on globalization, transnationalism, and cosmopolitanism, defining and identifying a national literature may seem self-defeating or irrelevant. Yet it is also true that nationalistic ideologies are on the rise: India and the United States are just two of the many examples of nation-states where nationalism has led to many political and sociocultural changes in the past decade. What, then, is the role of such political shifts in the study and canonization of literature? The question of national literature, especially in multinational states such as Canada and India, is complicated by the political discourses of citizenship, imperialism, and multilingualism. As David Damrosch has argued, "we have habitually constructed our national traditions in narrow and inconsistent terms, playing a double game of language and geography that has policed internal and external boundaries alike" (27). In Canada, an officially multicultural and bilingual nation, writers' choice of language has long been a debated issue. Canada has a rich heritage of literature produced in its two official languages, English and French. Equally interesting, and not always acknowledged, are the contributions of writers who create in non-official languages, or what I call heritage languages. In fact, as it is widely known, Canada's policy of bilingualism has constructed an environment of linguistic hegemony: English and French have the official status; non-official languages are considered the "other." Canadian writers have written in many heritage languages for over a century, but their reception is far from encouraging. In such circumstances, what is the role of heritage-language literary texts in Canada? How do they fit into definitions of the country's national literature? One needs to consider these questions while being mindful that defining Canadian literature is complex; many writers and scholars, including Robert Lecker and Margaret Atwood, have tried to characterize it with varied approaches (see also Kamboureli and Miki).

Literature written in heritage languages not only challenges the English/French linguistic and cultural hegemony but also serves to archive early identities and encounters between newer and more established "mainstream" communities, as well as to record the "development" of intercultural identities that result from these interactions. As such, as I have argued elsewhere, "limiting the vision of Canadian literature merely to those texts written in English and French places non-productive limits on the vision of a nation-state where literature is produced in many languages" (Sayed 218). Besides, in 2016 approximately 7.7 million Canadians reported a mother tongue other than English or French and

19.4 percent of people reported speaking more than one language at home (Statistics Canada, "Linguistic Diversity" 1). Taking as examples South Asian diaspora literatures in Canada written in heritage languages, especially Hindi, Urdu, Gujarati, and Punjabi, this chapter aims to examine the place of minority or heritage languages in the canon of Canadian literature, and the role of translation in furthering the expansion of a canon. I argue that literature produced in heritage languages adds to the plurality of Canadian literature and should be analyzed with new epistemological approaches rooted in decolonial methodologies and techniques.

Multilingual Literature in Canada
An overview of multilingual literature in Canada, mainly in the South Asian context, will help contextualize the issue. Canada has a long history of authors writing in non-official languages including but not limited to Gaelic, Icelandic, Yiddish, Hungarian, Polish, Italian, German, Spanish, Armenian, Estonian, Czech, and Ukrainian. Writers who have written in some of these languages include Josef Škvorecký, Pablo Urbanyi, Nicholas Prychodko, Arved Viirlaid, and Saad Elkadem among others. Some of the critical and scholarly works documenting the contributions of these writers include *Canadian Fiction Magazine* (see issue numbers 36 and 37), *Exile*, and *Canadian Ethnic Studies*. Watson Kirkconnell, from 1937 to 1965, reviewed Canadian literature in languages other than French and English annually in the *University of Toronto Quarterly*. J. Michael Yates published *Volvox: Poetry from the Unofficial Languages of Canada in English Translation* in 1971.

My research has focused on writers of South Asian origin who write in Hindi, Gujarati, Punjabi, and Urdu.[1] The history of South Asian migration to Canada dates back to the end of the nineteenth century. Archival evidence shows that approximately 5,000 South Asians arrived between 1904 and 1908. A 1908 amendment to the Immigration Act, known as the Continuous Journey Regulation, prohibited entry into Canada to those who did not arrive directly from their country of origin. After the subsequent *Komagata Maru* incident in 1914, when a group of 376 South Asians from the British Raj were denied entry into Canada, immigration from South Asia almost came to a halt. It regained momentum in the 1960s after Canada re-opened immigration to non-Europeans. As per the 2016

Canadian census, 1.9 million Canadians, approximately 5.6 per cent of the populace, identify themselves as of South Asian origin, making them the largest visible minority group in Canada (Statistics Canada, "Data Tables"). Some migrated directly from South Asia, while others arrived through the process of "double diaspora" via East Africa, the Caribbean, or other global locations. Among those who came to Canada were many talented writers and filmmakers. The earliest record of publication activity of South Asian Canadians goes back to 1911 with the English-language newspaper *The Aryan*, as well as a Punjabi language newspaper *Sansar* (Johnston 31–32). Early migrants wrote mostly in their heritage languages, such as Punjabi, Hindi, and Urdu. Those who came after the 1960s created mostly in English, but heritage-language writers continued to produce and publish either in local community newspapers and magazines or outside of Canada (see Khan and Sugunasiri).

Literature in heritage languages invites us to think about the nations within a nation-state and the global impact of Canadian literature. South Asian diasporas globally are distinct from other diasporas, such as the English and the French for instance, given their history of multiple displacements. Whether people moved across continents as a result of indentured labour or were internally displaced within South Asia as a result of Partition, they carried with them the complexities of their South Asianness defined not only by their gender and class but also by the politics of religion and caste that is unique to the region, and the use of multiple languages. Yet, as Vijay Mishra has argued, South Asian diasporas, across history and regions, both "the older diasporas of classic capitalism and the mid- to late twentieth-century diaspora of advance capital to the metropolitan centres of the Empire, the New World and the former settler colonies...are interlinked" (421). In fact, as Ananya Jahanara Kabir contends, one of the commonalities in South Asian diasporic literature is that it has many characteristics of a literature of trauma: "Whether the text evokes the old diaspora, the new diaspora, the transnational condition or Partition migration—that which is left behind, and which has scarred the subject formed in and through displacement, emerges as the nation: a phantom, yet palpable, force that is political as much as, and indeed because, it is emotional" (392). Similarly, South Asian diaspora subjects carry with them the burden of the colonial past and share a postcolonial sensibility and identity of a displaced diasporic subject. Thus, South Asian writers in Canada bring a unique historical and global context that enriches the transnationality and polyvocality within Canadian literary culture.

Although South Asian writers in Canada have been writing in heritage languages since the early twentieth century, almost none of their writing is to be found in anthologies of Canadian literature. A study of Canadian university syllabi also shows that Canadian literature is studied and taught predominantly in the two official languages, although attempts have been made to include literatures in Indigenous languages, especially after the findings of the Truth and Reconciliation Commission of Canada (Sayed 216). Ronald Sutherland, in the 1990s, argued that scholars need to pay greater attention to the growing body of South Asian Canadian literature:

> *Perhaps the richest and most rapidly growing new component of Canadian literature is the work being produced by the writers of South Asian affiliations. Whether they write in Hindi, Urdu, Punjabi, other languages, or English, they constitute an intriguing dimension. I can already see thematic parallels with other Canadian works—a duality of attitude toward nature, a special sense of exile. But there are also fascinating contrasts, the expected result of a cultural conditioning so vastly different from that of most native Canadians. And, of course, the great variety among South Asians themselves concords with the existing diversity of Canadians and Canadian literature. (73–74)*

Considering that our understanding of nation, space, and identity has shifted considerably since the early days of Canadian literature, it would seem that the movement would be toward broadening the canon, but that is not the case. Lecker, in his article on some of the early anthologies of Canadian literature, provides a detailed account of how our understanding of Canadian literature has continuously changed. He reminds us that the editors of the early anthologies were motivated by a number of personal and political circumstances: "evangelical nationalism, political allegiance, literary alliances, and the desire to profit from shifting perceptions of the country and its literature as Canada moved past

Confederation and towards the twentieth century" (93). These editors, Lecker further suggests, "were drawn to contemporary writers and saw their work as evidence of progress in a new land; but at the same time, they were driven by nostalgia and a desire for imperial connection, which prompted them to celebrate the historical and classical at the expense of the modern. Their anthologies were always compromised, as was their vision of the nation" (94). The number of writers working in South Asian languages has consistently increased in Canada into the twenty-first century. Many literary journals and newspapers continue to be published throughout Canada in a number of South Asian languages. Thus, the process of anthologizing Canadian literature also needs to move beyond the early narrow confines to the contemporary.

Urdu writing in Canada is one of the most developed in South Asian writing in heritage languages. The Urdu Society of Canada, which gathered people with interest in Urdu literature and language, was formed in the 1970s in Toronto; the society was functional until the mid-1980s and organized many conferences and poetry readings. Several literary journals and news magazines in Urdu were also launched in the 1970s and 1980s: *Fortnightly Crescent*, *Weekly Jung*, and *Eastern News* are some examples. The first Canadian conference on Urdu literature was organized in Toronto in 1982. M.H.K. Qureshi produced a report of Urdu literary activity in Canada in 1990. Currently, the Canada Urdu Association, established in 1997, active in Surrey, British Columbia, organizes bi-monthly literary readings; there are also a number of other smaller and informal groups across Canada that organize events celebrating Urdu literary contributions.

Some of the most notable Urdu writers are Shakila Rafiq, Ashfaq Hussain, and Ikram Brelvi. Rafiq is an Urdu short story writer of Pakistani origin now based in Toronto. She has published seven collections of short stories. Khalid Sohail, a scholar of Urdu literature, in his introduction to his collection of translations of Rafiq's work, identifies her writings as "reflect[ing] the struggles and challenges, dilemmas and dreams of women in the South Asian culture." Her short stories have been translated into Hindi, Sindhi, and English. Ashfaq Hussain Zaidi, known as Ashfaq Hussain in Urdu literary circles, is one of the most recognized names among Urdu-reading Canadians. Originally from Pakistan,

Hussain is a poet and has hosted a number of Urdu programs on radio and television platforms in Canada. He is also a renowned scholar on the works of Faiz Ahmed Faiz, one of the most noted Urdu poets globally. In 1982, Hussain launched a journal, *Urdu International*, which subsequently published thirteen issues. A collection of some of his Urdu poems translated into English, *That Day Will Dawn*, was published in 1985. Another noted Urdu writer, Ikram Brelvi, primarily a novelist, immigrated to Canada from Pakistan in 1976. Before moving, he was an established writer in the Indian subcontinent. His novels, such as *Naya Ofaq* (*New Horizon*), *Gardish* (*Misfortune*), *Pul Siraat* (*Treacherous Path to Heaven*), and *Hasrat-i-Tameer* (*Desire to Build*), all published between 1947 and 2007, have been popular among Urdu readers in Canada and South Asia. Other Urdu writers include Jawaid Danish, Kishwar Ghani, Irfana Aziz, Tazeen Hina, Wali Alam Shaheen, and Aziz Ahmed, to name just a few.

Punjabi literature in Canada is the oldest and the most prolific. It has received more recognition than other language groups, mainly due to the efforts of the community and availability of some translations into English. Sadhu Binning, Ajmer Rode, Surjeet Kalsey, and Ravi Ravinder are well-recognized names among Punjabi readers. Rode's play *Komagata Maru* (1984) and Binning's play *Samundari Sher Nal Takkar* (*The Battle with the Sealion*, 1989) are known both in and outside of Punjabi-speaking South Asian communities. Kalsey, in 1978, wrote an MA thesis focusing on Punjabi poetry in Canada, and followed it up with a collection of poems in 1992, published in Delhi. To recognize literary contributions in Punjabi, the Dhahan Prize for Punjabi literature was established in 2014. The prize is awarded by the Canada India Education Society in partnership with the Department of Asian Studies in the Faculty of Arts at the University of British Columbia.

Similarly, Gujarati writers are also a productive group in Canada; they have been active since the 1950s. Virendra Adhiya wrote "Letter from Canada" in *Kumar*, a leading Gujarati literary journal published in India in the 1950s. These "letters" carried information about sociocultural and political aspects of Canada. Jay Gajjar, Keshav Chandaria, Smita Bhagwat, Rashida Damani, Firoz Khan, and Shailesh Desai are some writers who create in Gujarati and are known in the community both in Canada and in Gujarat. Additionally, Hindi writers such as Suresh Goyal have a large readership in India; his Indian readers look forward to his short fiction, which generally has a Canadian setting, in literary and popular magazines. These writers, especially those who focus on Canadian life, provide a glimpse into Canada for the non-Canadian reader. Also, many Gujarati and Hindi literary groups as well as community newspapers and magazines are active across Canada.

Collectively, South Asian Canadian writers have published novels, short stories, poetry, essays, and plays in a number of languages. Their subject matter has focused both on Canadian and non-Canadian issues; for instance, many of the early writers were concerned with matters of immigration, racism, identity, alienation, and nostalgia for the homeland.[2] Several of Hussain's poems highlight the trauma of immigration; Gajjar has written stories celebrating Canada Day and St. Patrick's Day; Rafiq's stories have unpacked the plight of senior citizens in Canadian long-term care homes. Irrespective of setting and thematic concerns, they are recognized authors in their culturally specific communities in Canada and abroad. Yet most of these authors struggle to find funding and publication venues. They self-publish overseas or in community newspapers in Canada. Often, they distribute their books via community networks. This lack of support, acceptance, and recognition is a result of ongoing assumptions about what constitutes Canadian literature.

Canada, India, and National Literatures
The linguistic structure of Canada, and the colonial assumption that the country is founded on two cultures—English and French—has deprioritized the history of Indigenous communities as well as that of those considered ethnic minorities. Thus, the understanding of Canadian literature has mostly remained confined to literatures written in English and French. The Official Languages Act of 1969 furthered the acceptance and cultural recognition of these two languages as official and effectively subordinated other languages to a marginalized status. The implementation of the Canadian Multiculturalism Act in 1988 and newly invigorated discourses around the nation-state saw the emergence of Indigenous and new immigrant writers who were eventually included, celebrated, and recognized through literary awards, reviews, and scholarly critiques, rendering Canadian literature more diverse than ever

before. Nonetheless, the focus has remained on literature in the official languages. As dialogues about the nation, identity, integration, and multiculturalism continue to generate debates, scholars situate and resituate Canadian literature and culture not only within the framework of these debates but also broadly in the context of postcolonialism, globalization, diaspora, and transnationalism. Many recent works by scholars such as Smaro Kamboureli, Cynthia Sugars, Laura Moss, Roy Miki, Rosemary Chapman, Imre Szeman, and E.D. Blodgett, among others, have identified the changing trajectories of Canadian literature and Canadian literary and cultural history. Certainly, "because the contexts and concerns of the nation-state and its various institutional structures have shifted under the pressures of globalization and neoliberalism, the foundations and assumptions of Canada's national(ized) literature have been exposed to critique...[and] the institutional signature of the field has begun to shift directions" (Kamboureli and Zacharias xi). Diana Brydon has suggested that there is "the need to rethink Canadian literature beyond older forms of nationalism and internationalism, and toward multiscaled visions of place—local, regional, national, and global—each imbricated within the other" (14).

However, the above-mentioned scholars have not adequately pushed for inclusion of multilingual literatures, or what many scholars have called "literatures of lesser diffusion." John Robert Colombo, in his introduction to *The Poets of Canada: An Anthology of Poetry in Non-official Languages*, remarks that "the so-called ethnic writers [creating in non-official languages] have played a much more important role in the literary history of this country than has generally been recognized" (13). Likewise, Jars Balan, in 1982, noted that "undoubtedly the most significant gap in our knowledge is Canadian literature in languages other than English or French, which has been excluded from most discussions and assessments of Canadian letters" (ix). Michael Batts also lamented the state of acceptance of heritage-language writing: "Writers in non-official languages are doubly disadvantaged inasmuch as they are little known outside their own ethnic group in Canada, and at the same time they are generally ignored by literary critics and historians in their home country" (764). We thus have to ask, Who are "the best arbiters of what is most valuable about a country's national literature"? (Braz 131). Since these linguistic cultures do not have "the power and prestige to determine what constitutes superior literary production" (Braz 131), they are left out of the canon of Canadian literature.

This is not to say that no attempts have been made to include multilingual literature. Some critics have argued that writers writing in languages other than English and French should be included in the definition of "Canadian literature." For instance, Kirkconnell, in *Canadian Overtones* published in 1935, and in the review sections of the *University of Toronto Quarterly* published from 1937 to 1965 mentioned earlier, introduced the idea of a national literature that included writers writing in "other languages." Similarly, years after Kirkconnell's intervention, in 1996, Natalia Aponiuk, in an article in *Canadian Ethnic Studies*, wondered if writers writing in "minority languages" will become part of the Canadian canon (2). J.M. Bumsted, a Canadian historian, suggested that "anyone who lives and/or writes and/or publishes in Canada must be accepted as a Canadian" (18). In contrast, responding to Edward Mozejko's question of whether the minority writers (those writing in non-official languages) belong to their nationalities or Canada, Blodgett proposed that "they are, in fact, both, but being both, they can be exclusively neither one nor the other" (*Five-Part Invention* 211). In fact, Blodgett, as early as 1988, in his article "Canadian Literature Is Comparative Literature," argued that he did "not subscribe to the cultural domination of Canada by the anglophone majority" and was hopeful about the "importance of other cultures and languages in Canada" (908). He reasoned that "the ethnic in the largest sense, that is, the several distinct cultures of Canada, makes Canada cosmopolitan," which allows "the literatures of Canada [to] belong to Weltliteratur" (909–10). Despite such arguments, which have been raised sporadically, sustained efforts have not been made to critically study literature in heritage languages.

Canadian literary history has mostly been constructed around the concept of a nation-state, primarily focusing on anglophone and francophone writing. Blodgett asserts that "not all literary history is explicitly organized around the nation. It may emphasize, for example, an author or group of authors, a region, or a province. Somewhere, however, the nation is present, if only implicitly, and in most instances the nation is the dominant" (*Five-Part Invention* 4). Literary history, he argues, "has a didactic purpose that is aimed at constructing the idea of nation, and it does so by giving it a certain form in both time and space. It requires clarity of origin and precise delimitation. As history, it constructs a past by selecting texts (canonization) and commemorating events so that the nation may be imaginatively shaped by the reader in such a way as to acquire meaning" (10). The Canadian nation-state, then, in the context of its literary history, and by extension, the canon of Canadian literature, has been imagined by selecting texts in English and French, and occasionally commemorating events from colonial history. Such compartmentalization is not unique to Canada.

India, a country with hundreds of languages and thousands of dialects, a truly multilingual society, has many parallels with Canada. It has not been easy to define national literature in India, just as in Canada. Amiya Dev, one of the best-known scholars of comparative literature in India, cites Swapan Majumdar, author of *Comparative Literature: Indian Dimensions*, who argues that "Indian literature is neither 'one' nor 'many' but rather a systemic whole where any sub-systems interact towards one in a continuous and never-ending dialectic. Such a systemic view of Indian literature predicates that we take all Indian literatures together, age by age and view them comparatively" (qtd. in Dev). In Canada, the canon of Canadian literature, as mentioned earlier, is rooted in colonial history, which marginalizes multilingual literature as it developed its own nationalist literary canon. Perhaps Canada could use the model of Indian literature and think of its multilingual literature as subsystems that all work toward a continuous Canadian literature. That is, Canadian literature does not have to be a hegemonic singular asserting its bilingual nation-state identity, but rather a polyvocal, truly global, and decolonial model of "interliterary process and a dialectical view of literary interaction" (Dev). Such a model would recognize and appreciate the coexistence of the global polyvocality within Canada. However, the model has its limitations. In India, it seems to have sought to palliate the crisis of putting all its various multilingual traditions under the single umbrella of "Indian literature." As Revathy Krishnaswamy notes, these attempts "[obscure] the exclusionary gestures through which anticolonial nationalisms have often consolidated themselves in these postcolonial spaces, erasing in the process the myriad subnational, subaltern, and regional cultural formations fighting to assert their own identities there" (404). Critiquing India's Sahitya Akademi's (Literary Academy) project of a ten-volume history of Indian literature, Krishnaswamy writes, "in the wake of globalization and the rise of various social movements in India, such nationalistic literary projects have come under attack for replicating the exclusionary gestures of both colonialist and anticolonial nationalist historiography, as well as for marginalizing or assimilating various regional, linguistic, caste, class, and gender struggles into a nationalist literary agenda" (403–04). In a similar vein, if the model were to be understood in the Canadian context, assimilation of Indigenous and ethnic minority writers would remain an issue. Thus, one needs to think about Canadian literature without erasing the uniqueness of all the literary traditions within a nation-state.

National literatures have at times been defined based on the content of the text. A question that is often asked of Canadian literary texts is, Does this literature focus on Canada? Queries have also been raised about the subject matter, the length of a given writer's stay in Canada, and the quality of heritage-language literature. In a globalized, cosmopolitan, interconnected, twenty-first-century world, questions about the subject matter seem irrelevant. Can we really argue that Brelvi's novels with a focus on Pakistan and Afghanistan have no bearing on us in Canada? Or that if a writer was not born in Canada, but has lived in Canada for five, ten, or, in some cases, over forty years, they still are not Canadian enough because they write in non-official languages? If similar criteria were to be used to establish Canadianness, how would one justify Mavis Gallant's inclusion in the majority of anthologies of Canadian literature when she spent most of her life in Paris? Just as Gallant considered herself a Canadian, Brelvi and many other authors who live in Canada, and write in their heritage languages, consider themselves Canadians. Thus, the emphasis on geographical and spatial limitation is narrow and exclusive. Such a view of Canadian literature would fail to be "celebrative of inter-lingualism, inter-literariness, and interculturalism," terms that Avadhesh Kumar Singh used for comparative literature in India (28).

One option is to consider the concept of literary cosmopolitanism. Explaining Goethe's concept of world literature, Antoni Monterde writes, "the fact that no individual national literature can exist without relating to the rest—and to alterity, in a broader sense—or dooming itself to extinction, no matter how strong that literature considers itself, determines the organic unity of literatures" (413). If one were to think of literary cosmopolitanism in the context of Canadian literature, considering literature in the two official languages without taking into account multilingual literature means not only missing the connection among various linguistic traditions within Canada but also failing to bear in mind its broader link to world literatures.

The Role of Translation

So, the question remains: As much as some of the multilingual writers mentioned above are celebrated in their homelands and in their diasporic communities, why have they not been included in Canadian literary history? One could argue that their works have not been mentioned in literary histories of Canadian literature because most of them are not available in translation, English or French. At the same time, such an argument furthers the hegemony of English and French and makes multilingual literature worthy of mention only through the medium of translation into a hegemonic language. If literature written in non-Western languages ought to be translated into a Western language for it to be noted in history, it only speaks to "the long legacy of the colonial empires and their logics of Anglicization (or Westernization) and Orientalization" (Mufti 147). Yet Albert Braz reminds us that "there is no avoiding the fact that writers in peripheral tongues face a major obstacle in their attempt to gain literary acclaim: the limited circulation of their languages" (120). Thus, translation has a role to play in expanding the canon of Canadian literature. As many scholars of comparative literature have argued,[3] one needs to be mindful that translation is a medium for literary exchange and makes it possible for us to study literature from various cultural and linguistic backgrounds. Translations have limitations, and they may lose or change the original textual meaning, or may alter the style and other nuances of literary texts. Nonetheless, Pascale Casanova's assertion that translation "is one of the principal means by which texts circulate in the literary world" (xiii) needs to be taken into consideration. Similarly, Damrosch has noted, "If you're writing in English or French, you're going to get more attention than if you're writing in Slovakian...We really need to look at work that's being done in Italian, Chinese, Korean, Japanese, and in Eastern Europe—in translation if we can't read it in the original—and we need to be getting more translations of things that aren't translated…One of the things world literature has to talk about is its own uneven playing field" (qtd. in Lenfield).

Comparatists could fill the gap left in the canon through compilations and translations by putting to use their multilingual talents. As has been argued in the Bernheimer Report on the state of comparative literature as a discipline, "Comparative literature should be actively engaged in the comparative study of the canon formation and in reconceiving the canon" (44). Nonetheless, canonization is a political process as traditionally the power structures of race, class, and gender have played a significant role in deciding what is included or excluded from a canon. Thus, Bernheimer's point that "attention should also be paid to the role of non-canonical texts, reading from contestatory, marginal, or subaltern perspectives" is an important one to note. Such readings, he notes, "given prominence recently in, for example, feminist and postcolonial theory, complements the critical investigation of the process of canon formation—how literary values are created and maintained in a particular culture—and vitalizes the attempt to expand canons" (44). While it may sound counterintuitive to have to translate texts in order for them to be noticed, if translation brings attention to multilingual writers and expands the horizons of Canadian literature, it may be a useful exercise. For instance, Josef Škvorecký's *The Engineer of Human Souls*, originally in Czech, once translated, won the Governor General's Award in 1984.

As I have argued elsewhere, "assessing and compiling literatures in a number of languages can be a daunting task, but certainly one worth undertaking" (Sayed 218). Like many other multilingual countries, "India provides us with an example of how this might be done on a national scale. Indian literature is produced in a number of languages and cross-linguistic translations are encouraged through funding and awards provided by various literary academies." Similarly, "Canadian writers, translators and scholars need to push for more funding to encourage more literature in heritage languages and translations of those works." Canadian literary historians will then take note of the heritage-language literature, and it will create possibilities for teaching these works in

Canadian classrooms. Comparatists could pay more attention to translation projects specially focused on heritage-language writing. This task has its own challenges. Damrosch, speaking of world literature, asserts that "the three intertwined problems are that the study of world literature can very readily become culturally deracinated, philologically bankrupt, and ideologically complicit with the worst tendencies of global capitalism. Other than that, we're in good shape" (456). Works in non-official languages usually do not get translated unless there is a guarantee of economic returns. Nonetheless, an active attempt to translate could allow us to do what Krishnaswamy has said in the context of world literary knowledges:

> *There can be little doubt that at the level of epistemology the comparative study of different literary traditions can expand our common storehouse of aesthetic concepts and produce important insights about the nature of literature/literariness and the ways in which different societies/cultures view these categories. It also may lead us to discover what aesthetic concepts are universal, what concepts are limited to certain cultural traditions, and what concepts are unique to a particular tradition. We may likewise find that some literary features are common or shared by all languages, that some are limited to literatures written in certain languages, and that some are unique to a particular linguistic or literary tradition. These and other (unforeseen, unforeseeable) discoveries may further enable us to craft a more thoughtful response to the question of universals than the one we have at present. (415)*

Another possibility to ponder is self-translation, a practice that Ngũgĩ wa Thiong'o and many others have followed. Most of the writers writing in heritage languages are proficient in English (and occasionally French). If the writers were to choose to translate their own work, this would not only make it accessible to non-speakers of the language, but also, as Arianna Dagnino has argued, help in the effort to "'majorize' a minority language by using their bilingualism and self-translational practices to expose the power dynamics at work within specific national contexts and linguistic communities" (384).

The issue of accessibility and acceptance of literature is not going to be resolved completely through a resort to translation only. We must also take into consideration that the works written in Eastern languages and using a cultural context that may be foreign to scholars assessing works in English and French, or Western traditions more broadly, cannot be analyzed without an understanding of non-Western theory models.[4] Krishnaswamy contends that we need a "radical re-vision[ing] of...what counts as theory" (401). She suggests establishing a system of "world literary knowledges...the purpose of which is to open up the canon of literary theory and criticism to alternative ways of conceptualizing and analyzing literary production" (408). This system would ensure, she argues, that "regional, subaltern, and popular traditions, whether latent or emergent, may be studied, analyzed, and evaluated as epistemologies of literature/literariness alongside the traditions of poetics that currently constitute both the canon (Euro-American) and the counter-canon (Arabic, Sanskrit, Chinese, Japanese) of literary theory" (408). Further, it would "mean that conceptualizations of literature/literariness may be approached as historically and culturally situated knowledges (or ideologies)—but without foreclosing the possibility that an open-ended, cross-cultural study of literary knowledges from around the world might at some point disclose certain literary or aesthetic features that characterize our shared humanity" (408). Thus, if one were to assess the quality of writing, heritage-language literature would have to be analyzed on terms that are not derived directly from hegemonic Western literary traditions. Heritage-language literature has a varied approach, appeal, and readership. Analyzing it from a Eurocentric perspective, one in which "the world [is] seen, described and mapped from European perspectives and interests," will not help in moving toward decolonial scholarly praxis which can lead to a more equitable representation of literary works in any given canon; such a canon will help us imagine a world within and beyond our national boundaries (Mignolo ix).

Conclusion

It is important for Canadian comparatists to read Canadian literature globalectically and explore national literatures from a multicultural and multilingual angle. Ngũgĩ writes that "the globalectical approach is...a method of both organizing and reading literatures: any text can lead the reader from the 'here' of one's existence to the 'there' of other people's existence and back" (42). Ngũgĩ further argues that "a globalectical imagination also calls for changes in attitudes to languages: monolingualism suffocates, and it is often extended to mean monoliterature and monoculturalism" (42). Canadian literature comprises multiple literary traditions, including the Indigenous, settler, and new immigrant narratives. Referring to Hugh MacLennan's novel *Two Solitudes*, Blodgett argues that "all writing that emerges from the minority languages and cultures of Canada constitutes its own solitude, and a history of Canadian culture is perforce a history of many solitudes" (224). While the question of what constitutes national/Canadian literature has been debated for over two centuries (see Lecker), and does not seem likely to be resolved any time soon, one could certainly argue that in this age of diversity it is beyond time that Canadianists acknowledge multiple solitudes and move toward a more inclusive model of Canadian literature. To study multiple literary and linguistic traditions side by side needs new epistemological approaches rooted in decolonial methodologies and techniques. Relegating multilingual literatures to the margins is a colonial exercise that situates literatures in French and English at the centre and accords them more power. Such "powers of domination produce system-*effects* and are experienced as pressures at a range of locations across the social, cultural, literary, and linguistic fields" (Mufti 96). New translations will also add a fresh chapter to comparative literary studies in Canada, which currently is focused mainly on the comparison of English and French literature. In order to decolonize the canon of Canadian literature, the contribution of literature in heritage languages needs not only to be acknowledged, but it ought to be actively promoted. Unless there are programs and funding in place for translation of multilingual literature, Canadians, and the world at large, will fail to see literary diversity and established and emerging multilingual voices.

NOTES

1. South Asian Canadian writers have also been actively writing in Bengali, Tamil, and other South Asian languages. While each of these is a minority language in Canada,

internationally they are prominent vectors of linguistic expression. For instance, globally, Hindi is spoken by more than 260 million, Urdu by approximately 70 million, and Punjabi by nearly 100 million. Hindi is also the national language of India and Urdu that of Pakistan.

2. While I identify some prominent authors writing in South Asian heritage languages and the form and content of their writing, this list is not meant to be expansive. It is outside of the scope of this chapter to expound in detail on the form and content of South Asian Canadian literature as its focus is mostly on a broader institutional perspective; nonetheless, as I have noted throughout this section, the literature is produced in multiple genres (poetry being prominent), and like other literary traditions, the content varies from author to author based on their country of origin, diasporic journeys, and lived realities.

3. See Emily Apter's *Against World Literature: On the Politics of Untranslatability*, for instance.

4. For further information on including non-Western theoretical premise(s) in literary analysis, see Hamid Dabashi's *Can Non-Europeans Think?*

WORKS CITED

Aponiuk, Natalia. "'Ethnic Literature,' Minority Literature,' 'Literature in Other Languages,' 'Hyphenated-Canadian Literature'—Will It Ever Be Canadian?" *Canadian Ethnic Studies*, vol. 28, no. 1, 1996, pp. 1–7.

Apter, Emily. *Against World Literature: On the Politics of Untranslatability*. Verso, 2013.

Atwood, Margaret. *Survival: A Thematic Guide to Canadian Literature*. House of Anansi, 1972.

Balan, Jars. Introduction. *Identifications: Ethnicity and the Writer in Canada*, edited by Jars Balan, Canadian Institute of Ukrainian Studies, 1982, pp. ix–xii.

Batts, Michael. "Multicultural Voices." *Encyclopedia of Literature in Canada*, edited by William H. New, University of Toronto Press, 2002, pp. 764–69.

Bernheimer, Charles, et al. "The Bernheimer Report, 1993: Comparative Literature at the Turn of the Century." *Comparative Literature in the Age of Multiculturalism*, edited by Charles Bernheimer, Johns Hopkins University Press, 1995, pp. 39–48.

Blodgett, E.D. "Canadian Literature Is Comparative Literature." *College English*, vol. 50, no. 8, 1988, pp. 904–11.

———. *Five-Part Invention: A History of Literary History in Canada*. University of Toronto Press, 2003.

Braz, Albert. "Chosen Literatures: Core Languages, Peripheral Languages, and the World Literary System." *Mosaic: A Journal for the Interdisciplinary Study of Literature*, vol. 47, no. 4, 2014, pp. 119–34.

Brydon, Diana. "Metamorphoses of a Discipline: Rethinking Canadian Literature within Institutional Contexts." *Trans.Can.Lit: Resituating the Study of Canadian Literature*, edited by Smaro Kamboureli and Roy Miki, Wilfrid Laurier University Press, 2007, pp. 1–16.

Bumsted, J.M. Introduction. *A/Part: Papers from Ottawa Conference on Language, Culture, and Literary Identity in Canada*, edited by Bumsted, *Canadian Literature*, Supplement No. 1, 1987, pp. 7–20.

Casanova, Pascale. *The World Republic of Letters*. 1999. Translated by M.B. DeBevoise, Harvard University Press, 2004.

Colombo, John Robert, editor. *The Poets of Canada: An Anthology of Poetry in Non-official Languages*, Hurtig Publishers, 1978.

Dabashi, Hamid. *Can Non-Europeans Think?* Zed Books, 2015.

Dagnino, Arianna. "Translingual Practices and Alternatives: Literary Studies in the Age of Global Mobility." *Canadian Review of Comparative Literature*, vol. 46, no. 2, 2019, pp. 380–91.

Damrosch, David. "National Literatures in the Age of Globalization." *ADE Bulletin*, no. 149, 2010, pp. 26–37.

Dev, Amiya. "Comparative Literature in India." *CLCWeb: Comparative Literature and Culture*, vol. 2, no. 4, 2000, https://docs.lib.purdue.edu/clcweb/vol2/iss4/10/.

Johnston, Hugh. *The Voyage of the Komagata Maru: The Sikh Challenge to Canada's Colour Bar*. University of British Columbia Press, 1989.

Kabir, Ananya Jahanara. "Literature of the South Asian Diaspora." *Routledge Handbook of South Asian Diaspora*, edited by Joya Chatterji and D.A. Washbrook, Routledge, 2013, pp. 388–99.

Kamboureli, Smaro, and Roy Miki, editors. *Trans.Can.Lit: Resituating the Study of Canadian Literature*. Wilfrid Laurier University Press, 2007.

Kamboureli, Smaro, and Robert Zacharias. Preface. *Shifting the Ground of Canadian Literary Studies*, edited by Kamboureli and Zacharias, Wilfrid Laurier University Press, 2012, pp. xi–xviii.

Khan, Nuzrat Yar. *Urdu Literature in Canada: A Preliminary Survey*. Ottawa: Department of Secretary of State of Canada, Multiculturalism, 1988.

Kirkconnell, Watson. *Canadian Overtones*. Columbia Press, 1935.

Krishnaswamy, Revathi. "Toward World Literary Knowledges: Theory in the Age of Globalization." *Comparative Literature,* vol. 62, no. 4, 2010, pp. 399–419.

Lecker, Robert. "Nineteenth-Century English-Canadian Anthologies and the Making of a National Literature." *Journal of Canadian Studies*, vol. 33, no. 1, 2010, pp. 91–117.

Lenfield, Spencer Lee. "A World of Literature: David Damrosch's Literary Global Reach." *Harvard Magazine*, Sept.–Oct. 2019, www.harvardmagazine.com/2019/09/david-damrosch.

Mignolo, Walter. Foreword: Yes, We Can. *Can Non-Europeans Think?* by Dabashi, pp. viii–xlii.

Mishra, Vijay. "The Diasporic Imaginary: Theorizing the Indian Diaspora." *Textual Practice*, vol. 10, no. 3, 1996, pp. 421–47.

Monterde, Antoni Martí. "World Citizenship and *Weltliteratur*: Revisiting the Origins of Comparative Literature." *Canadian Review of Comparative Literature*, vol. 46, no. 3, 2019, pp. 399–422.

Mufti, Aamir R. *Forget English!: Orientalisms and World Literatures*. Harvard University Press, 2016.

Ngũgĩ wa Thiong'o. "A Globalectical Imagination." *World Literature Today*, vol. 83, no. 3, 2013, pp. 40–42.

Qureshi, M.H.K. "Urdu in Canada." *Toronto South Asian Review*, vol. 1, no. 1, 1982, pp. 82–97.

Sayed, Asma. "Towards a Globalectical Reading of Comparative Canadian Literature." *Canadian Review of Comparative Literature*, vol. 41, no. 2, 2014, pp. 216–19.

Singh, Avadhesh Kumar. "Comparative Literature in India in the Twenty-first Century." *The English Paradigm in India: Essays in Language, Literature and Culture*, edited by Shweta Rao Garg and Deepti Gupta, Palgrave Macmillan, 2017, pp. 7–30.

Sohail, Khalid. *Shakila Rafiq's Legacy*. 2015.

Statistics Canada. "Data Tables, 2016 Census, Visible Minority (15), Immigration Status and Period of Immigration (11), Age (12) and Sex (3) for the Population in Private Households of Canada, Provinces and Territories, Census Metropolitan Areas and Census Agglomerations, 2016 Census – 25% Census Data," *2016 Census of Population*, 17 June 2019, Statistics Canada Catalogue no. 98-400-X2016191.

——. "Linguistic Diversity and Multilingualism in Canadian Homes," *Census in Brief*, 31 Aug. 2017, https://www12.statcan.gc.ca/census-recensement/2016/as-sa/98-200-x/2016010/98-200-x2016010-eng.cfm.

Sugunasiri, Suwunda H.J. *The Search for Meaning: Literature of Canadians of South Asian Origin*. Department of the Secretary of State of Canada, 1988.

Sutherland, Ronald. "The Mainstream of Canadian Literature." Vassanji, *Meeting of Streams*, pp. 69–77.

Vassanji, M.G. "Am I a Canadian Writer?" *Canadian Literature*, no. 190, 2006, pp. 7–13.

Vassanji, M.G., editor. *A Meeting of Streams: South Asian Canadian Literature*. Toronto South Asian Review Press, 1985.

Yates, Michael J., editor. *Volvox: Poetry from the Unofficial Languages of Canada, in English Translation*. Sono Nis Press, 1971.

"No Nation Now but the Imagination"
No Caribbean Nation without the Dutch Caribbean

DORIS HAMBUCH

THE COVID 19 PANDEMIC has highlighted the continued authority of nation-states. It showed that in times of extreme threat, national governments appear as primary agents of protection and aid. In response to the pandemic, many countries closed their borders and "repatriated" their citizens. Newscasts provided regular updates of measures taken by individual governments. This scenario emphasized the shortcomings of phenomena such as transnationalism and globalization in addressing the needs of peoples, and it altered the important argument made by Shalini Puri in *The Caribbean Postcolonial* that "transnationalist agendas...are poorly served by denying the continuing, though discernibly declining, power of the nation-state" (6). The alteration relates to the idea of the decline. The recent global crisis has, it seems, proven the contrary, that for all the efforts to create international unions and collaborations, power and indeed supremacy does, in the end, remain with the nation-state. In literary studies, however, as this chapter's title emphasizes, the imagination allows for ideals that reality denies. Aesthetic representations, in Puri's terms (1), may contrast with political ones. Poetics may complement politics. In this vein, the following argument renews Puri's claim that "the Caribbean's cultural, economic, and geopolitical coordinates make it both urgent and difficult to imagine Caribbean community identity" (12). I posit that any community, whether potential or actual, should aim for inclusivity, and my focus on Dutch Caribbean writers addresses a systematic neglect in the conception of Caribbean community identity. I suggest that however complicated the political status of the individual entities in the region may be—ranging from independent neocolonial states to overseas departments—the cultural identity of all of them would be strengthened through the establishment of a "Caribbean Nation," as long as it is inclusive.

In anglophone literary criticism, cross-Caribbean studies emerged towards the end of the twentieth century, with J. Michael Dash's *The Other America: Caribbean Literature in a New World Context* and Silvio Torres-Saillant's *Caribbean Poetics: Towards an Aesthetic of West Indian Literature*. These works ignore the Dutch Caribbean, possibly because both scholars are from the discipline of Romance languages. In "Displacements in Contemporary Caribbean Writing" (2000), I advocate the inclusion of writers from Suriname and the so-called ABC islands, the Netherlands Antilles, in comparative Caribbean discourse. Two decades later, with the exception of Torres-Saillant's *Intellectual History of the Caribbean*, there has not been much progress in this regard, as single-authored books—for example, Carol Boyce Davies's *Caribbean Spaces: Escapes from the Twilight Zones* and Yolanda Martínez-San Miguel's *Coloniality of Diasporas: Rethinking Intra-colonial Migrations in a Pan-Caribbean Context*—show. The fact that such studies fail to even acknowledge their exclusions prompts an investigation of the circumstances that render Dutch Caribbean thought absent from anglophone cross-Caribbean studies.[1] This chapter examines the status of Dutch as a means of exploring the various ways that cross-Caribbean discourse stands to gain from closer attention to the Dutch-speaking part of the region. In the process, it highlights selected poets from across the region who are representative of different generations: Frank Martinus Arion (1936–2015) from Curaçao, Astrid Roemer (1947) from Suriname, Lasana M. Sekou (1959) from Sint Maarten, and Radna Fabias (1983) from Curaçao. Selected passages from the work of these authors illustrate their concerns with and contributions to an imagined Caribbean Nation. The larger entity, for this contribution to *National Literature in Multinational States*, is imagined in order to advocate inclusion of the marginalized in general, and of Dutch Caribbean artists in their regional discourse in particular.

Sandra Messinger Cypess analyzes the distinction between Latin American and Caribbean Studies in *Reimagining the Caribbean: Conversations among the Creole, English, French, and Spanish Caribbean*. Cypess's detailed overview of departments and programs across universities in the United States suggests that the omission of the Dutch Caribbean from cross-Caribbean studies owes in no small part to North American academic practices. The "language hierarchy" in the respective programs begins with Spanish and does not tend to include "Dutch, Papiamentu, or Haitian Creole" (Cypess 2). The collection, co-edited by Valérie K. Orlando and Cypess, lists neither "Dutch," nor any Dutch Caribbean locations in its index, although reference is made to the language in the above quoted passage. While it is obvious that such an anthology cannot be all inclusive, one would at least expect its introduction to prevent readers from forgetting the existence of Aruba, Bonaire, Curaçao, Saba, Sint Eustatius, Sint Maarten, and Suriname. Instead, the "polyvalent nature of the Caribbean" there comprises only "English, Spanish, French, and [French] Creole" (2). The omission is to some extent due to the persistent lack of translations, but more effort could be made to propagate and include those texts that are already translated. In support of Rose Mary Allen's claim that Dutch Caribbean intellectuals offer significant contributions to a comprehensive understanding of the region (95), this chapter demonstrates how more attention to Dutch Caribbean literature and more mediation via translation could enrich the field of Caribbean studies. To that effect, it situates the national literatures of the Caribbean within the wider context of an imaginary Caribbean Nation, and argues that such a construct loses its raison d'être when it becomes exclusive. At the same time, the positing of a larger entity that invites a broader sense of belonging should raise awareness of, and help eliminate, potential exclusions.

In geographical terms, the Caribbean region comprises the archipelago between the Caribbean Sea and the Atlantic Ocean, as well as several bordering continental countries such as Guyana, French Guiana, and Suriname. While nationalism has played a crucial role for independence movements in individual Caribbean countries throughout the twentieth century, the vision of a "Caribbean Nation," which prioritizes regional identity, has always accompanied the process of decolonization. This vision manifests itself in much of the region's literature. Jamaican Edward Baugh sums up the relationship between Caribbean writers and their "imagined community" (Anderson) when he describes how the St. Lucian Nobel laureate Derek Walcott considered himself "a St. Lucian first and last," but that there is "no necessary conflict between his considering himself this and, at the same time, a West Indian and a member of the boundary-less guild of poets" (Baugh 157). Walcott's line from "The Schooner *Flight*" that features in this chapter's title, best illustrates such a multilayered sense of home: "I had no nation now but the imagination" (Walcott 350). It should be clear that there is a discrepancy between the local poet's imagination and that of the politicians responsible for the current geographic divisions. For the present argument, the focus is on the Caribbean Nation as imagined by the region's poets.

The borders in the Caribbean result from its history of colonization. They were imposed rather than determined by an indigenous population. Colonization, however, did not only lead to the spread of European languages and culture; it also brought people of African and eventually Asian heritage to the area. It has made every Caribbean country a "multinational state" in its own right. The entire region shares the history of colonial wars and the resulting cultural diversity. The literary representation of this shared diversity led to a concept known as "Caribbeanness" in English-language criticism. Linked to the idea of "creolization," with its origin in French Caribbean thought, Caribbeanness encapsulates the region's unique version of cultural diversity. Aart Broek explains how, after the Second World War, Dutch Caribbean writers such as Pierre Lauffer and Cola Debrot advocated such a sense of regional cultural identity in opposition to the colonizer's dominance (Broek 44). During this time, most of the former British colonies, became independent nation-states. Within the Dutch Caribbean, only Suriname, Dutch Guiana until 1975, followed their examples.

Elleke Boehmer's *Empire, the National, and the Postcolonial, 1890–1920* demonstrates how "around the turn of the nineteenth into the twentieth century, certain early anti-imperial and nationalist movements, and nationalist and anti-colonial leaders and writers, found inspirational solidarity and instructive models in *one another*'s work and experience" (1–2).[2] The movements in question achieved different outcomes throughout the Caribbean region. French Guiana, Guadeloupe, and Martinique remain French Overseas Departments, while Saint Barthélemy and Saint Martin count as French Overseas Collectivities. Suriname became an independent country in 1975. Aruba, Curaçao, and Sint Maarten form constituent countries within the Kingdom of the Netherlands. Bonaire, Sint Eustatius, and Saba count as special municipalities. When Wim Rutgers concludes his survey of literary magazines in the Netherlands Antilles with the prediction that better collaboration across the region could "contribute greatly to the formation of a truly Antillean nation" (567), the nation in question refers to the Dutch Antilles. The following inquiries suggest that it would be fruitful to extend an imagined entity's borders beyond the reach of an individual colonial power, and beyond language barriers. A useful way to do this is to look at the language choices of individual poets. Regardless of constitutional status, the reality of a unique creolized culture finds its expression in language variation throughout the entire Caribbean region. Curaçao is indeed at the forefront of linguistic independence with Papiamentu serving not only as an official language next to Dutch and English, but also as a language of instruction, as well as of mass media.

Allen's discussion of Curaçaoan intellectuals in "Toward Reconstituting Caribbean Identity Discourse from within the Dutch Caribbean Island of Curaçao" identifies creolization as a major theme. Relying on the sociologist René Römer's view, she states that "creolization in Curaçao emerged from the tensions and contradictions arising from the admixture of the white, Protestant, West-European culture of the Dutch, the Iberian culture of the Sephardic Jews, and the various African cultures, which over the course of time developed their own distinctive character" (Allen 99). Allen draws a parallel between Römer and the Curaçaoan author Frank Martinus Arion, who reflects on this vision in his linguistic scholarship and in his creative writing. Better known as novelist, he is the author of the long poem "Stemmen uit Afrika" (Voices from Africa),[3] which, as the title suggests, echoes the *négritude* sentiment of Martiniquan Aimé Césaire's *Cahier d'un retour au pays natal*.

It was Césaire's student Édouard Glissant who became the most prominent theoretician of creolization. Initially used in the Caribbean to refer to any mixed background including European descent, "creole" came to refer to all forms of regional transculturation. Departing from his understanding of creolization, Glissant defined Antillanité in *Caribbean Discourse* as derived from a system of multiple interrelated cultures (*"une multi-relation"*; 249), and Caribbeanness expresses the anglophone version of this understanding. The Cuban writer Antonio Benítez-Rojo later applied chaos theory to the idea of creolization in *La isla que se repite* (*The Repeating Island*). Around the time of this text's publication, the late 1980s, discussions of multiculturalism led James Clifford in his *Predicament of Culture* to use the Caribbean region as model of a hybrid society. The sentence quoted here from Dash's *Other America* became something like a slogan for Caribbeanists: "We are all Caribbeans now in our urban archipelagos" (Clifford qtd. in Dash 6). Many Caribbean authors, at that time, had indeed moved to European or North American metropoles, and one needs to distinguish whether texts about regional identity originate within the Caribbean or its so-called diaspora.[4] In general, regardless of their location, those poets who foreground Caribbean origins in their work often favour the "utopia of a Caribbean nation" (Van Haesendonck 3) that Kristian van Haesendonck refers to in *Caribbeing: Comparing Caribbean Literatures and Cultures*. In his introduction to this anthology, Van Haesendonck points out Arion's exasperation with the reality of Caribbeanness (2). Much of the Curaçaoan's creative writing nevertheless celebrates and advocates the vision of a common regional identity.

One does well to contrast the seductive nature of an imagined, utopian Caribbean Nation with the sobering concept of Belinda Edmondson's "Caribbean romances." In a collection by the same title, Edmondson cautions that the "Caribbean that has developed in scholarly discourse... sometimes seems to have a life of its own" and that the debates about concepts such as Caribbeanness "have such power to shape the way the region now imagines itself that they have become mythic" (2). Every part of the region has its own intra-ethnic conflicts, a theme that will be discussed in the context of Roemer's *Suriname Trilogy*. Rivalries exist between the individual Caribbean countries and in particular between islands still governed by the same European power. Yet there is undeniable strength in the recalling of common ground, in collective memory, and in communal collaboration. Cross-regional co-operation has potential on the economic level and offers invaluable opportunities in a cultural context, as Caribbean scholarly associations, journals, magazines, and festivals demonstrate. The poets themselves are well aware of the utopian character of a unifying vision, as Walcott's conceit of the imagi*nation* illustrates. Puri reminds readers that Anderson's "imagined community" also "posits a tension between fact and fiction" (20). Arion invents the fictitious island Amber to project his ideal of an independent country. The threat of a volcano eruption symbolizes potential shortcomings in Arion's scenario.

De laatste vrijheid (The ultimate freedom), set mainly in Amber, is the best example of Arion's belief in Caribbeanness. The novel's protagonist Daryll Guenepou, described as "typically Curaçaoan," combines in his heritage Dominican, Colombian, Aruban, and Surinamese ancestry (Arion, *De laatste* 73). His ex-wife Aideline is from Sint Maarten, with relatives in Anguilla, St. Croix, St. Kitts, and Nevis (108). Daryll's family name emphasizes his African origin and establishes the relevance of language.[5] Guene was a secret language spoken by slaves on plantations in Curaçao. In one of his contributions to A. James Arnold's *History of Literature in the Caribbean*, Arion explains the connection between Guene and Papiamentu ("Value of Guene"). Ineke Phaf-Rheinberger, who illuminates the Guene word *pou*'s derivation from Portuguese *pau* (wood), explains how this kind of name choice reveals Arion's expertise in the "'deep Papiamentu' connected with several African-Portuguese languages" (Phaf-Rheinberger, *Air of Liberty* 132).

Daryll and Aideline leave Curaçao because the former is not allowed to teach in Papiamentu there. They move through the Caribbean in search for a place that could develop its Caribbean identity via independence from the colonial power. The couple is explicit in their aim to explore new aspects of Caribbean culture (Arion, *De laatste* 96). The independence movements that play a crucial role throughout their search are not all part of the Dutch Caribbean. In Grenada, where they meet the revolutionary Maurice Bishop, they are joined by Guyanese Jan Carew and Barbadian George Lamming (99). Until Bishop's execution in 1983, followed by the Reagan-led invasion, Grenada served as role model for many Caribbean intellectuals. Arion contrasts Grenada's potential with V.S. Naipaul's negative vision of the region in *De laatste vrijheid* (100). Before they move to Grenada, however, Daryll and Aideline live in independent Suriname. Phaf-Rheinberger emphasizes the autobiographical element when pointing out that Arion himself, with Trudi Guda, had moved to Suriname for ideological reasons (Phaf-Rheinberger, *Air of Liberty* 135).

After the fictional couple's return to Curaçao, they split ways. Daryll and their twins find the utopian Amber after Aideline leaves to pursue her career as composer in Amsterdam. Aideline's work, now emerging from the Caribbean diaspora in Europe, continues to rely on her Antillean origin. In fact, she is the character who provides most of the intertextual references to Caribbean literature, in particular to Walcott's *Omeros* and V.S. Naipaul's *Guerrillas*. *De laatste vrijheid* enters a dialogue with the work of several other Caribbean writers, mainly from the anglophone part of the region. One may note at this point that the region's linguistic borders are at times as arbitrary as the geographical ones. Walcott's home, St. Lucia, still shows a strong French influence, obvious in place names such as Anse La Raye, Choiseul, Gros Islet, and Vieux Fort, as well as in the poet's use of French Creole. Broek explains that the first Dutch Antillean literature was published in Spanish (Broek 10). Lasana M. Sekou, from Dutch Sint Maarten, writes predominantly in English. Sint Maarten shares the same island with the French "overseas collectivity" Saint Martin. Torres-Saillant makes reference to the Sint Maarten–based Nigerian scholar Fabian Badejo, who confirms that most inhabitants of Sekou's home island have proficiency in English, Dutch, Spanish, and Papiamentu (Torres-Saillant, *Intellectual History* 188). Papiamentu itself once moved from a Portuguese- to a Spanish-based Creole, which explains the alternative spelling Papiamento.

Arion served as head of the Curaçao Language Institute in the 1980s and published in Papiamentu on occasion. Daryll, his protagonist in *De laatste vrijheid*, is happy to settle in Constance, the capital of Amber, where his friend Bernard Cheri serves as minister of education and is about to introduce Creole as an official language of instruction. As small as an audience for Creole literature may be, readers of Dutch are also comparatively few in numbers globally. When Allen asks, in her article on Cuaraçaoan intellectuals, why French Caribbean authors do not suffer the same neglect (95), one may look to Arturo Desimone for an answer: "Unlike other imperial languages of the Caribbean—French, Spanish, English—the Dutch language possesses no similar international audience" (Desimone). Therefore, the subjects of Allen's inquiry "have become part of the Dutch-Caribbean canon and their scholarship has become recognized in the Netherlands, [but they] have not become recognized as contributors to Caribbean thought beyond the Dutch-Caribbean academic sphere" (Allen 95). Studies by Phaf-Rheinberger and Torres-Saillant are rare, notable exceptions that may lead the way to remedy this situation.

Two decades ago, I wrote that it would take many more initiatives like Hilda van Neck-Yoder's special issue of *Callaloo* devoted to the Dutch Caribbean to generate inclusive intellectual exchange within and about the Caribbean region (Hambuch, "Walcott vs. Naipaul" 95). Unfortunately, there has not been a sufficient number of such projects in the meantime, though several editors of anthologies do deserve praise for their efforts to include texts from the Dutch Caribbean. The *Oxford Book of Caribbean Verse* (Brown and McWatt) features translated poems by Arion and four Surinamese poets. It further includes a text by Nydia Ecury from Aruba, as well as one by Sekou, who has received recognition for his initiatives as founder of a regional publishing house and a book fair. Translations of stories by Roemer can be found in *Green Cane and Juicy Flotsam: Short Stories by Caribbean Women* (Esteves and Paravisini-Gebert) and the *Oxford Book of Caribbean Short Stories* (Brown and Wickham). Particular praise is due to M.J. Fenwick for inclusions of original texts along with English translations in *Sisters of Caliban: Contemporary Women Poets of the Caribbean (A Multilingual Anthology)*.

A short Papiamentu text by Curaçaoan Gladys Do Rego in Fenwick's collection discusses women's position within the context of cultural and national identity. The poem's speaker fails to recall her people's collective memory via history books and monuments, or within "the nation's soul"

(Fenwick 298, "den kurasou di nos patria"). A long poem by Puerto Rican Olga Nolla, in the same collection, provides a more explicitly feminist critique of the concept of nationalism (Fenwick 251–56). An obsession with nation-building has often been attributed to male Caribbean politicians and writers of the twentieth century.[6] Metaphors involving women's bodies are a result of this male-dominated discourse, as examples from Sekou's poetry illustrate. Florencia V. Cornet discusses the work of five Curaçaoan women writers who express what she calls a "cosmopolitan patriotism" (196), a sentiment that can be seen in contrast to the nationalism of their male predecessors. Throughout publications that are unfortunately not readily available for international audiences, writers such as Diana Lebacs, Myra Römer, and Mishenu Osepa Cicilia represent "transnational collective plurality and difference" (Cornet 175). This kind of cosmopolitan patriotism challenges the negative consequences of exaggerated nationalism, including dictatorships, political persecution, and massacres. Examples from Fabias's *Habitus* and Roemer's *Suriname Trilogy* illustrate this kind of challenge.

In April 2012, on the occasion of Peepal Tree Press's twenty-fifth anniversary, Leeds Metropolitan University hosted a conference titled "Narrating the Caribbean Nation: A Celebration of Literature and Orature." The only contribution revolving around the Dutch Caribbean explored Roemer's *Suriname Trilogy* as a fictional record of a country's formation within the kind of postcolonial environment discussed in the preceding paragraphs. Arion's character in *De laatste vrijheid* moves to Suriname, if only temporarily, because of this country's constitutional independence. Roemer's trilogy, consisting of *Gewaagd leven* (Risky living), *Lijken op liefde* (Looks like love), and *Was getekend* (Something signed), weaves intriguing plotlines around the historical events that led to the independence movement's success in 1975 and that also prompted upheavals and mass migration. As Phaf-Rheinberger asserts in the second part of Arnold's *History of Literature in the Caribbean*, Roemer's trilogy "displays a breathtaking effort to (re)write foundational history from a postcolonial perspective of its own" (Phaf-Rheinberger, "Contemporary Surinamese Novel" 538).

The second of the three novels is the one most focused on post-independence developments. It is also the only one in which precise dates are significant, as the plot projects an event into the immediate future, at the end of the millennium. Traumatic historical moments are remembered during the preparations for a cleansing tribunal to take place on the eve of 2000: "The approaching year 2000 has given Suriname the opportunity to enter the coming century absolved from history. After violent ethnic conflicts, the elected government has asked the people in a referendum about two 'terrible questions': the affair with the Netherlands and the investigation of the December massacre" (Roemer, *Lijken* 22). To use the word "verhouding" with regard to the relationship between ex-colony and -colonizer means to present this relationship as one between lovers. Indeed, the novel is dedicated to "lovers and their beloveds," and the intimate merges with the public throughout the narration.

Since Roemer's trilogy is concerned with the independence of one specific country within the projected Caribbean Nation, the mixed-cultural background of her characters reflects on ethnicities rather than, as in *De laatste vrijheid*, ancestry from across the region. Onno Mus, the protagonist of the first novel, *Gewaagd leven*, is the grandson of a white European man and his mistress from a *Bosneger* (Maroon) village in Galibi. Cora Sewa, the third-person narrator in the second novel, is the daughter of a Hindustani from Nickerie and an Afro-Surinamese from the Para district. In the last novel, Ilya can "call himself the son-of-that-red-Bush Negro-and-that-white-nurse, everybody can still see that he is indeed a saltwater-Chinese" (Roemer, *Was getekend* 28). While these characters are thus representative of Caribbean creolization, their stories also illustrate a reality of inter-ethnic disputes and at times violent conflicts. The Surinamese, at the end of *Lijken op liefde*, cannot enter the new millennium "absolved from history, despite their efforts" (245). On a personal level, however, Roemer's protagonist Cora, a housekeeper by profession, does succeed in clearing up a great deal of secrecy. Seen in a comparative sense, and with regard to the mentioned feminist premise, the female narrator's mission is fulfilled whereas the male politicians' is not.

In an extensive study of decolonization in the Dutch Caribbean, Gert Oostindie and Inge Klinkers trace political developments across the region, beginning with the 1791 Haitian Revolution (9). According to their findings, statistics demonstrate that living standards and political stability are higher in the non-sovereign Caribbean entities. "Small wonder then,"

Oostindie and Klinkers write, "that the urge for independence in these territories is weak, and indeed it seems that Caribbean decolonization may well have reached its final *dénouement* with the present status quo" (9). At the time of publication, about five million Caribbean citizens were living in one of the non-sovereign parts of the region, Puerto Rico, the French overseas departments, the Netherlands Antilles and Aruba, the British Caribbean Overseas Territories, and the U.S. Virgin Islands. Despite ongoing debates and frequent referendums, none of the listed locations has, to this day, changed the status of political dependence significantly.

The following section highlights the work of a poet who continues to advocate independence, and in this case independence would mean the union of a single island currently governed by two different European powers, the Kingdom of the Netherlands and France. Lasana M. Sekou uses a traditional saying about the unity of St. Martin as epigraph to his recent collection *Hurricane Protocol*, "The gale doesn't stop at the frontier" (v). It may surprise, then, that this book, inspired by hurricane Irma's devastation and combining written text with Lacambalam illustrations from the Maya codex, conveys much less of a nationalist ethos than Sekou's earlier work. *The Salt Reaper: Poems from the Flats* makes a strong case for an independent St. Martin that would unite the Dutch-governed North and the French-governed South of the island. The collection is divided into two parts, the first comprising poems written before and the second after the turn of the millennium. Poems in the first part are riddled with notions of the "Mothernation" (4), "Freedom" (9), "our nation's business" (5), "meh country" and "the nation-birth of republic" (9), as well as "the captive nation" (23). Contexts identify St. Martin rather than the entire region as the nation in question here. The second part begins with a comparatively long text titled "cradle of the nation" (47), which recalls various aspects of the region's history. It signals a break with preceding activism as it creates a more cosmic scope in which a reader could situate other parts of the region, after all.

Sekou was born in Aruba, raised mainly in Sint Maarten, and holds postsecondary degrees from North American institutions, including an MA in mass communication from Howard University (Sekou, *Salt Reaper* 114). After his return from the United States, he founded the House of

Nehesi, a publishing initiative for which Torres-Saillant reserves a prominent place in the closing of his second edition of *Caribbean Poetics*:

> *During the golden years when the Cuban Revolution enjoyed economic stability, Casa de las Americas encouraged literary creativity in the region...Today the socialist government that supported that initiative no longer enjoys its former prosperity and the neoliberal states that abound in the rest of the region have not exhibited a comparable commitment to ameliorating the bane of Caribbean fragmentation by forging bridges of artistic and intellectual communication across the various divides of language and geography. Therefore, it may have to fall upon enlightened private advocates like Sekou to endeavour to create structures, their magnitude notwithstanding, that may contribute to bringing the multilingual voices of the Caribbean to speak within hearing range of one another, thereby affording us a fuller, larger, more complex, hence truer, view of the body of utterances we call Caribbean literature. (351)*

Besides founding the House of Nehesi, Sekou also participated in the inauguration of the St. Martin book fair. His success with these initiatives led to a recognition for "literary excellence in the service of Caribbean unity" (Sekou, *Salt Reaper* 114). The multilingual character of Sekou's work, it would seem, symbolizes the hybrid nature of a Caribbean Nation even if English is predominant. *The Salt Reaper* features all the languages Badejo considers native to Sint Maarten (Torres-Saillant, *Intellectual History* 188). A single poem such as "Title Deed," for example, combines several of these languages in the context of nation-building:

> to born the day of democracy in the nation-birth of republic
> and no longer swear that there is no greater reward
> than the heaven which awaits those
> wie willen holland houden
> vie who be more french than the french
>
> luister allemaal
> listen everybody

escuchan pueblo

écoute tout le monde *(Sekou 9)*

This passionate call for attention is then followed by the kind of metaphor that characterizes nationalist poetic discourse as sexist. "Soft as the whisper may be," the poem continues, "your period is calling you / like a girl come of age" (9). Other poems are more graphic yet, with the "earth-womb / of the Mothernation" and "a new banner of colors / in the nipples of the future" (4). "Freedom," Sekou writes in a poem with that title, "is my bitch to keep" (24), and alternates later in the text to "is my kept sweet piece / not some venal virgin" (26). Grounded in the oral/spoken word tradition, these lines lend themselves to some of the kinds of inquiries that rap and hip-hop have provoked. They are beyond the scope of the present study. For investigations into the discourse of nationalism, however, the respective metaphors confirm the notion that this discourse is male dominated. In its worst manifestation, nationalism may lead to dictatorships and, although not all women leaders may qualify as benign, their names do not come as readily to mind as examples of dictators.

The last poet that this chapter highlights, Radna Fabias, in fact makes a strong statement about a dictator's masculinity in a short poem titled "04:40."

> *there was no wall the wall that did not*
> *exist did not fall*
> *the man with the false moustache is not*
> *a dictator and this is not a moustache*
> *there were no explosives it was no*
> *war nothing exploded (Fabias 521)*[7]

A reference to the notion of "fake news" may not be avoidable in the interpretation of this poem that sets out to deny everything from the war to the dictator's moustache. The text's power lies in its abstraction. It identifies neither place nor historical figures, only a specific time seems suggested in the title. The time, "04:40," indicates the early morning hours before dawn, the historically preferred time for many military attacks. The denial may imply a secret operation, but it may also refer to erroneous reporting via media and/or historiographers. The most relevant elements for the present argument are the two repeated nouns, the wall and the moustache. The moustache underlines the dictator's virility, and the wall provokes connotations of infamous examples of misguided nationalism, such as in the context of Korea's division, or the Berlin Wall. In the Caribbean context, this poem recalls the Colonial Wars as much as recent dictatorships. Roemer's *Lijken op liefde* depicts Suriname's December massacre as one historical example, and the Dutch word "lijken" means both "to look like" and "corpses." Not all texts in Fabias's debut collection are equally abstract. With a series of poems titled "travel guide," which describe Caribbean scenes, *Habitus* moves between concrete and abstract locations. It is expressive of the same cosmopolitan patriotism that Cornet ascribes to the women writers in her study.

Unlike single-authored books, anthologies have a greater chance to be more inclusive, as Arnold's massive three-volume *History of Literature in the Caribbean* and Van Haesendonck's more recent *Caribbeing* show. A unique effort is made in *Reshaping Glocal Dynamics of the Caribbean: Relaxiones y desconexiones / Relations et déconnexions / Relations and Disconnections* with the inclusion of critical essays in the various languages at home in the Caribbean region. In line with the trilingual subtitle, the introduction to this collection features an English epigraph by Walcott, one in Spanish by Mayra Santos-Febros, and one in French by Glissant. The omission of Dutch, which recalls Desimone's statement on this language's global status, and Creole epigraphs is at least accompanied with an apology. With the aim to "shed light from an explicitly comparative, historical, and contemporary perspective" on creative expression in the Caribbean, the editors Anja Bandau, Anne Brüske, and Natascha Ueckmann apologize for the lack of critical essays in the other languages: "Contributions in other languages spoken in the Caribbean, such as Dutch or the Creole languages, would have put at risk the general accessibility of their contents" (8n11). As in Fenwick's collection of primary texts, bilingual presentations of essays in the omitted languages might set important signals in follow ups on Bandau, Brüske, and Ueckmann's seminal anthology.

Although Torres-Saillant remedied the previous oversight of Dutch Caribbean writers in his 2006 *Intellectual History of the Caribbean*, his 2013 edition of *Caribbean Poetics* does not develop inquiries into these writers' oeuvres sufficiently. The revised edition of *Caribbean Poetics*, commissioned by Peepal Tree Press, reserves updates for the afterword. There, the reader finds references to Dutch Caribbean authors such as Jit Narain, Anton de Kom, and Cynthia McLeod, but they appear very much like an afterthought. This also applies to the above quoted applause for Sekou's publishing efforts in the concluding paragraph. The introduction of the updated edition of *Caribbean Poetics* repeats the earlier version's goal to provide "close readings of major figures from three of the Caribbean's linguistic blocs," without identification of the excluded fourth (Torres-Saillant 20). There is much room for future comparative Caribbean studies to create the kind of "hearing range" envisioned by Torres-Saillant (351). Special attention should be paid in this endeavour to Allen's conviction that intellectuals from Aruba, Bonaire, Curaçao, Saba, Sint Maarten, Sint Eustatius, and Suriname "have brought forward, from a Dutch-Caribbean perspective, new, useful and important aspects of the diverse and complex Caribbean reality" (95). These aspects relate to multilingualism and the significance of Creoles, as well as to geographic confusion over Leeward and Windward locations along with intra-Caribbean migration (Allen 101). They furthermore relate to multiple variations of national identity within and without the Kingdom of the Netherlands.

In her warning not to underestimate the impact of what she calls a "national unconscious" (19), Puri relies on anthropologist John Borneman's distinction between nationalism ("willed adherence to a community") and nationness ("praxis of belonging;" Borneman qtd. in Puri 19). Arguing that there is an unconscious pursuit of nationalism, even in discourses that claim to denounce the latter, she interprets nationness as "the ways in which everyday practices and subjective meanings are shaped by national culture, ideologies, and state policies" (28). To accept the concept of "national unconscious" means to admit that no individual is immune to a certain degree of national belonging. Awareness of this fact indeed facilitates participation in a given community. In the spirit of nationness, one does well to consider one's belonging beyond the immediate state or country, and situate the one among the many of an imagined larger union. A Trinidadian, Puerto

Rican, Aruban, or Martiniquan who ponders belonging to the construct that is the Caribbean Nation not only takes note of the common ground among parts of the region. This person also relativizes specific issues in a new context, recognizes the impact of the larger entity on the smaller, and vice versa. Only the consideration of the larger union draws attention to systemic exclusion. After all, the popular saying that one should not lose sight of the forest while focusing on the trees is very similar in Dutch, French, Spanish, and English.[8]

NOTES

1. Puri's *Caribbean Postcolonial* is a notable exception. In her first footnote, Puri apologizes for the "marginalization that arises from the number of local Dutch Caribbean contact/languages, the paucity of translations, and the Netherlands' own relative marginality to the centers of European power" (223). These three reasons reoccur throughout this chapter.
2. Lea Reade Rosenberg scrutinizes this historical period and its consequences in the context of the anglophone Caribbean in *Nationalism and the Formation of Caribbean Literature*. She relies on Kamau Brathwaite's definition of creolization, constituting both acculturation and interculturation, to explain this concept's relevance for independence movements: "creolization was constituted by struggles among Caribbean social groups for power and legitimacy as well as by a contest for power between colony and metropole" (Rosenberg 7). Aesthetic representations of the Caribbean Nation tend to gloss over such historical facts.
3. Translations are my own unless otherwise indicated.
4. Puri further demonstrates striking differences that depend on whether the Caribbean intellectual participating in the creolization discourse hails from an independent nation-state, or from a place like Puerto Rico, Guadeloupe, or Martinique (34).
5. It is telling that Kamau Brathwaite uses the designation "Nation Language," now an encyclopedia entry, in his attempt to elevate the status of Caribbean English.
6. The most famous Caribbean nationalists, like Grenada's Maurice Bishop and Trinidad's Eric Williams, have tended to be men. So were the intellectuals who described concepts such as creolization and Caribbeanness. Rosenberg considers Una Marson an exception in this context (1). See, for example, Luis Fernando Restrepo's "Closure and Disclosure of the Caribbean Body: Gabriel García Márquez and Derek Walcott," in Arnold, vol. 3, pp. 251–66, for further literary representations of resulting gendered discourse.
7. er was geen muur de muur die er niet / was is niet gevallen / de man met de foute snor is geen / dictator en dat is geen snor / er waren geen explosieven het was geen/ oorlog er is niets ontploft

8. The Dutch version is "door de bomen het bos niet meer zien," the French "l'arbre cache souvent la forêt," and the English "not to see the forest for the trees." The Spanish "los árboles no le dejan ver el bosque" is less popular than the other three.

WORKS CITED

Allen, Rose Mary. "Toward Reconstituting Caribbean Identity Discourse from within the Dutch Caribbean Island of Curaçao." *Freedom, Power and Sovereignty: The Thought of Gordon K. Lewis*, edited by Brian Meeks and Jermaine McCalpin, Ian Randle, 2015, pp. 94–110.

Anderson, Benedict. *Imagined Communities: Reflections on the Spread of Nationalism*. 1983. Verso, 2006.

Arion, Frank Martinus. *De laatste vrijheid*. De Bezige Bij, 1995.

———. "Stemmen uit Afrika." *Antilliaanse Cahiers*, vol. 3, no. 1, 1957, pp. 1–56.

———. "The Value of Guene for Folklore and Literary Culture." Arnold, vol. 2, *English- and Dutch-Speaking Regions*, pp. 415–19.

Arnold, A. James, editor. *A History of Literature in the Caribbean*. John Benjamins, 1994–2001. 3 vols.

Bandau, Anja, Anne Brüske, and Natascha Ueckmann, editors. *Reshaping Glocal Dynamics of the Caribbean: Relaxiones y desconexiones / Relations et déconnexions / Relations and Disconnections*, Heidelberg University Press, 2018.

Baugh, Edward. "Derek Walcott and the Centering of the Caribbean Subject." *Research in African Literatures*, no. 34, vol. 1, 2003, pp. 151–59.

Boehmer, Elleke. *Empire, the National, and the Postcolonial, 1890–1920*. Oxford University Press, 2002.

Brathwaite, Kamau. "National Language." Concise Oxford Companion to the English Language. *Encyclopedia.com*, 24 Jan. 2022, https://www.encyclopedia.com/humanities/encyclopedias-almanacs-transcripts-and-maps/nation-language.

Broek, Aart G. *The Colour of My Island: Ideology and Writing in Papiamentu (Aruba, Bonaire & Curaçao); A Bird's-Eye View*. In de Knipscheer, 2009.

Brown, Stewart, and Mark McWatt, editors. *The Oxford Book of Caribbean Verse*. Oxford University Press, 2005.

Brown, Stewart, and John Wickham, editors. *The Oxford Book of Caribbean Short Stories*. Oxford University Press, 1999.

Césaire, Aimé. 1939. *Cahier d'un retour au pays natal*. Présence Africaine, 1956.

Cornet, Florencia V. "Dutch Caribbean Women's Literary Thought: Activism through Linguistic and Cosmopolitan Multiplicity." *Wagadu: A Journal of Transnational Women's and Gender Studies*, vol. 18, 2017, pp. 175–202.

Cypess, Sandra Messinger. "Approaching the Caribbean from a Latin American Perspective." *Reimagining the Caribbean: Conversations among the Creole, English, French, and Spanish Caribbean*, edited by Valérie K. Orlando et al., Lexington, 2014, pp. 1–22.

Dash, J. Michael. *The Other America: Caribbean Literature in a New World Context*. University Press of Virginia, 1998.

Davies, Carol Boyce. *Caribbean Spaces: Escapes from the Twilight Zones*. University of Illinois Press, 2013.

Desimone, Arturo. "The Divided Dutch Antillean Writer and the Unifying Force of Translation." *sx salon*, vol. 23, 2016, http://smallaxe.net/sxsalon/discussions/divided-dutch-antillean-writer-and-unifying-force-translation.

Edmondson, Belinda, editor. *Caribbean Romances: The Politics of Regional Representation*. University Press of Virginia, 1999.

Esteves, Carmen C., and Liesbeth Paravisini-Gebert, editors. *Green Cane and Juicy Flotsam: Short Stories by Caribbean Women*. Rutgers University Press, 1991.

Fabias, Radna. *Habitus*. E-book, De Arbeiderspers, 2018.

Fenwick, M.J., editor. *Sisters of Caliban: Contemporary Women Poets of the Caribbean (A Multilingual Anthology)*. Azul Editions, 1996.

Glissant, Édouard. *Le discours antillais*. Seuil, 1981.

Hambuch, Doris. "Displacements in Contemporary Caribbean Writing." PHD dissertation, University of Alberta, 2000.

———. "Walcott Versus Naipaul: Intertextuality in Frank Martinus Arion's *De laatste vrijheid* (The ultimate freedom)." *Journal of Caribbean Literatures*, vol. 3, no. 2, 2002, pp. 89–101.

Martínez-San Miguel, Yolanda. *Coloniality of Diasporas: Rethinking Intra-colonial Migrations in a Pan-Caribbean Context*. Palgrave Macmillan, 2014.

Oostindie, Gert, and Inge Klinkers. *Decolonising the Dutch Caribbean: Dutch Policies in a Comparative Perspective*. Amsterdam University Press, 2003.

Orlando, Valérie K., and Sandra Messinger Cypess, editors. *Reimagining the Caribbean: Conversations among the Creole, English, French, and Spanish Caribbean*. Lexington, 2014.

Phaf-Rheinberger, Ineke. *The 'Air of Liberty': Narratives of the South Atlantic Past*. Rodopi, 2008.

———. "The Contemporary Surinamese Novel." Arnold, vol. 2, *English- and Dutch-Speaking Regions*, 2001, pp. 527–41.

Puri, Shalini. *The Caribbean Postcolonial: Social Equality, Post-Nationalism, and Cultural Hybridity*. Palgrave Macmillan, 2004.

Roemer, Astrid. *Gewaagd leven*. De Arbeiderspers, 1996.

———. *Lijken op liefde*. De Arbeiderspers, 1997.

———. *Was getekend*. De Arbeiderspers, 1998.

Rosenberg, Lea Reade. *Nationalism and the Formation of Caribbean Literature*. Palgrave Macmillan, 2007.

Rutgers, Wim. "Literary Magazines and Poetry in the Netherlands Antilles." Arnold, vol. 2, *English- and Dutch-Speaking Regions*, 2001, pp. 563–68.

Sekou, Lasana M. *Hurricane Protocol*. House of Nehesi, 2019.

———. *The Salt Reaper: Poems from the Flats*. House of Nehesi, 2004.

Torres-Saillant, Silvio. *Caribbean Poetics: Towards and Aesthetic of West Indian Literature*. Cambridge University Press, 1997.

———. *Caribbean Poetics: Towards and Aesthetic of West Indian Literature*, 2nd ed. Peepal Tree Press, 2013.

——. *An Intellectual History of the Caribbean*. Palgrave Macmillan, 2006.

Van Haesendonck, Kristian. "Introduction: Caribbeing – Setting a New Comparative Agenda for Caribbean Studies." *Caribbeing: Comparing Caribbean Literatures and Cultures*, edited by Kristian van Haesendonck et al., Rodopi, 2014, pp. 1–17.

Van Haesendonck, Krisitan, and Theo D'Haen, editors. *Caribbeing: Comparing Caribbean Literatures and Cultures*. Rodopi, 2014.

Walcott, Derek. *Collected Poems 1948–1984*. Faber & Faber, 1986.

Rediscovering the Republic
The Work of Joan Daniel Bezsonoff

JERRY WHITE

"Com es pot ser català amh un nom rus i un passaport francès?"
(How can you be Catalan with a Russian name and a French passport?)
—JOAN DANIEL BEZSONOFF, Els taxistes del tsar *(93)*

FRANCE POSES A PARTICULAR PROBLEM for the topic of this collection. Most readers will likely know that the French republican model sets the standard for creating a singular national identity. In the popular press of the last decade or so, this has largely played out in terms of debates over *laïcité* and immigration, particularly immigration from France's former North African colonies, all of which are majority Muslim. Important as these debates have been, they have also obscured a longer-running set of tensions that goes back right to the moment of the Revolution: between a unified (and de facto Paris-led/metropolitan) identity based in *liberté/égalité/fraternité* and the multilingual, multicultural reality of the French state. That state is, despite the outward appearance so relentlessly maintained by its government elite, a composite, one that is made up of groups that exist across the boundaries of states (the Catalans, the Basques, the Flemish) as well as groups that are distinct to French territory (such as the Bretons, the Occitans, and to some extent the German-speaking Alsatians). The work of the French novelist Joan Daniel Bezsonoff, all of which is written in Catalan, offers the opportunity to examine these tensions in some detail, and to see them as just that, tensions, and possibly creative ones. What is being created by these tensions is a different approach to French identity. Bezsonoff's novels have a radically territorial approach to Frenchness inasmuch as they are invested in what is going in France herself and are either hostile to the colonial project (as his work that engages with Algeria or Indochina demonstrates) or generally uninterested in parts of the Catalan-speaking world that are not also part of France (as the absence of Catalonia, by which I mean, the devolved region of Spain, demonstrates).

Contemporary students of the concept of the nation could be forgiven for finding this "radically territorial" approach surprising. But it is one of the unspoken assumptions of this collection that this concept "nation" still has analytical value in our globalized world, and moreover that it need not be conflated with narrow concepts of ethnic exclusionism. Nations are, to be sure, composites; they are also tentative structures that change over time; it is equally certain that, to follow Benedict Anderson's now absurdly well-worn formulation, they are acts of imagination, and such acts also change over time. But none of this—composite, tentative, imagined—is simply synonymous with "incoherent," "illegitimate," or "meaningless." Despite the fact that all of this implies that nations could be described as "limited" (that is, as containing people who do and do not belong), there is no reason to see that simple confirmation of a finite status as synonymous with a pejorative sense of "exclusionary." In seeing national identity as both meaningful and malleable, I am strongly influenced by George Orwell's question from *The Lion and the Unicorn*: "What can the England of 1940 have in common with the England of 1840? But then, what have you in common with the child of five whose photograph your mother keeps on the mantelpiece? Nothing, except that you happen to be the same person" (5).

This concept of national identity as territorial, flexible, and so on may seem to be out of place most of all in France. On this issue, I think that France gets a "bad rap." Or perhaps it is only, following Orwell again (this time in *The Road to Wigan Pier*), that like Christianity and socialism the worst advertisement for French republicanism is its adherents. In 2018, I edited a special section of *Dalhousie French Studies* devoted to Catalan culture in France, and part of my goal there was to broaden the concept of "French identity." I did so not by rejecting French republicanism, which might seem to be the logical strategy, at least if one believes that this model of social organization is hopelessly hostile to minorities. I do not believe that, so I chose to try to recover more sympathetic and what I would argue are fuller understandings of the concept. One such understanding can be found chez Richard Kearney, a key figure in Irish political philosophy with strong Europhile tendencies. He writes that "there is, I believe, a great need for a novel appreciation of the universalist dimension of republicanism, as we move towards greater integration with the common house of Europe and the wider world. And there is a corresponding need for a re-appreciation of its localist dimension, if we are even to realise the possibilities of a participatory democracy which the project of a decentralised Europe of the regions will, if achieved, open up" (37). This dual heritage—the universal and the regional—is at the heart of republican conceptualizations of national identity. It is that conception that, I will strive to show in this chapter, is alive and well in the literary work of Joan Daniel Bezsonoff. Such a conception of national identity is, I believe, *plus catholique que le pape*; that is to say, it embodies the real pluralist and universalist force of the republican ideal, without the centralizing, chauvinistic tendencies that have become synonymous with the word *Jacobinism*, especially in Catalan.

That was a term that Llorenç Planes used, although to describe a Barcelona-centred approach rather than a Parisian one. Planes was a key architect of the Catalan movement in France, and in 1974 he published, under the imprimatur of his magazine *La Falç*, a booklet called *El petit llibre de Catalunya-Nord: Lluita per un "Rosselló" català*. Planes's polemic set out the terms of the debate that would follow, in both French and Catalan, about the place of Catalans in French society. Like many Catalan speakers in France, he felt marginalized by a Paris-based French nationalism that would recognize him only as French, and also by a Barcelona-based nationalism that assumed that the only Catalans worth talking about were in Spain. He saw these both as forms of Jacobinism, writing that "The difference between Parisian Jacobins and Barcelonan Jacobins is that one assumes that this is France, and no more than France, and the other assumes that this is Catalonia, and no more than Catalonia. Because they both believe that they have the right to do here the same things that they do in other places and to disregard the people who live there year-round, negating the specificity of Catalunya Nord, specifically that which gives us, whether we want it or not, our particular history" (97).[1] The invocation of Jacobinism, both with its familiar Parisian resonances and in the less-familiar form of *"els jacobins barcelonins,"* is meant to draw attention to the revolutionary zeal that does indeed define a lot of the nationalist movement in Catalonia. But what it also calls to mind is the post-Revolutionary France's experience of consolidating a new national identity, one that put republican universalism in the place of an older, quasi-feudal system that, nevertheless, made space for ethnic and linguistic difference. Because that space had historically been codified as a series of informal and often inequitable relationships between minor royals (dukes of Brittany, for instance) and the French crown, it came to stand for the sort of backward and oppressive views that the Revolution was meant to wipe out. Post-Revolutionary governments thus took to replacing local patois (which would have included Catalan) with a Parisian standard of French, all in the name of building a new society where all citizens would be equal before the state, a state that would be unfailingly blind to the sorts of religious, cultural, or linguistic differences that the French crown had earlier used to its strategic advantage (Michel de Certeau's work *Une politique de la langue* is the seminal treatment of this subject). This sort of rigorous blindness to difference now seems to be synonymous with a French republican model that is so often explained in the mainstream anglophone press as being incompatible with multiculturalism. Novelists such as Bezsonoff, both soaked in republican universalism and drawing attention to the multicultural reality of France, offer a rebuke to such oversimplifications.

It is worth a few words to explain the geographical term Planes uses, "Catalunya Nord." It is surprisingly contentious. The term refers to the Catalan parts of France, that is to say the regions around Perpignan that make up most of the Département des Pyrénées Orientales, especially (although not exclusively) the area known as Roussillon. There is certainly a very strong consciousness on the part of residents there of being Catalan (and Catalan flags are to be found flying from most public buildings), but the language, while present, is fairly weak. Alà Baylac Ferrer's 2016 book *Le catalan en Catalogne nord et les pays catalans* quotes figures that have 1.3 per cent of the region's population claiming it as their *"langue habituelle,"* 9.1 per cent claiming it as their *"langue initiale,"* 35.4 per cent claiming to be able to speak it, and 61.1 per cent claiming to be able to understand it. The Barcelona-based Institut d'Estudis Catalans, which serves as a kind of Académie française for the Catalan language, insists on grammatical grounds that the correct appellation is "Catalunya *del* Nord."[2] But anyone who has spent any time with Catalan speakers in France knows that this term has no currency; *"Catalunya Nord"* is what flows off northern tongues naturally. These kinds of regional differences in language account for a certain low-level tension between these two parts of what is known as *"Els països Catalans,"*[3] one that is not unlike the tensions between Acadians and Québécois, or Chicanos and Mexicans.

When I edited the aforementioned section of *Dalhousie French Studies*, I entitled it "La France catalane." Its introduction explained that this title came in part from a desire to sidestep the "Catalunya (del) Nord" disagreement (since my Catalan was not sufficiently polished to really give me the right to an opinion on the matter), and so I preferred to make up a term that *nobody* would accept. But I also explained there that the title stemmed from the section's basic thesis, which was that French Catalan identity is still *French*, that is to say an important part of the culture of the nation-state we call France. This thesis is certainly shared by key figures of Catalan culture in France, as can be seen in statements like Pere Verdaguer's, who in his 1974 book *Defensa del Rosselló català* wrote of the early meetings of the Grup Rossellonès d'Estudis Catalans that "For Marcel Oms, who participated in the conference, the folks from Roussillon were hopelessly French" (67).[4] I think one could also translate "*irremeiablement*" as "unmistakeably," and I think that in part because Verdaguer (who was born in Banyoles but came to France as a child with his refugee parents during the Spanish Civil War) uses the first-person form of the verb "to be": "*els rossellonesos som irremeiablement francesos*"—"*les roussillonnais sommes désespérément françaises.*" He was talking about his own people with some gentle irony, very aware of their difference from fellow Catalans to the south. The work of Joan Daniel Bezsonoff offers a chance to explain the literary manifestations of this tension in the republican reality of contemporary France.

Born in 1963, Bezsonoff (whose full name is Joan Daniel Bezsonoff i Montalat)[5] has never lived for any extended period anywhere except for France, and has also never written anything significant in any language other than Catalan. And he has written a significant amount: fifteen novels since the early 1990s, in addition to a sort of family history, two memoirs, and extensive journalism for newspapers based in the Principat de Catalunya, the devolved region of Spain whose capital is Barcelona and which, going forward, I am going to call the Principat. All of this writing is very self-consciously about life in France. Sometimes this is a regional matter; that is true of the memoirs he has published, such as 2009's *Un educació francesa* and 2015's *Guia sentimental de Perpinyà*, which are both about the city of Perpignan. Sometimes it is a national matter; that is true of the book I will pay closest attention to in this chapter, 2014's *Matar de Gaulle*, about the conspiracy to assassinate the French president in 1962. Just as often the question of writing specifically about life in France has been a global matter for Bezsonoff, a matter that directly engages the world outside of the Hexagon. He has, for instance, written novels about French colonialism in Algeria and Indochina, reflecting the experiences of his army-officer father. *Matar de Gaulle* is a kind of sequel to his 2011 book *La melancolia dels oficials*, which I will discuss below; *El fill del coronel*, published in 2017, is mostly about the Battle of Algiers of 1956 and is thus almost a "prequel" to *Matar de Gaulle*. This is all to say that Bezsonoff's relationship with France is certainly complicated, but he is just as certainly inseparable from that country. It is very difficult to think of him as a "Catalan writer" in the manner of one of his contemporaries in the Principat, such as the Barcelona-based Quim Monzó. I would concede that the term "Catalan writer" might *à peine* fit other writers who have built their careers in France, such as the aforementioned polymath Pere Verdaguer, whose work included novels, prose-poems, science fiction works, and anthologies, as well as regional history. But as I mention above, Verdaguer was born in 1929 in Banyoles, a small town outside of Girona; he came to France (where he died in 2017), with his exile parents, at the end of the Spanish Civil War, and he never entirely lost his connections to the Principat itself (something that does come out in some of his work). In terms of his nationality, second-person verb forms or not, Verdaguer was something of a hybrid figure. Bezsonoff, not to put too fine a point on it, is not. Bezsonoff is *French*.

This is most clear in his cycle of novels about the French colonial experience in Algeria and its aftermath. That historical narrative has some important connections to Catalunya Nord, inasmuch as many pieds noirs wound up in Montpellier, which as part of Occitania is adjacent (linguistically as well as geographically) to the Catalan parts of France. But it has special importance for Bezsonoff, whose father was a career officer in the French army, an institution that had an enormous impact on him as he grew up in the 1960s and 1970s. He wrote in the introduction to *El fill del coronel*, one of the later instalments of this cycle, that he "maintains a visceral connection with the French army" (11).[6] Acknowledging that its colonial past may seem at odds with someone so committed to an underdog culture like that of the Catalans, he contrasted it sharply with the armed forces known to his *cosins catalans* to the south: "There is quite a distance between the Republic's army and the form that the armed forces take in the Kingdom of Spain. This is the army of the republic, the nation's army, without any tradition of coups" (12).[7]

Bezsonoff goes on to evoke *une certaine tendance* in the French military sensibility that is also central to his view of French identity: a radical openness to the other, an openness that is, of course, central to republican idealism. Recalling some of the soldiers of his father's circle, he goes on in that introduction to *El fill del coronel* to claim that "Brigadier Patrice Clerc was delighted by Japanese poetry. Lieutenant Thierry Morice was fluent in Serbo-Croatian, German, Italian, and other languages of *Mitteleuropa*" (12).[8] Mitteleuropa and Eastern Europe have been Bezsonoff's other great concern. His 2007 "family history" *Els taxistes del tsar* tells the story of his Russian ancestors; he notes in *Ell fill del coronel* how "I was born in Catalan territory that was annexed by France, of a mother from Roussillon and a father who was half from Conflent and half from Russia" (11).[9] *El taxistes del tsar* is his exploration of that Russian side of his father's family history, in addition to being something of a personal meditation on how Russian, Catalan, and French identity can and often do not intersect: "But since nobody in France, except for the Besiers and a few raucous Spanish teachers, knows anything about Catalonia, I always thought I was Russian. They called me 'The Russian'" (33).[10] That widespread apathy to cultural difference that we have in the sentence's first clause is central to contemporary assumptions about French identity under a republican regime. But the second clause brings out the degree to which this is not really the case, either in terms of French demographics or of the popular acceptance of those demographic realities; they all called him "The Russian" after all. It is just that Catalonia, unlike Russia, is a "small" nation, and a particularly complicated one at that (as I explain in note 3). *La ballarina de Berlín* is more about Central than Eastern Europe, a hybrid work about a Polish army officer's experiences in late Weimar-era Berlin. But there is a very similar set of themes afoot here, a similar fascination for this tension between diversity and cultural belonging. The key aspect of Mitteleuropa culture is the reality of highly concentrated cultural, linguistic, and religious diversity, and it is a truism to say that it is no less recognizable as a distinct cultural formation because of this diversity. When it is evoked by Bezsonoff, it is hard not to see it as a sketch of what a diversity-engaged French republicanism might look like. Bezsonoff writes at one point in *La ballarina de Berlín* that "Commissar Kubitzky knew Berlin too well to not know that the Jewish community constituted an essential component, like the Irish in the United States, the Chinese in Indochina, or the Dutch in South Africa" (111–12).[11] The specific examples here are key. Each of these groups is unquestionably distinct, but that distinction also clearly survives within the citizenship regimes of republics; Irish Americans are just as certainly Americans as the Chinese community of Saigon are Vietnamese or the Afrikaners are South African. So it is, Bezsonoff's oeuvre shows us, with the Catalans of France. The key difference, of course, is the absence of migration; it is scarcely an exaggeration to say that France came to the Catalans rather than Catalans coming to

France. But the basic point still holds; there is no reason to see a minority as anything other than *"un component essencial"* of a national framework. To imply otherwise would be to contradict not only the concept of nation that I tried to put forward at the beginning of this chapter, but also one of the basic principles of republicanism, which is, following Kearney, its *universalism*.

La melancolia dels oficials' 2015 sequel, *Matar de Gaulle*, expands on this sense that France has always been a culturally complex place, partly because of its colonial history. Bezsonoff's presents the pied-noir experience as a kind of "close but not quite" version of multiculturalism; in *Matar de Gaulle* this becomes an omnipresent, if sometimes uneasy, multilingualism. At one point, Alain Vidal, the book's young protagonist, who eventually comes into the orbit of the Organisation armée secrète (OAS), recalls taking music lessons and wanting to learn some of the songs he had heard on Radio Montpellier:

> *Four times per week he took classes from the teacher Miguel Fontceha. Fontecha, almost Fonseca, like the song he was studying:*
>   Sad and alone
>   only Fonseca remains
>   Sad and tearful
>   the university remains.
> *The teacher said to him:*
>   Hey, buddy, I'm Basque. You're Catalan. I'll give you lessons for free. Pay me back when you're famous. We're just about countrymen, brothers, I mean come on... *(23–24)*[12]

The tone here is overly casual; it is not clear at all that Alain accepts this description of himself as more or less a *paisano* of a Basque teacher. Part of this is because there is also nothing in the text to suggest that Alain can understand Spanish past the words that he learns through the famous Salamancan songs he is learning. A few pages later, Bezsonoff is even more explicit about the complexity of the French Algerian soundscape, now given a density that makes the matter of understanding it all seem fully ridiculous: "Anatole would have wanted to have the class of Eddie Constantine, the voice of Luis Mariano, the *swing* of Frank Sinatra, the style of Henry de Montherlant, the French of Roger Peyrefutte, and the Afrikaans of Eugène Marais" (26).[13] That roll call takes in a French crooner originally born in the United States, a Basque singer of operettas, an American jazz superstar, a Belgian essayist, a French novelist, and a mad visionary scientist who wrote exclusively in Afrikaans. The Algeria that Alain feels part of is unmistakably French territory, as all of the pieds noirs with whom he hangs around never tire of pointing out. But it is a certain kind of French territory, one where difference is present in more complicated shades than the conventional French Arabic distinction would hold. What makes this pied-noir experience French is precisely this kind of difference, this membership in a community that is culturally distinct from the *indigènes* and yet also linked to an elaborate web of languages and cultural belongings that are not limited to simple-minded appeals to a Gallic heritage. Rather, the France that Bezsonoff sees as typical of the pied-noir experience is multilingual but only to a point; that community's collective inability to recognize its inherent complexity and the limits of that complexity is part of what leaves it open to a certain kind of atavistic violence, one that reached a fever pitch with the attempt on de Gaulle's life by the OAS in 1962.

Overall, then, the novel is about the emergence of the OAS, the ultimate challenge to the French state, and the degree to which it embodied a kind of doomed, apocalyptic vision, one that has strong resonances with the contemporary situation of nationalism. All to say that it is not a romantic defence of the Catalan experience, or the Catalan language, any more than it is a simple patriotic singing of the praises of French culture. For the most part, the Catalan language itself is usually in the background of the novel, rarely front and centre, as the great events of French history unfold around the Vidal family. But at one point, Alain is talking to a friend in the OAS, and recalls how

> *Lucien Delmas adhered to a strange political position. He wanted to reconquer Algeria as well as struggle for the incorporation of Roussillon into an independent Catalonia.*
> *"Why?" Alain asked him in Catalan, with his dodgy French.*

"Because Algeria is a French province and Roussillon is a Catalan region," *Delmas responded gravely in French, without thanking him for the effort of speaking Catalan. (130–31)*[14]

The implication here seems to be that a Catalan *risorgimento* is as much a part of a *"polític estrany"* as the notion that Algeria is just another part of France. This is a fairly good summary of the main line of politics in the Catalan parts of France. There is no question that an awareness of distinctiveness runs high; Roussillon is a *distinct* part of the country, if mostly for linguistic reasons: the historical presence and, most importantly, the persistence of a language that is not French. But not even the most fervent *catalaniste* political parties, which had a high point in the 1970s, ever advocated a position that would detach any part of France. Rather, they tended to speak either in the language of federalism or of classical republicanism.[15] This language of a reconquered Roussillon joined to an independent Catalonia is deliberately calibrated to sound ridiculous; pairing it with the continuation of French rule in Algeria is to place all of this political discourse onto the realm of the crackpot, the sorts of people who stage attempts on the life of a French president.

My goal with this textual exposition has been to demonstrate the degree to which Bezsonoff's *Matar de Gaulle* is a *French* novel; even when it invokes the Principat, it does so by centralizing perspectives and histories that are specific to *la république elle-même*. The part of this question relevant to this collection, really, is whether or not France is a "multinational" state. A simple answer would be to say that it probably is, although perhaps not in quite the same way that Spain or Canada are. In the popular press, analogies between Catalonia and Québec are very common, and while these are not the exact same situations, the politics are close enough to make the analogies understandable and useful. What must also be understood, though, is that Catalunya Nord does not find a perch in such analogies. It is not the Québec of France. It is not even the Catalonia of France! Radical movements in the Basque Country, by contrast, seek the creation of an independent Euskadi that incorporates the Basque parts of both Spain and France. The Breton separatist movement was, at its high point, seeking a comparably complete independence from France. Serious militants in both communities basically reject Spanish or French nationality, just as their counterparts in Québec and Catalonia reject Canadian or Spanish nationality. So it is difficult to imagine any novelist invested in these movements (such as Jacques Ferron, say) writing about Québec identity in the same way that Bezsonoff wonders about his *catalanité* in *Els taxistes del tsar*: "Catalanité allowed me to see identity clearly. I could take apart the souls involved. Officially, I have two French grandmothers, a French grandfather born of Spanish parents, and a Russian grandfather. Thanks to this Catalan sleight of hand, I am three parts Catalan. A fourth from Roussillon, a fourth from Conflent [a historically Catalan part of France], a fourth from Empordà [in Girona], but it's this Russian fourth that looks at me sideways [*lit.* with the smile of a skunk]. Who is this guy born in Perpignan, of Russian origins, who writes novels in Catalan?" (94).[16]

The invocation of clarity is clearly ironic; this is not exactly a battle cry from a born-again Catalan nationalist. Although it may seem paradoxical, the sense of Catalan identity on display here seems very specifically French: somewhat skeptical of picking apart one's ethnic belonging, along the lines of an author who would write that his *catalanité* meant he "*pogut desembullar les meues ànimes embolicades*." I specifically have in mind Alain Finkielkraut's invocation of Witold Gombrowicz in his 1987 book *La défaite de la pensée*: "He used the case of France as a corrective to Poles, who, fascinated by their 'Polishness,' were wearing themselves out trying to become the best examples of their history: 'Is a Frenchman more French if he sees nothing but France or less French? To be really French is to see something beyond France.' An admirable observation and one that explains why France for many years has attracted foreigners chased from their homes by the hateful stupidity of the *Volksgeist*" (*Defeat of the Mind*, 102).[17] Following this reasoning, I see Bezsonoff as French precisely because he sees something beyond France. In *Matar de Gaulle*, that novel about a figure who was literally a quasi-religious embodiment of the soul of undefeatable France, Bezsonoff sees Spain, Catalonia, South Africa, and Belgium. In *Els taxistes del tsar*, he cannot talk about being French without talking about being Catalan, but he cannot talk about being Catalan without also talking about France and Russia. The *Volksgeist* can find no purchase in his work.

Another way of explaining this is to invoke the way that Paul Willemen described the wave of Black British cinema of the 1980s (Isaac Julien, John Akomfrah, etc.): "Compared to US black films, black British films are strikingly British, yet in no way can they be construed as nationalistic. They are part of a British specificity, but not part of a British nationalism" (209). Bezsonoff's work is part of just this kind of non-nationalist French specificity, one that reaches out to other cultural communities outside of the nation-state itself, even though it does not present itself in terms easily understandable in classic "multinational state" terms, as with Canada/Québec, or Spain/Catalonia. Looking at Bezsonoff in this way can perhaps allow us to see the Americanness of Chicano writing instead of as some sort of annex of Mexico, and thus see American culture in a new way, or to see writing in the Irish language as a full, indispensable part of Irish literature and culture, and not some quaint folkloric relic best understood alongside comparably eccentric projects such as literature in Scottish Gaelic or Welsh. In the final analysis, this is the direction for a new kind of globalized literary and cultural study, one that acknowledges the reality of national belongings while equally acknowledging that such national formations are inherently complex: culturally plural, and often multilingual.

Furthermore, Bezsonoff's work poses the problem of when exactly comparison begins. If we were to set *Matar de Gaulle* alongside a novel like Adrien Bosc's 2014 *Constellation* (a historical fiction about a celebrity-packed transatlantic flight in 1949), would that be a comparative exercise? Or would it be a study in a single national literature, in this case French literature? How indispensable is cultural difference, or linguistic difference, to the process of comparison? This is a problem of a different order than the "Comparative Canadian Literature" discourse that loomed so large in the 1970s and 1980s, with major literary-historical works by figures such as Ronald Sutherland (whose 1971 study *Second Image* was seminal) and E.D. Blodgett. It was Blodgett who memorably wrote in a 1988 follow-up to his 1982 book *Configuration* that "If it is true that the present effort to unify Canada could in fact leave it in pieces, we should cultivate a co-operative separatism that would prevent the kinds of ideological unity that the international and centrist schools seek. Good fences, I believe, do indeed make good neighbours" (34–35). In a 2006 article titled, as an homage to Blodgett's essay, "Irish Literature Is Not Comparative Literature," I argued that the status of writing in Irish was very different: a matter of linguistic rather than cultural difference, where separatist aspirations of any kind (literary or political, destructive or co-operative) were simply non-existent. We can see something very similar in Catalunya Nord, and Bezsonoff makes for a particularly vivid example of this. Partly this is because many of his novels and memoirs are set in France or her former colonial possessions, and deal so vividly with the vagaries of French history. But even when he is writing about other places—Russia, Weimar-era Berlin—his work embodies a certain approach to the diversity-unity nexus that is inseparable from *la France actuelle*, at least a version of that republic as it could be.

NOTES

1. "La diferència entre els jacobins parisencs i els jacobins barcelonins és que els uns consideren que aquí és França, i només França, si els altres que aquí és Catalunya, i només Catalunya. Però tenen en comú de considerar que tenen el dret de fer aquí el que fan a altres llocs, prescindint de la població que hi viu tot l'any, negant l'especificat de Catalunya Nord, especificitat que ens ho donat, ho vulguin o no, la nostra historia particular." All translations from Catalan are mine.
2. I do not wish to belabour this overly, but the Institut has very precise grammatical reasons for insisting on this appellation: "es tracta gramaticalment d'un sintagma format per dos substantius, units necessàriament per la preposició" (grammatically speaking, it is a syntactic element [un sintagma] formed by two nouns, thus necessarily linked by a preposition). They also point out that North Korea (Corea del Nord) and North America (America del Nord) are named in the same fashion (see Institut d'Estudis Catalans, "Perpinyà"). The Institut d'Estudis Catalans's key document on the place names of La France catalane is a 2007 report titled *Nomenclàtor toponímic de la Catalunya del Nord*.
3. The term *Els països Catalans* refers to the territories where Catalan has historically been spoken and persists in some recognizable way: the Principat, Catalunya (del) Nord, Andorra, Valencia, Franja de Ponent (the Catalan-speaking part of the autonomous community of Aragon), the Balearic Islands, and the city of L'Alguer on the island of Sardinia (its Italian name is Alghero). Geopolitically, this is a very diverse group: regions large and small, devolved and non-devolved; a city; and a fully independent if very small country (the microstate of Andorra).
4. "Per a Marcel Oms, que assistia al col·loqui, els rossellonesos som irremeiablement francesos."

5. Bezsonoff does not generally spell his first name with a hyphen. Most of his novels have the name "Joan Daniel Bezsonoff" on the cover. Not always, though: *La presonera d'Alger* (2002) and *El fill del coronel* (2017) have "Joan-Daniel Bezsonoff" on the cover, and *Les rambles de Saigon* (1996) has "Joan-Daniel Bezsonoff i Montalat" on the cover.
6. "...conservi un vincle visceral amb l'exèrcit francès."
7. "L'exèrcit de la república dista molt de les formes armades del regne d'Espanya. Aquest és un exèrcit de la república, l'exèrcit de la nació sense tradició colpista."
8. "El brigada Patrice Clerc es delia per la poesia japonesa. El tinent Thierry Morice dominava el serbo-croat, l'alemany, l'italià i altres llengües de la *Mitteleuropa*."
9. "...vaig néixer en una terra catalana, annexionada per França, d'una mare rossellonesa i d'un pare mig conflentí mig rus."
10. "Però ja que ningú a França, més enllà de Besiers, llevat d'algun professor de Castellà rancuniós, no sap res de Catalunya, sempre s'han pensat que jo era rus. Em deien 'le Russe.'"
11. "El comissari Kubitzky coneixia massa Berlín per ignorar que la comunitat jueva en constituïa un component essencial, com els irlandesos als Estats Units, els xinesos a la Cotxinxina o les holandesos a Sud-àfrica."
12. "Quatre cops a la setmana seguia les classes del mestre Miguel Fontecha. Fontecha, quasi Fonseca com la cançó d'estudiantina:

    Triste y sola

    sola se queda Fonseca

    Triste y llorosa

    queda la universidad.

    El mestre li digué:

    Oye, chico, yo soy vasco. Tú eres catalán. Te daré lecciones gratuitas. Me pagarás cuando seas famoso. Somos casi paisano, unos hermanos, vamos..."
13. "L'Anatole hauria volgut tenir la classe d'Eddie Constantine, la veu de Luis Mariano, el swing de Frank Sinatra, l'estil de Henry de Montherlant, el francès de Roger Peyrefitte i l'afrikaans d'Eugène Marais."
14. "...en Lucien Delmas defensava un ideari polític estrany. Volia reconquerir Algèria bo i lluitant per la incorporació del Rosselló en una Catalunya independent.

    —Per què?—li havia demanat l'Alain en català, amb la seua erra francesa.

    —*Parce que l'Algérie est une province française et le Roussillon est une région catalane...*—va respondre amb gravetat Delmas en francès, sense agrair-li l'esforç de parlar català."
15. This republican element of Catalanist thought in France is an important part of the discussion found in my introduction to the special section of *Dalhousie French Studies*.
16. "La catalanitat m'ha permès aclarir-me la identitat. He pogut desembullar les meues ànimes embolicades. Oficialment, tinc dues àvies franceses, un avi francès nat de pares espanyols i un avi rus. Gracies al joc de mans català, soc tres parts català. Un quarts rossellonès, un quart conflentí, un quart empordanès, però queda aquest quart rus que

em mira amb un somriure mofeta. Qui és aquest home nascut a Perpinyà, d'origen rus, que escriu novel·les en català?"

17. "Il a donné en exemple à ses compatriotes fascinés par la 'polonité' et s'exténuant à devenir eux-mêmes des produits aussi emblématiques que possible de leur histoire collective: 'Un Français qui ne prend rien en considération en dehors de la France est-il plus français ? Ou moins français ? En fait, être français, c'est justement prendre en considération autre chose que la France.' Phrase admirable et qui explique l'attrait que la France a longtemps exercé dur les étrangers chassés de chez eux par la bêtise haineuse du *Volksgeist*" (*La defaite de la pensée*, 138–39).

WORKS CITED

Bezsonoff, Joan Daniel. *La ballarina de Berlín*. Empúries, 2017.

———. *El fill del coronel*. L'Avenç, 2017.

———. *Matar de Gaulle*. Empúries, 2014.

———. *La melancolia dels oficials*. Empúries, 2011.

———. *Els taxistes del tsar*. Empúries, 2007.

Blodgett, E.D. "Canadian Literature Is Comparative Literature." *College English*, vol. 50, no. 8, Dec. 1988, pp. 904–11.

———. *Configuration: Essays on the Canadian Literatures*. ECW, 1982.

Bosc, Adrien. *Constellation*. Stock, 2014.

De Certeau, Michel et al. *Une politique de la langue*. Gallimard, 1975.

Ferrer, Alà Baylac. *Le catalan en Catalogne nord et dans les pays catalans: Même pas mort!* Presses Universitaires de Perpignan, 2016.

Finkielkraut, Alain. *La défaite de la pensée*. Gallimard, 1987.

———. *The Defeat of the Mind*. Translated by Judith Friedlander. Columbia UP, 1996.

Institut d'Estudis Catalans. "Perpinyà acull la presentació del Nomenclàtor toponímic de la Catalunya del Nord." *El Butlletí de l'IEC*, vol. 114, 18 Oct. 2007, www.iec.cat/butletti/114/notices.htm#3.

———. *Nomenclàtor toponímic de la Catalunya del Nord*. Institut d'Estudis Catalans, 2007, https://publicacions.iec.cat/repository/pdf/00000044/00000018.pdf.

Kearney, Richard. *Postnationalist Ireland: Politics, Culture, Philosophy*. Routledge, 1996.

Orwell, George. *The Lion and the Unicorn: Socialism and the English Genius*. Penguin, 1984.

———. *The Road to Wigan Pier*. Penguin, 2001.

Planes, Llorenç. *El petit llibre de Catalunya-Nord: Lluita per un "Rosselló" català*. Edicions La Falç, 1974.

Sutherland, Ronald. *Second Image: Comparative Studies in Québec/Canadian Literature*. New Press, 1971.

Verdaguer, Pere. *Defensa del Rosselló català*. Curial, 1974.

White, Jerry. "Irish Literature Is Not Comparative Literature." *English Studies in Canada*, vol. 32, nos. 2-3, summer-fall 2006, pp. 115–40.

———. "'Y a-t-il des Catalans en France pour pouvoir y espérer l'avènement d'un cinéma catalan ?': Introducing *La France catalane.*" *Dalhousie French Studies*, no. 113, winter 2019, pp. 3–23.

Willemen, Paul. *Looks and Frictions: Essays in Cultural Studies*. British Film Institute, 1993.

A Multinational Narrative in a Case Study of Translating an Eastern Christian Play

CLaRa A.B. JOSePH

PRO-NATIONALIST FORMS OF REPRESENTATION ignore the differences within and favour a monolithic nation. Gayatri Spivak studies this problem in her influential essay "Can the Subaltern Speak?" (279). As early as 1987, one of the few arguments that Benita Parry approves of in the work of Homi K. Bhabha concerns nationalism's tendency to substitute the problem of "representing difference" with "the demand for different and more favorable representations" (46). Tejaswini Niranjana, in her oft-cited work *Siting Translation: History, Post-structuralism, and the Colonial Context*, recognizes, among others, the above critics and concludes, "The post-colonial translator must be wary of essentialist anti-colonial narratives; in fact, s/he must attempt to deconstruct them, to show their complicity with the master-narrative of imperialism" (167). In this chapter, I focus on the problem of the essentialist anti-colonial narrative, but note how Niranjana too is implicated in conceiving of the nation as less heterogeneous than it is.

Niranjana proceeds to analyze translations of a medieval, religious, poem in Kannada and contends that (Indian) "indigenous religious texts" are threatened by Christianity: "We see here one of the typical moves of a colonial discourse that translates indigenous religious texts, castigates the native for not being faithful to the tenets of their (translated) religion, then claims that the native religion is incapable of sustaining its devotees, and proposes 'conversion' as a path of salvation" (181). In reaching this conclusion, Niranjana accepts the colonial presumption that the "West" referred to in the *vacana* (verse) is the space west of Africa and Arabia and that Christianity is a colonial intrusion in India. Although she is discussing South India, she is unable to discern the plausible influence of a neighbouring region in the West, but within India, on the Saivites. (The Bhakthi movement, for instance, originated in regions that form present-day Tamil Nadu and Kerala.) Nor does she acknowledge a pre-colonial Christian tradition in that West within India. In this chapter, I consider this general problem of essentialist but anti-colonial narratives in terms of representation and reflexivity as processes within translation studies and as illustrated in the translation of a Thomas Christian play.[1] I want to do this in the course of reflecting on my experience of translating an Eastern Christian play from Malayalam to English. While acknowledging that it needs ongoing effort to rid oneself of essentialist anti-colonial narratives, I suggest that a mimetic and self-oriented perspective in the practice of translating tends to essentialize at the expense of alterity within the nation. That is, such a translation often relies on dominant or hegemonic cultural representations and ignores or marginalizes the multinational in the multinational state. I contend that representation and reflexivity as counter-tactics to the incursions of power in a multi-national state can prove to be implicitly insufficient for representing minority communities.

Mar Joseph Cariattil, by Geo Thadikkatt, traces the struggles and victories of communities and leaders of the Indian Church of the Thomas Christians during the period of Portuguese colonial and ecclesiastical control in the eighteenth century. This is a historical drama centred on important Church figures and key events that took place in the Thomas Christian community in the eighteenth century. The eighteenth century was a period of extraordinary turmoil: the first half of the century was marked by dissenting groups among the Thomas Christians ruled separately by Rome's Sacred Congregation for the Propagation of the Faith (*Sacra Congregatio de Propaganda Fide*)—generally referred to as *Propaganda Fide* or the Propaganda, the Portuguese Padroado, and the so-called schismatics, the Jacobites, who were products of the Coonan Cross Oath of 1653 that, according to most scholars, created the first known formal split in the Thomas Christian community. The second half of the eighteenth century saw the rise of leaders such as Archbishop Joseph Cariattil, whose name appears as the title of the play, his assistant and confidante, Malpan Thomas Paremmakkal, and Mar Thoma VI (alias Dionysius I), the archbishop of the Jacobite group of Thomas Christians. The play focuses on the latter part of the eighteenth century and on these figures and, therefore, represents the resistant stance of the Thomas Christians against Portuguese colonizers. The plot centres on the extraordinary attempts made by Cariattil and Paremmakkal to attain two major goals of the Thomas Christian community: (a) obtain preferably an indigenous administrator or at the very least a sympathetic foreign administrator by persuading both the Propaganda (Rome) and the Padroado (Portugal), and (b) bring about the reunification of the Thomas Christians with the support of Mar Thoma VI. The colonial administrators interpreted these moves as downright anti-colonial. In retrospect, we can deduce the two goals of the Thomas Christians as essential steps in the eventual formation of a multinational state.[2] The insuperable obstacles that both the Propaganda and the Padroado posed for the Thomas Christians and the partial victory that the latter claimed make most of the play. These ought to be at least subplots in canonical narratives of the nation or the multinational state; instead, they are ignored in narratives of Church history and Indian history. Thadikkatt's play somewhat disrupts that trend by representing the Thomas Christian community whose activities at the micro level give us a preview of a multinational unit—Kerala.

The play was staged only once, in 1983—the year of composition—and that too before an exclusive audience of priests and seminarians, as part of India's Independence Day commemorative celebrations in Kerala. However, the archival significance of the play arises from the fact that it is based on India's first travelogue, *The Varthamanappusthakam* (1786) and its historical significance. The genre of the travelogue and this history have shaped the play. In the foreword, the playwright confides that the historical events of the late eighteenth century in which Cariattil played a pivotal role and the relevance of the countless persons, places, and events posed a major challenge: "The main concern was how to reduce all of this to a two or a two-and-a-half-hour-long play" (Thadikkatt 5).

In translating this play, I found myself going through processes of being introduced and reintroduced to the related historical and cultural details, re-examining my westernized worldview in its relationship to the target narrative, and being sensitive to unexpected demands. These, briefly, are methods of representation, reflexivity, and a turn to the other. I propose that the main problem a translator encounters when translating a minority language text into English is at basis an ethical problem because the phases of representation and reflexivity are self-oriented, not other-oriented. I intend to examine this problem in the context of a close reading of the play, of course, but also within the framework of colonial and diasporic contexts: colonial because the original events took place (as I have noted) during the period of Portuguese ecclesiastical and temporal domination and the play itself was performed during the post-colonial period; diasporic because the target audience of my translation is the English-speaking diasporic St. Thomas Christian Indian community. I expect that the confluence of colonial, diasporic, and translation studies that I examine in this project will prompt practitioners of translation studies and scholars of literary studies to reassess their considerations of issues of representation and reflexivity as counter-tactics, in view of their potential to reimagine and redefine the nation or, as in the case of India, the multinational state.

Representing, Not Quite and Then Some
Problems of representation are usually viewed in terms of mimesis: What is being presented? How accurate is the representation? How do I capture that accuracy in translation? Mimetic representation involves the linguistic as well as cultural phase of translation studies. In the case of Thadikkatt's play, it considers questions such as how to preserve the genre of the Malayalam play; how to sustain the nuances of the dialogue, the intricacies of the plot, the relevance of the setting, and the life of the

characters; how to narrate the community and the nation.[3] In doing so, mimetic representation also responds to the problem, identified by Anisur Rahman as "the status of marginalized discourses in *bhasha* [regional] literatures and the need to make space for them in English translation." If Sanskrit and, later, Urdu took over the literary scene in India as the dominant or *"marg"* language, European colonialism ensured that that status went to English. Hence the anxiety over the translation of regional literatures to English. Rahman, however, cautions that a translation of the *bhasha* cannot be understood under the general term "postcolonial." He writes, "This engagement may best be viewed in terms of the specific Indian context rather than the broad and amorphous postcolonial context, which incorporates too many shades of postcoloniality without necessarily identifying any of the precise locations precisely" (169). In the context of the Indian national scene, issues of linguistics underlying the *bhasha* to *marg* conversion are closely linked to matters of cultural specificity that would find themselves at the core of not only a Eurocentric understanding of the translation but—I would add—also a postcolonial perspective that unwittingly homogenizes cultural representation in the name of, for instance, a nation. The problem of representation as a counter-tactic to colonialism, in this sense, is that mimetic representation is not quite doing its job.

Here is an instance of the kind of problem that mimetic representation poses in the original play. In a review of the play that appeared in the largest *bhasha* daily, *Deepika*, on August 20, 1983, the anonymous reviewer writes, "We usually see exaggeration and incomprehensibility when historical truths are truthfully represented through the medium of art. Avoiding such issues, doing full justice to truthfulness, seminarians at Vadavathur St. Thomas Apostolic Seminary presented the historical play *Mar Joseph Cariattil* in the seminary auditorium" (Thadikkatt 7, translation mine). The reviewer goes on to praise the "originality" and the "extraordinary imagination" and "realism" displayed in the play, all the while acknowledging its fidelity to historical truth. However, even so, the reviewer doubts if "the ordinary lay community can swallow the historical facts contained in the play" (7). The producers had restricted the staging of the play to the seminary grounds. All the same, the reviewer recommends that it be staged before a wider public to permit at least some unbiased awareness of historical truth. According to this reviewer, the play has succeeded in the realm of mimetic representation of history. Yet, for various reasons and, significantly, amidst celebrations of the nation's independence from colonial rule, this representation can find only a limited and selective audience—priests and seminarians. The success of the representation, in other words, becomes the precise reason for censorship so that, for all practical purposes, including the fear of splitting the nation in the face of the (imperfect) Indian Christian, the laity are forbidden to see the play.

As colonialism became increasingly a distant memory, by 1983 it was important that the foibles of priests, even foreign ones, should be kept from the laity, for fear of scandal and a split within the church surely, but also for the sake of prudence in a newly independent nation with a Hindu majority. During the period of European colonialism, the Thomas Christian Church had gone through disunity (Friekenberg 42) and even schism, beginning with the historic event of the Coonan Cross Oath in 1653 that, according to Church historians, rejected the foreign ecclesiastical control over their community (Kollaparambil n.p.; Thekkedath 100–07). In the play, we see that in his conversation with the so-called schismatic Jacobite bishop, Mar Thoma VI, the protagonist—the Catholic priest and professor, Cariattil—lays the blame squarely on the Jesuit and Carmelite ecclesiastical rulers of their church for the schism (Thadikkatt 34). Under the Padroado, the Jesuits held sway over their church in the sixteenth and early seventeenth centuries, and soon after that the Carmelites gained dominance, during Dutch colonial rule, when both the civic and ecclesiastical powers of the Portuguese were curbed. Mar Thoma VI concurs that two religious orders were culpable for the mess in which the Thomas Christians found themselves. Cariattil and Mar Thoma VI know only too well that the problem did not start with but rather continued in their own generation. Soon they would face unrelenting opposition to any application for reunification of the two churches from Bishop Sales, a Carmelite and a Catalan. The play blatantly presents Sales's greed for power as the main reason for his opposition to the reunification. In the process and for effect, in another scene, Sales's predilection for the Carmelite customs of rosary and novena are contrasted with the St. Thomas Christians'—supposedly loftier—practices of scripture reading and fasting, for instance, as apparent and trivial reasons for any opposition to reunification. When Sales flings the scroll of the application for reunification submitted on behalf of Mar Thoma VI, however, Cariattil exposes Sales's fear of losing the jurisdiction to Mar Thoma VI. Though historical, these are events and conversations meant in 1983 for a "mature" audience, namely priests and seminarians, not the laity of the nation. All the same, theoretically, the worry that the Thomas Christian community might disintegrate when it accosts the laxity or unscrupulousness of its past and present administrators is unfounded because, and I elaborate on this phenomenon in my article "Nation Because of Differences," the generative elements of a nation evolve from the fissures. The present collection of articles underscores that the fissures are indeed the inherent characteristics of a multinational state.

The spotlight, shifted onto controversies, effectively opens up opportunities to reassess the relationship between Christianity and the formation of the multinational state. Another sensitive topic that the play deals with is how to solve the problems that would arise from the fact that the Jacobite Church had married priests. Salomi, the daughter of a Jacobite priest, raises this point with the concern and bluntness of a teenager: "If father joins the Catholic Church, will he abandon mother?" Her mother, Mariamma, alert to the realities of a patriarchal society, adds, "When I think of that I feel awfully scared. All I have is four daughters...If he forsakes me what will I do?" (Thadikkatt 30). The dialogue effectively brings to mind the tragic experience of the Thomas Christians who, in the late sixteenth century, witnessed the colonially and ecclesiastically forced separation of wives and children from husbands and fathers who were priests. The forced separation and sanctions continued into the following centuries whenever priests lapsed. In the play, all this comes only after an introductory reminder by a relative of Mar Thoma VI, Kunjappi Tharakan, that not only among the Jacobites but among the rest of the Thomas Christians too there had been many married priests. After almost four hundred years of the imposition of the rule of celibacy over the Catholic priests, under the Latinized Church of the Thomas Christians, these discussions were simply too uncomfortable, even controversial, to be made public at any time, let alone during the Independence Day celebrations. By presenting the controversies to, albeit, a religious community,

Thadikkatt sets in motion a reconsideration of the characteristics and role of Christianity in nation formation. Otherwise, the continuation of clerical celibacy among sections of the Thomas Christians would simply feed into the dominant nation narrative of Portuguese colonization by celibate Western missionaries and thereby increase instances of profiling Indian Christians as supporters of colonialism. The narrative of the married Christian or Catholic priest would, on the other hand, highlight Eastern Christianity and, thus, unsettle the nationalist narrative. A translation of the play into English has the potential to increase the visibility of Eastern Christianity and its suppressed history of anti-colonialism. It may cause further fissures in local narratives that tend to align with hegemonic national narratives and, thereby, shine light on the possibility of a more nuanced multinational state. A translation into the *marg*, English, has the potential to free the play from some of the limitations described earlier. The religious and secular characteristic of the English language and of English literature has the potential to, as it were, push the play onto other stages and into other audiences. Of course, a translation into any language will offer a whole set of new readers. In the case of the English translation of the play, for example, English's (both the language's and the literature's) "protestant" and—often—"anti-papist" history and culture serve to dull some of the anxiety surrounding the ontology of married clergy as well as the fact that priests err. Moreover, the secularly westernized and diasporic context of the target audience that otherwise comes from the history and culture linked to the original also helps to relax some of the puritanical elements of reception. These new cultural and structural aspects to some extent create an environment that is conducive to attention away from the historical self, heretofore dominated by ecclesiastical concerns and to the detriment of everything else. Yet Umberto Eco cautions, "It is extremely important to study the role of translation within the context of a receiving culture, but from this point of view a translation becomes a purely internal affair of the target language, and all the linguistic and cultural problems posed by the original become irrelevant" (21). In other words, the liberal ideologies of a diaspora into which the translated text enters cannot simply ignore the issues of language and context that marked the Malayalam play. Certainly, as a countertactic, representation in the translation appears to resolve some of the censorship issues faced within the Indian nation; nevertheless, as the next section shows, a certain *paradigm* of censorship sets in.

Dialoguing with Oneself, with Goodwill and Reflexivity
If translation into English can create new opportunities, on the other hand, English can have a severely alienating effect in the post-colony. In the conclusion of his essay "Jasmine," V.S. Naipaul narrates how as a young man visiting British Guiana he once encountered the familiar scent of a flower he had known from childhood. He never learnt its name and so enquired of his host, "an elderly lady of a distinguished Christian Indian family" (368). "Jasmine," was the reply. Naipaul continues, "The old lady cut a sprig for me. I stuck it in the top buttonhole of my open shirt. I smelled it as I walked back to the hotel. Jasmine, jasmine. But the word and the flower had been separate in my mind for too long. They did not come together" (368). One cannot help wondering how Naipaul, coming as he does from a distinguished Hindu Indian family, could have gone through the jasmine-filled pujas at home or in temples without a name, any name for this flower. But, when he did put a familiar flower to the English name, he was struck by alienation: "they simply did not come together." If Wordsworth's "daffodil" (364) held its sway over him, it was because he had never really accosted one in the fields of his native Trinidad. The fiction brought on by words and books, which he relished to the core, threatened to vanish at the strike of reality.

The cure for this—this need "to make an instant adjustment" between fantasy and reality—was, according to Naipaul, to "adapt" (364). He was going to reject the domination of daffodils in English literature; instead it appears that, like a (nationalist) visitor of his, he was going to have "sapodilla-skinned women groaning like bamboos in high wind" (364) and insert the name of a street in Port of Spain, where he had been brought up (365). He was not going to do adaptations of the colonial kind—rewriting source texts for new readers; rather, his counter-tactic would be to make the English language his own in Trinidadian or West Indian literature. In his novel *Midnight's Children*, Salman Rushdie suggests that such transformation of the English language is "chutneyfication." Chutneyfication challenged linguistic imperialism (see Phillipson) and opted for nativization and hybridization (Nayar 29). With all the accompanying problems of appropriation, exoticization, influence, and marginalization (Nayar 30), issues also of ethnography, Naipaulian adaptation or Rushdian chutneyfication was a significant use of the English language and the creation of an important national literature.

Not surprisingly, in translation studies, one of the counter-tactics to the incursions of power in a nation is reflexivity. Walter Benjamin's comment—"Translation is so far removed from being the sterile equation of two dead languages that of all literary forms it is the one charged with the special mission of watching over the maturing process of the original language and the birth pangs of its own" (256)—in some ways points to the reflexivity of the translator. This is a translator who, like Naipaul, is conscious of the burden of translating, who is conscious of the purpose to "liberate the language imprisoned in a work in his re-creation of that work" (Benjamin 261). Likewise, for me this burden translated itself as, "Does this translation make sense for my readers?" It thus became for me a gnawing botheration about my style as the translator and the problem of "getting it right," of ensuring the balance between specifics and universals.

My efforts to solve worry spots in fact replaced specifics with universals. The most obvious one is an instance of replacing a proverb with its raw denotation. In a scene marked by fiery exchanges between esteemed representatives of the Propaganda—including none other than the famous Cardinal Borgia (who later became prefect of the Propaganda) and the representatives of Mar Thoma VI (i.e., Cariattil and Thoma Paremmakkal), the following ensues. Borgia directs the two visitors to return to India and simply wait for the decision by the Propaganda on Mar Thoma VI's application for reunification. Realizing that not only would the wait be endless but also that the decision (if it arrived at all), by all indications so far, would be unfavourable, Cariattil's companion, the priest Paremmakkal, responds, "We too may be obliged to take a decision" (Thadikkatt 55). Borgia asks, "And what can that be... Is it to go to Portugal and work against the Propaganda again?" (55). Paremmakkal responds with a proverb: "*Kananirikkunna pooram kandariyukayanu nallathu*" (78). To transliterate, "it is better to see the *pooram* [festival] first hand." The proverb concerns a non-Christian scenario of India, the *pooram* or the festival of the goddesses. Paremmakkal is undoubtedly referring to the age-old Arattupuzha Pooram that was visited by the numerous deities of the neighbourhood, which preceded the modern Thrissur *pooram* designed by Raja Rama Varma, the king of Cochin from 1790 to 1805, and dedicated to Lord Siva, known locally as Vadakkunnathan (the Lord of the South). In *Glimpses of Nazraney Heritage*, George Menachery comments that "there is no proper Hindu god or goddess honoured during these festivals" (23), suggesting that Christianity entered the shores of Kerala before Hinduism proper. In his introduction to Menachery's book, M.G.S. Narayanan counters this reading, pointing out that it is based on a Western view of Hinduism that equates only "Vedic Brahmanism as Hinduism" (10). The exchange between Menachery and Narayanan—on respective native roots—is the other side of the history of the Thomas Christians that is not referenced either in the play or *The Varthamanappusthakam* or within colonial studies in Christianity. If Paremmakkal's portion of the dramatic dialogue cannot escape this insinuation, the contextual significance is the spectacular nature of the *pooram*. The festival is marked by great ostentation and is, indeed, a sight to behold. Paremmakkal's response references this display. In one sense, Paremmakkal's words simply mean, it is useless to venture to describe the festival; it is better seen in person. This invitation to a grand spectacle, however, is extended to someone who comes across as a racist and a highly conservative member of the Propaganda. In the context of the exchange, thus, it is neither an invitation nor an instance of enculturation. It simply stands for the exclamatory threat: "Just wait and see for yourself!" My translation is that non-specific and sufficiently universalized statement that takes into account the needs and literacy level of the extended multinational state, the diaspora.

Lawrence Venuti might point this out as an instance of domestication, the fluent (not resistant) variety (*Translator's Invisibility* 19). It is a bad word in his glossary. Venuti tends to agree with Henri Meschonnic (and Friedrich Schleiermacher too) that erasing the alien nature of a foreign text by doing what I did spreads the dominant ideology (in this instance, of ignoring the complex history of the foreign/other) in the name of "transparency" ("Translating Derrida" 257). Whereas it is not unusual to opt for universalisms in order to make a translation translate to a different society, the diaspora in this case, my point is that reflexivity appears to have a limited reach and tends to remain within the circumference of the self: the effort is successful in bringing the original to the target audience; but such self-oriented concerns may not necessarily, to echo Schleiermacher, take the audience to the original. To an extent, reflexivity—notwithstanding immense goodwill—results in dialoguing simply with oneself.

The phase of translator reflexivity permits a Naipaulian correction of course; it seeks out the gaps, brings the author to the reader, and thus considers logical universals as well as outstanding cultural specificities. It is concerned with receptivity. This is reflected in, at this stage, the obsession to get it right, a critical awareness of the style of the translator; the search for universals and culture specific aspects; the search for shared ground and a dialogue; and overall goodwill. Yet its problem is the self: self-censorship and seeking out shared grounds. Reflexivity, as an examination of conscience, has a tendency to remain rooted in the self and in efforts to understand the other in the image of the self. However, it is also a phase that Paul Ricoeur would call oneself as another. Politically, this is also the problem of the (majoritarian) state that tends to overwhelm the multinational state and its constituent differences—its minorities.

It can accordingly be pointed out that the censorship imposed on the original, preventing laity outright from any access to the staging of the play, manifests only differently in the translation of the play as a product of reflexivity. A certain paradigm of censorship sets in instead. This paradigm leads to the homogenization of who or what is represented and, as in the instance of the *pooram*, the universal replaces the specific and thus miscarries as a counter-tactic. When the peoples of Africa are represented as "Africans," the paradigm of censorship is in play to ensure that stereotypes remain so that the subject is treated and dealt with, for instance in hirings, incarcerations, and so on, as "Africans," and—at this moment in history—not according to slightly more favourable labels, such as Nigerian, Sudanese, Jamaican, capitalist, or communist.[4] Similarly, in the reflexive phase of the translation, the paradigm of censorship ontologizes the dominant ideology, in this case, the ideology of "India" as a homogenized entity that permits elisions of the *pooram*.

Turning to the Other, with a *Sthuthi*

In this section and in response to the obstacles posed by both representation and reflexivity, discussed above, I consider the opportunities available in that which is untranslatable: the priority of the "nation" in the context of European colonization, a close-up of the accommodation of internal differences in the multinational state, and the possibilities of a multinational India in the diaspora form the focal points.

There is a Thomas Christian ritual that is part of the family prayer and also marks meetings and greetings. This ritual is known as the *sthuthi*. It functions within a hierarchy, where the subordinate person "gives the *sthuthi*," uttering "*sthuthi* to Jesus the Messiah" (*eesho mishiyakku sthuthi ayirikkatte*), and the receiver of the *sthuthi* responds, "forever be the *sthuthi*" (*ellayippozhum sthuthi undayirikkatte*). The word *sthuthi* simply means "praise." In this sense, the giver of the *sthuthi* says, "praise be to Jesus the Messiah" and the respondent says, "praise be forever." This transliteration, however, cannot provide the specifics of the Thomas Christian context involving hierarchy and giving/taking. The Malayalam phrases are *sthuthi kodukkuka* (to give the *sthuthi*) and *sthuthi vanguka* (to receive the *sthuthi*). Elders teach and remind their young ones to "give the *sthuthi*" when meeting a priest or another elder. The priest or elder "receives the *sthuthi*." They acknowledge receipt of the *sthuthi* by saying the respondent's formula. The *sthuthi*, thus, is addressed at once to God and the fellow human being. In fact, the *sthuthi* cannot be uttered unless in the presence of fellow human beings; it has to be given and received by persons. It would be appropriate to cite the Jewish French philosopher Emmanuel Levinas here to describe the *sthuthi* as the rendezvous of two human beings, specifically the self and the other, where God passes through: "The existence of God is sacred history itself, the sacredness of man's relation to man through which God may pass" (Levinas and Kearney 18).

We come across this giving and receiving of the *sthuthi* in the play. On most occasions the giver of the *sthuthi* spells out the formula, the receiver acknowledges the *sthuthi* but does not necessarily utter the formula. For instance, when a mother and daughter receive (Thadikkatt 30), and later bid farewell to (32) Mar Thoma VI by giving the *sthuthi*, the bishop in response touches his ring on their forehead both times, while the former remain much obliged for the opportunity to give the *sthuthi* and are grateful for the blessing in return. Similarly, when a priest, Chacko, someone who had just arrived to see Cariattil, gives the *sthuthi* to Sales, who is having a heated conversation with Cariattil, Sales only nods in response (39). Conventionally, these responses of the bishops are sufficient in view of their relatively high place in the hierarchy. It is likely that Mar Thoma VI would have silently recited the formula in response. One is not entirely sure that Sales would have done the same, not necessarily because he was not a Thomas Christian, but because Cariattil had been talking to him about Mar Thoma VI's desire to reunite the Thomas Christians, and Sales was anxious to convince him that Mar Thoma VI was a schismatic. Moreover, Sales suspected that Cariattil was friendly towards Mar Thoma VI. His own instructions to Cariattil were otherwise and therefore Sales queries: "We had told you not to give extraordinary respect to him. You know that he is a schismatic, don't you?...That in his presence you should sit down as his equal and that you should reply firmly to his questions" (39).

Thadikkatt has not manufactured this event. The following excerpt from the English translation of *The Varthamanappusthakam*, by Placid Podipara, provides some insight:

Several times he [Mar Thomas VI, alias Mar Dionysius I, the bishop of the Jacobite/Old Party] requested the late Vicar Apostolic Msgr Florence, the bishop of Areopolis and Msgr Salvador dos Reis to receive him into the Church. But they did not. While he was making inquiries as to how he could realise his desire, he heard that the Padres had quarrelled with Bishop Sales and that the assembly of the churches had conducted the bishop from Verapoly to Alangat under the leadership of Malpan Cariattil. He hoped, therefore, that he could realize his desire through Malpan Cariattil. From Niranam he wrote to Alangat to Malpan Cariattil and to Bishop Sales praying that Malpan Cariattil might go to Niranam to console him.

Bishop Sales was not much pleased with the letter of Mar Thomas. But being an insincere man he concealed the wickedness of his heart and resolved to send Malpan Cariattil to Niranam. He, however, instructed the Malpan not to show any respect to Mar Thomas, to sit

> in his presence with no hesitation and to give harsh replies to all his demands. (Podipara 57–59)

Here, Paremmakkal sums up the immediate history pertaining to the attempts made by the Thomas Christians for unity, the rejection of their proposal by the European missionaries of both the Propaganda and the Padroado, and the hypocritical ways of Sales himself. E.R. Hambye writes that although Sales was initially reluctant, he later changed his mind and sent Cariattil to promote a dialogue. Therefore, he writes that Cariattil went to Niranam and met with Mar Dionysios I there "at the request of Bishop Francis of Sales" (Hambye 68). However, Paremmakkal's version insinuates that Sales meant to go through the motions of talks towards unity while having no intention whatsoever of bringing it to fruition. In fact, Paremmakkal explains, the bishop categorically instructed Cariattil to show no respect towards him: "to sit in his presence with no hesitation and to give harsh replies to all his demands" (Podipara 59). Accordingly, Sales's plan was perhaps to make it possible to report to Propaganda that on receiving Mar Thoma VI's request for unity he had indeed proceeded as per required procedures but that the talks—through no fault of his— had broken down. In "Mar Joseph Cariattil: Life and Activities," Charles Payngot, having consulted several archival sources, describes the event as follows: "Sales deputed Cariattil to visit Mar Thoma with the specific instruction not to show any signs of respect to him. Therefore, he went to the residence of Mar Thoma on March 18, 1777 and behaved there not as Sales told him to do but as he had learnt from his parents" (Payngot 43). My point is that Sales's instructions to Cariattil on how to conduct himself as an emissary of the colonizer, who must "sit down as his equal," would have no place for the *sthuthi*. But when the *sthuthi* is given and received God passes through, in between the giver and the receiver, and, thus, the *sthuthi* already signifies the multinational state in the face of European colonization.

In the translation, where *sthuthi* remains, the audience or reader becomes privy to the pedagogy of the other. This can be explained through a Levinasean framework, where the giver of the *sthuthi*, who is always at a relatively lower position in the hierarchy, can be tentatively labelled "the other," whereas the receiver of the *sthuthi*, who is relatively higher up in the hierarchy, can be labelled "the self." This is because the self is always the location of power. There is no contradiction here. The self is always the receiver of the *sthuthi* and the other, the giver. The giver of the *sthuthi*, it so happens, sometimes—and this in the presence of someone inferior—receives the *sthuthi* from the latter. Here, the earlier "other" becomes the "self." Thus, ultimately, everyone is obliged in the face of the other. The *sthuthi* is not simply an announcement of difference (not a ritual of colonial/Western Christianity, not a *Namaste*, etc.), but a compelling invitation, at once a command and a beseeching to assume responsibility for the other. The *sthuthi* summons this core of sociality— response-ability/responsibility—for the other and, in doing so, admits of the differential (and theological) in the multinational state.[5] I suggest that the *sthuthi* as a foreign element becomes for the readers (whether the diaspora or the indigenous and settler communities) an illustration of the relationship between the self and the other where the self is as it were eternally obliged to the morally superior other, that is, the otherness of the other and, therefore, nation space.

Since the role of a person as *sthuthi*-giver or *sthuthi*-receiver switches as befits the context that bestows positions in the hierarchy (one's role as a giver or receiver of the *sthuthi* is determined by whether one is encountering a junior or senior), ultimately everyone is obliged in the face of the neighbour, the other. The relationship is one of giving and receiving always. This is the unchanging context. Here, the receiver is always obliged in the face of the other/giver of the *sthuthi*. The Thomas Christian and anyone else who enters the space of the *sthuthi*, the diasporic and the diasporic's neighbour, are bound by the same responsibility, the same theology of the Messiah, Suffering Servant of Isaiah 53 (Levinas 33; Joseph, "Mahatma Gandhi" 464). The *sthuthi* requires the Thomas Christian in the diaspora to be accountable for the life and death of the indigenous person. The *sthuthi* also obliges the mainstream community to look into the face of the Thomas Christian as other. Postcolonial scholars find themselves without a paradigm to comprehend the Indian *sthuthi* as a Christian gesture because they presume that Christianity is a Western and colonial religion (Fanon 41; Sugirtharajah 111; Viswanathan). The untranslatability of the *sthuthi* compels the reader to look into the face of the other, forcing a re-vision/revision of the multinational state of India.

The untranslatability of the *sthuthi* functions as a synecdoche for the otherness, the alterity, of the other. The untranslatability is also translation's counter-tactic as a multinational narrative that voices its silenced margins. It is also the opportunity that Niranjana's reflections on her own translation of the *vacana* perhaps misses.

In conclusion, this chapter has pointed to the problem of essentialist anti-colonial narratives in a multinational state. The issue of presenting anti-colonial narratives in essentialist ways is lodged in the process of representing, even if self-reflexively, the stereotypical nation with its minorities and margins fading into oblivion. The historical play *Mar Joseph Cariattil* highlights the efforts of the Thomas Christian community in forming a nation in the eighteenth century. The process of translating this play from Malayalam to English foregrounds the ethical problem in that methods of representation and reflexivity rely heavily on the perspectives and preferences of the translator, that is, the self. The potential then, I have argued, lies in that which cannot be translated, for it impels the translator and the reader to encounter alterity. This space of the other is the often-ignored constituent part of the multinational state, which—for the purposes of this chapter—importantly connects the eighteenth-century national struggles of minorities, such as the Thomas Christians, and twentieth-century understandings of the nation and its diaspora. In the above ways, both translation studies and literary studies direct the reader of books and events to comprehend the multinational state in the face of the other.

NOTES

1. The Thomas Christians, a community of about nine million chiefly located in Kerala, India, claim to be descendants of those converted by the Apostle Thomas.
2. Those who view India as a pluralist union (not multinational) state tend to interpret the nationhood of India as more the product of the grip of the centre than an organic push of its diverse parts (for instance, see Basta et al.).
3. Here, I extend to translation studies arguments, made by Paul D. Morris, Matthew Tétreault, and Asma Sayed in this collection, on the role literary productions play in defining the nation.
4. In "Nigeria's Other Civil War" (this volume), Albert Braz considers how both Nigeria and Biafra failed to recognize the rights of ethnic and cultural groups in nation narratives.

5. Wayne Norman observes that minorities have been given little political autonomy and, therefore, it is not easy to draw a correlation between "minorities getting more autonomy and their expanding nation-building efforts" (74) for autonomy. However, Norman continues, multinational states with a lengthy period of democracy are less likely to demand secession. Whereas the relevant groundwork of minority politics in its relationship to a majoritarian nation remains conjectural at best, the instance of the untranslatable I introduce gestures at once towards a religio-social minority's desire for autonomy and their budding sense of nationalism in the period of eighteenth-century European colonization.

WORKS CITED

Basta, Karlo, John McGarry, and Richard Simeon. *Territorial Pluralism: Managing Difference in Multinational States*. University of British Columbia Press, 2015.

Benjamin, Walter. "The Task of the Translator." 1968. *Walter Benjamin: Selected Writings*, vol. 1, 1913–1926, edited by Marcus Bullock and Michael W. Jennings, Belknap Press of Harvard University Press, 1996, pp. 253–63.

Eco, Umberto. *Experiences in Translation*. Translated by Alastair McEwen, University of Toronto Press, 2001.

Fanon, Frantz. *The Wretched of the Earth*. Translated by Constance Farrington, Grove Press, 1961.

Friekenberg, Robert Eric. "Christians in India: A Historical Overview of Their Complex Origins." *Christians and Missionaries in India: Cross-Cultural Communication since 1500*, edited by Robert Eric Friekenberg, Wm. B. Eerdmans Publishing Co., 2003, pp. 33–61.

Hambye, E.R. "Mar Joseph Cariattil." *Homage to Mar Cariattil: Pioneer Malabar Ecumenist*, edited by Charles Payngot, Oriental Institute of Religious Studies, India Publications, 1992, pp. 65–73.

Joseph, Clara A.B. "Mahatma Gandhi and Emmanuel Levinas: What's Wrong with Worshiping the Christ?" *International Journal of Hindu Studies*, vol. 18, no. 3, 2014, pp. 451–90.

———. "Nation Because of Differences." *Research in African Literatures*, vol. 32, no. 3, 2001, pp. 57–70.

———, translator. *Mar Joseph Cariattil (A Church History Play)*. 2015. TS.

Kearney, Richard. "Introduction: Ricoeur's Philosophy of Translation." *On Translation*, by Paul Ricoeur. Routledge, 2006.

Kollaparambil, Jacob. *The St. Thomas Christians' Revolution in 1653*. St. Joseph's Press, 1981.

Levinas, Emmanuel. "Signification and Sense." 1972. *Humanism of the Other*. Translated by Nidra Poller, University of Illinois Press, 2006, pp. 9–44.

Levinas, Emmanuel, and Richard Kearney. "Dialogue with Emmanuel Levinas." *Face to Face with Levinas*, edited by Richard A. Cohen, SUNY Press, 1986, pp. 13–33.

Menachery, George. *Glimpses of Nazraney Heritage*. SARAS, 2005.

Naipaul, V.S. "Jasmine." 1972. *Concert of Voices: An Anthology of World Writing in English*, 2nd. ed., edited by Victor J. Ramraj, Broadview Press, 2009, pp. 363–68.

Narayanan, M.G.S. Introduction. *Glimpses of Nazraney Heritage*, by George Menachery, SARAS, 2005, pp. 9–14.

Nayar, Pramod K. *The Postcolonial Studies Dictionary*. Wiley Blackwell, 2015.

Niranjana, Tejaswani. *Siting Translation: History, Post-structuralism, and the Colonial Context*. University of California Press, 1992.

Norman, Wayne. *Negotiating Nationalism: Nation-Building, Federalism, and Secession in the Multinational State*. Oxford University Press, 2006.

Paremmakkal, Thomman. *The Varthamanappusthakam: An Account of the History of the Malabar Church between the years 1773 and 1786 with special emphasis on the events connected with the journey from Malabar to Rome via Lisbon and back undertaken by Malpan Mar Joseph Cariattil and Cathanar Thomman Paremmakkal*. 1786. Orientalia Christiana Analecta 190, translated and edited by Placid J. Podipara, Pontificium Institutum Orientalium Studiorum, 1971.

Parry, Benita. "Problems in Current Theories of Colonial Discourse." *Oxford Literary Review*, vol. 9, nos. 1–2, 1987, pp. 27–58.

Payngot, Charles, ed. *Homage to Mar Cariattil: Pioneer Malabar Ecumenist*. Oriental Institute of Religious Studies, India Publications, 1992.

Phillipson, Robert, editor. *Linguistic Imperialism Continued*. Orient Blackswan Private, 2009.

Podipara, Placid J., translator and editor. *The Varthamanappusthakam: An Account of the History of the Malabar Church between the years 1773 and 1786 with special emphasis on the events connected with the journey from Malabar to Rome via Lisbon and back undertaken by Malpan Mar Joseph Cariattil and Cathanar Thomman Paremmakkal* [1786], by Thomman Paremmakkal, Orientalia Christiana Analecta 190, Pontificium Institutum Orientalium Studiorum, 1971.

Rahman, Anisur. "Indian Literature(s) in English Translation." *Journal of Postcolonial Writing*, vol. 43, no. 2, 2007, pp. 161–71.

Ricoeur, Paul. *Oneself as Another*. Translated by Kathleen Blamey, University of Chicago Press, 1992.

Rushdie, Salman. *Midnight's Children*. Jonathan Cape, 1981.

Spivak, Gayatri C. "Can the Subaltern Speak?" *Marxism and the Interpretation of Culture*, edited by Cary Nelson and Lawrence Grossberg, University of Illinois Press, 1987, pp. 271–313.

Schleiermacher, Friedrich. "On the Different Methods of Translating." *Translation/History/Culture: A Sourcebook*, edited and translated by André Lefevere, Routledge, 1992.

Sugirtharajah, R.S. *Postcolonial Reconfigurations: An Alternative Way of Reading the Bible and Doing Theology*. SCM Press, 2003.

Thadikkatt, Geo. *Mar Joseph Cariattil (Sabhacharithra Nadakam)* [Malayalam]. Oriental Institute of Religious Studies, 1983.

Thekkedath, Joseph. *History of Christianity in India*, vol. 2, *From the Middle of the Sixteenth Century to the End of the Seventeenth Century (1542–1700)*. Church History Association of India, 2001.

Venuti, Lawrence. "Translating Derrida on Translation: Relevance and Disciplinary Resistance." *The Yale Journal of Criticism*, vol. 16, no. 2, 2003, pp. 237–62.

———. *The Translator's Invisibility: A History of Translation*. Routledge, 2008.

Viswanathan, Gauri. *Outside the Fold: Conversion, Modernity, and Belief*. Princeton University Press, 1998.

Nigeria's Other Civil War
Ken Saro-Wiwa and Ogoni Nationalism

ALBERT BRAZ

I don't think anybody can suggest to another person,
Please drop your culture; let's use mine.
　—CHINUA ACHEBE, There Was a Country

ONE OF THE MOST COGENT CRITIQUES of the idea that every sociological nation should have the right to sovereignty is that the process would be endless, with polities fragmenting into ever smaller units. Yet, as the example of Nigeria illustrates, history suggests that strife is inevitable unless nation-states accommodate the ethnonational diversity within their own borders. In the late 1960s, less than a decade after becoming independent from Great Britain, Nigeria descended into a devastating civil war that left over two million people dead. The fratricidal conflict between Nigeria and the breakaway Republic of Biafra is usually linked to the former's heterogeneous ethnonational make-up. But the hegemonic Federal-Igbo premises of the Nigerian Civil War have been contested from other perspectives as well, including the nationalist writings of the Ogoni minority writer Ken Saro-Wiwa.[1] In both his fiction and non-fiction, Saro-Wiwa makes a compelling case that Biafra was no more willing to consider the pluralism within its so-called national space than Nigeria had been with its own. It was precisely because of Biafra's purported indifference to the "national" rights of collectivities such as the Ogoni that Saro-Wiwa refused to support its drive for independence, underscoring the risks run by multinational states when they pretend to be unitary ones.

It is easy to understand why many Nigerians (and not only federal politicians and bureaucrats) might be reluctant to grant collective rights to every ethnonational group in the country. With anything between 250 (Achebe 25) and 300 "independent ethnic nationalities" (Adesanmi 226), and over 300 "warring languages" (Adesanmi 227), Nigeria would be a challenging territory in which to develop a unified consciousness at the best of times. It obviously does not fit the Herderian model that what makes a "distinct community...a *nation*" is that it has "its own national culture as it has its language" (Herder 284). But Nigeria also complicates the more recent thesis that all texts from the so-called third world must be read as *"national allegories"* (Jameson 68). Like the works of so many other post-independence Nigerian authors, Saro-Wiwa's writings often reveal that there is more than one nation in a given text.

Kenule Beeson (Ken) Saro-Wiwa[2] is today best known as an environmental activist, indeed, as an environmental martyr. He was born in the Niger Delta in 1941 and, along with eight other Ogoni activists, was executed in 1995 after what is generally deemed a show trial (Soyinka, *Open* 145–48). Saro-Wiwa, however, was not eliminated by the dictatorial government of General Sani Abacha and its multinational corporate allies, notably Shell Oil, just for opposing the despoliation of the Niger Delta, but specifically Ogoni territory. That is, his struggle was an ethnonational one. "It's one thing campaigning for the environment," he stressed late in his life, "it's another campaigning for the environmental rights of the Ogoni people. This is what gives me the kicks. Specificity" ("Letters and Poems" 103). Moreover, he fought his battle largely through his writings. Saro-Wiwa was a prolific and versatile writer, who composed novels, plays, poems, short stories, and television series, to say nothing of newspaper columns and non-fiction. In order to disseminate his books, he even became a publisher, an activity that "assisted" him in his "struggles for the rights of the oppressed minorities in Nigeria" (Saro-Wiwa, "Notes" 259; see also Neame 153–56). While referring to a variety of his texts, such as his 1989 memoir about the Nigerian Civil War *On a Darkling Plain* and his 1995 prison diary *A Month and a Day*, I will focus chiefly on his 1985 anti-war novel *Sozaboy*.

Saro-Wiwa's eldest child and namesake, Ken Wiwa, once remarked that, under more propitious circumstances, his father "probably would have been a comedian or an actor" (qtd. in Cohen). There is certainly much humour in Saro-Wiwa's fiction, starting with his phenomenally popular sitcom *Basi and Company*, a satirical comedy that during its five-year run between 1985 and 1990 was watched by a third of all Nigerians, "making it arguably the most successful local television show ever produced in Africa" (Pegg 701). Yet even *Basi*, which avoided ethnic humour since it tends to target minorities, was overtly political. As Saro-Wiwa elucidated at the time, he used his series "to excoriate" his co-citizens, by showing them that "rich Nigerians, especially of the political class, have the 'Basi' complex" and are "hustling con men" (qtd. in Brooke). In particular, Saro-Wiwa favoured the polemic, a literary genre that he claims most Nigerians were unused to and that he describes as "an aggressive attack on or refutation of the opinions or principles of another. A polemicist is one skilled or given to polemics. He is not thereby a cannibal or a butcher, but an artist" (*Similia* 166).[3] Saro-Wiwa's adoption of a polemical style reflects his belief that a "good book or piece of writing is one that gives the reader nightmares" and that "a writer's mission must be to cheer and challenge" (166). But it is also likely the result of the fact that his writings are infused with at least two nationalisms, Nigerian and Ogoni, identities that are not always easy to reconcile.

Saro-Wiwa's competing Nigerian and Ogoni nationalisms, to which could be added his staunch identification with the Niger Delta as a whole, elucidate another striking feature of his work, its dual anti-colonialism. Although Saro-Wiwa is conscious of the lasting impact of Nigeria's colonial past, most conspicuously highlighted by the country's artificial creation by Great Britain, he does not attribute Nigeria's inequities solely to foreign colonialism. He also traces them to what he calls "Indigenous colonialism" (*Darkling Plain* 11 ff.), which he maintains has placed

Nigeria's smaller ethnonational groups at the mercy of the three dominant ones, the Hausa-Fulani in the North, the Yoruba in the Southwest, and the Igbo in Saro-Wiwa's Southeast. These are the so-called Wazobians, whose leaders convey "the impression that Nigeria consist[s] of three ethnic groups instead of three hundred or thereabouts" (21; see also 147). In a newspaper column about *On a Darkling Plain: An Account of the Nigerian Civil War*, Saro-Wiwa affirms that in his memoir he "make[s] it clear that Nigeria is not a federation of geographical regions, not a federation of religions, nor a federation of administrative units. It is a federation of ethnic groups, and until this is properly understood, if at all, we will not be about to establish a stable federation" (*Similia* 98). Like his compatriot Wole Soyinka, for whom Nigeria is a country of "many nations" (*Open* 48), Saro-Wiwa considers his homeland a "welter of nationalities" (*Darkling Plain* 47) and contends that "the only way the majority of Nigerians can be protected against indigenous colonialism by the major ethnic groups...is through the development of the language and culture of each ethnic group" (*Similia* 106). Thus, if future civil wars are to be averted, it is imperative that all ethnonational groups, regardless of size, be part of the national dialogue.

In his provocative essay "The Language of African Literature: A Writer's Testimony," Saro-Wiwa discloses that it was only after he completed his undergraduate studies at the University of Ibadan, in the heart of Yorubaland, that he discerned "the true nature of Nigerian society as an agglomeration of peoples and cultures, much like the rest of Africa" (154). His childhood experience had been circumscribed by the world of the Ogoni, who then comprised about half a million people. His universe began to expand in secondary school, when he found himself "the only Ogoni boy" at Umuahia's then prestigious but Igbo-dominated Government College and "learned the necessity of being a good Nigerian" (153, 154; see also *Darkling Plain* 44). Saro-Wiwa points out that in his "Ogoni home, the idea of Africa never arose. It is not an Ogoni concept. Nor was Nigeria" ("Language" 155). But by the mid-1960s, Nigeria had definitely become real to him, as the existential crisis that befell the country forced him "to choose between Nigeria and Biafra" (155), a decision that he did not appreciate having to make. He ultimately sided with Nigeria, since he felt that "biafra [sic][4] offered nothing new," being

"Nigeria in a different name" (*Darkling Plain* 88), and would result in "the possible continued enslavement of the Ogoni people" (*Month* 17). He alleges that the Igbos "banked on being able to bully their minority neighbours into submission while convincing the outside world that those minorities had willingly agreed to go with them" (*Darkling Plain* 231). The lack of consultation with peoples like the Ogoni by both Nigeria and Biafra before the outbreak of what would become the Civil War of 1967–1970 persuaded him that "colonialism is not a matter only of British, French, or European dominance over Africans. In African society, there is and has always been colonial oppression" ("Language" 155), which is "harsh and crude" and "as detestable as European colonialism" (156). As he writes in his poem "Victory Song,"

> *You have raped my land*
> *Black brother, silenced my song*
> ...
> *Vampire, tyrant, rapist*
> *Black brother of the same womb*
> *But cruel as the flares that burn*
> *Poisonous gases into our skies.* ("Letters and Poems" 142)

By then, Saro-Wiwa had also become convinced that the Civil War was "mostly about the control of the oil resources of the Ogoni and other ethnic groups in the Niger River Delta" (*Month* 39; see also 44, 59, and 126).[5] So he comes to deeply resent what he calls the "Biafran propaganda [which] invariably claimed that the Biafrans were one. But this was a lie. A hoax. I saw it as my responsibility to fight that lie" ("Language" 155), which he proceeds to do with every means available to him.

Saro-Wiwa has been censured for his lack of sensitivity toward the Igbos and their justifiable fears of genocide, but there is much that is positive about his nationalism. For one, his "vision of Nigeria as a confederation of equal and autonomous ethnic groups encompassed all Nigerians, not just the Ogoni" (Pegg 705). As he declared during his imprisonment in 1993, his "primary concern as a man and a writer" was "the development of [a] stable, modern Nigeria which embraces civilised values" and "where no ethnic group or individual is oppressed"

(*Month* 56). Saro-Wiwa was clearly aware of the example of the former Ijaw police officer Isaac Adaka Boro, who, in a 1966 bid to gain control of the region's natural resources, "took up arms against Nigeria" and declared the Niger Delta Republic (*Similia* 133; see also *Darkling Plain* 30). Although it may be true that the reason the Nigerian government risked executing Saro-Wiwa was that he had failed to learn from Boro and "bring all the devastated and marginalised people of the Niger Delta into the forefront of [his] struggle," the fact remains that "the story of Saro-Wiwa...is the discourse of all [of Nigeria's] micro-ethnicities" (Okome xvi, xxiii). No less important, the Saro-Wiwa–led Movement for the Survival of the Ogoni People (MOSOP) advocated for "Ethnic Autonomy, Resource and Environmental Control," but insisted on "the path of non-violent struggle" (Saro-Wiwa, *Month* 98, 133). Finally, his steadfast support for the Ogoni and their fight for collective rights did not blind him to the shortcomings of nationalism, including Ogoni nationalism. This is never more evident than in *Sozaboy: A Novel in Rotten English*.

Sozaboy, which has been described as the Nigerian Civil War's "enduring literary monument" (Boyd), is a fascinating text for a variety of reasons, beginning with its demotic language. As the subtitle indicates, it is written mainly in a stylized Pidgin, Nigeria's unofficial but much disparaged national tongue, reflecting the author's desire to capture the ways of being and seeing of common people. Perhaps the best way to characterize *Sozaboy* is as a comedic meditation on war. At the centre of the narrative is a young apprentice truck driver whose name the reader gradually learns is Mene. The soldier of the title, Mene becomes totally identified by his involvement in the war. This is a role about which he is extremely ambivalent but which he cannot escape, due to external forces as much as internal ones.

Like a virus, war infiltrates Sozaboy's world, a somnolent (and fictitious) nine-village kingdom in the Niger Delta in the environs of Port Harcourt, or Pitakwa, as it is called in the text. At the outset, the whole collectivity is thrilled by the prospect of a conflagration. To quote the novel's signature opening one-sentence paragraph, "Although, everybody in Dukana was happy at first" (Saro-Wiwa, *Sozaboy* 1). The reason the denizens of Dukana are out dancing in the streets at the news that "the old, bad [civilian] government have dead, and the new government of soza and police have come" is that they are convinced this will mean the end of their troubles, or at least of systemic bribery (1). However, the situation soon becomes murky. To begin with, Mene's boss informs him that the inspector whom they have been bribing daily just to be able to do their work, instead of being demoted by the new government, is "bigger and bigger man" (2), suggesting that if things are about to change, it is probably not for the better. Then waves of people start streaming back to Dukana, since they are "killing plenty" elsewhere in the country (16). Most disconcerting, there is the realization that if there is a war, there must be soldiers, as there will be casualties. The people of Dukana will not be allowed to be bystanders, particularly Mene.

Saro-Wiwa's depiction of his protagonist's metamorphosis into Sozaboy is nothing short of brilliant. It has become common to posit that men fight for atavistic reasons, supposedly being programmed to offer their bodies as "weapon[s] of war" (Sainte-Marie 167). Mene's martial journey, though, is anything but uncomplicated. This is apparent when he dreams that the military has come to town to conscript new soldiers and he narrowly evades their grasp by jumping into the river, for he is "afraid of the sozas" and does "not want to join" them (Saro-Wiwa, *Sozaboy* 47). Mene agrees with Dukana's other young men that "to be a soza is not good thing...Because soza is stupid useless anmal who will just shoot and kill and then he can also be shoot and kill. Only stupid person who want to die quick can be soza" (43). More importantly, this is also the view held by his beloved mother, who raised him by herself, being "both [his] father and mother," and who thinks that his spasmodic desire to be a soldier is "foolish nonsense" (55, 56). In contrast, Mene's girlfriend Agnes is adamant that he must become a soldier if he wishes to marry her. A waitress that he met recently at a bar in Pitakwa, she tells him in no uncertain terms, "When trouble come, I like strong, brave man who can fight and defend me" (19; see also 37, 43, 54, and 59). Mene himself is torn, not only because he is infatuated with Agnes and desperately wants to wed her, but because he likes the "uniform...very much," believing that it will lead his compatriots to see him as a "good man and strong" (53, 104). In addition, he is cognizant of the need to have Dukana representation in the Army. Mene does not think much of Dukana's leaders, from Chief Birabee, the kingdom's monarch, to Pastor Barika, the head of its most important religious congregation, the Church of Light of God, considering all "dese chiefs...useless people" (5). Yet he too shares the general concern that "If Dukana man is not soza..., these sozas will continue to come here to beat our people" (43). In truth, even his mother is not opposed to Mene becoming a soldier. She just feels that if the war breaks out, "it is better to be in your own house and fight it" (67), possibly against both enemy and friendly troops.

Given his name, Sozaboy is of course destined to join the Army. But this hardly settles matters, as he is not at all certain who is "the Enemy" (54), despite being repeatedly told by officers, "We shall overcome. The Enemy will be vanquished. God is on our side" (78). Also, during the war, he continues to be assailed by the old questions, not the least, "Why are we fighting?" (90). This is a query to which he never manages to find a satisfactory answer, notwithstanding all the trials he undergoes. Among these are being complicit in the death of his abusive captain by a comrade and then helping his colleague try to persuade their superiors that it was the "enemy" who did it (109); removing his "soza uniform" and running for his life after his company is bombarded and nearly wiped out (112); and denying being "a soza" upon becoming a prisoner of war, an eventuality that leads to his donning the "enemy uniform" (122, 126). Most troubling for Sozaboy is that during the conflict he keeps coming across a soldier, known as Manmuswak (Man Must Eat), who seems to change sides at will, being one moment with the Army and the next with the enemy, and back again. Sozaboy cannot stop thinking about Manmuswak, whether he is awake or asleep. Manmuswak not only has the power to read his mind but appears to know everything about him, from his role in the killing of his captain to his desertion. "Sozaboy, just wait for me," the mysterious stranger torments him, "I am Manmuswak and you must fear me. As everybody who have hear my name in war front must fear me. Because I am soza and I am war. I have no friend and I can fight anybody whether whether" (121). Perhaps Manmuswak is not so much a mercenary as the spirit of war itself, the embodiment of warfare when driven by nothing beyond the instinct for survival, and power, and Sozaboy simply cannot escape him, or rather it.

Ironically, it is after Sozaboy becomes a driver for the enemy that he is able to pay a furtive visit to Dukana, hoping to see his mother and

Agnes. But he discovers that the town has been abandoned and, when he spots an old friend who has been hiding in the bush, the latter thinks he is a "ghost," since the townspeople were told that "everybody was killed" when Sozaboy's company was shelled (131). The friend's reaction to Sozaboy's return is a portent of his ultimate fate. After searching in vain for his mother and Agnes in a series of ever more grim refugee camps, Sozaboy is delivered to the enemy by a group of "Dukana people," at the urging of none other than Chief Birabee (159). He is imprisoned again, threatened to be "buried alive" along with other prisoners of war (160), and lined up to be summarily executed (167). Somehow, Sozaboy survives the war and decides to go back home. But when he gets there, he finds his mother's house demolished and his mother and Agnes nowhere in sight. Even more bewildering, everyone runs away from him. Sozaboy subsequently learns from another friend that the town is being decimated by an epidemic of kwashiorkor, lethal to children, and that the residents hold him responsible for it. More specifically, they have come to believe that because his mother and Agnes were killed during the aerial attack that levelled the family home, Sozaboy is determined to avenge their deaths by making sure that "everybody in Dukana must die too" (178). Their suspicions are confirmed when they consult their juju, or shaman, and are told that the deaths in Dukana will only end if they perform a series of sacrifices and kill the "ghost" of Sozaboy, who purportedly has returned from the dead because he was not buried properly after his company was eviscerated (180). Sozaboy finds the reasoning of his compatriots unfathomable but discerns that, as a soldier, he "cannot just stay in Dukana and allow people to come and kill me like goat or rat or ant" (181). The only explanation he has for what he considers this collective madness is that the war unhinged Dukana. To quote the novel's closing words, as he surreptitiously hastens out of town, "And I was thinking how I was prouding before to go to soza and call myself Sozaboy. But now if anybody say anything about war or even fight, I will just run and run and run and run and run. Believe me yours sincerely" (181). With that, he scampers out of his birthplace, with no idea of where he is going.

It must be noted that there is a crucial component of *Sozaboy* to which is difficult to do justice, which is Saro-Wiwa's pervasive use of humour in what is an exploration of devastating human loss and duplicity. This challenge, I suspect, is intrinsically linked to the text's genre. As Milan Kundera asks of Jaroslav Hašek's *The Good Soldier Švejk*, "Isn't it astonishing that this comic novel is also a war novel? What has happened to war and its horrors if they've become laughing matters?" (10). Or, equally apropos: What has happened to comedy? (Kundera 12). In the case of *Sozaboy*, part of Saro-Wiwa's humour lies in the fact that the collectivity that claims the hero as its own throughout most of the narrative expels him from its midst, without recourse or appeal. At the end, the protagonist is alone. After having gone through hell numerous times on behalf of his people, he is an individual without a community.

Yet, in many ways, the conclusion of *Sozaboy* is foregrounded from the beginning of the novel, especially through Saro-Wiwa's portrayal of his protagonist's responses to the leadership of Dukana, political as well as religious. While Dukana may not have been able to avoid becoming entangled in the war, given its marginality, the situation is not helped by either Chief Birabee or Pastor Barika. As mentioned earlier, from the start, Mene is openly dismissive of both leaders. He describes Birabee as "the most afraid" individual in Dukana and a "very coward man" (4), and can barely contain his derision as he watches how the seemingly omnipotent chief is always "smiling that idiot foolish smile...whenever he sees soza or police or power" (45). Mene is no less caustic toward Barika but for more personal reasons, failing to grasp why the cleric keeps warning the people of Dukana about the end of the world when Mene has yet to get his driver's licence or to sleep with a woman. This is a resentment that Saro-Wiwa captures with dexterity. As Mene listens to Barika blathering on about the imminence of doomsday, Saro-Wiwa has him observe to himself that "Pastor Barika is useless man...He is useless man inside useless church. I know it, but I cannot tell him. I just keep quiet" (4). In the process, Saro-Wiwa also shows the reader how Mene, and presumably other residents of Dukana, feels about his leaders, even if he has learned to keep his thoughts to himself.

Sozaboy could thus be interpreted as an unconditional condemnation of nationalism. In the moment of crisis, there is no communion of spirits in Dukana. There is also no place to contest the dominant ways of running the kingdom. Yet, as one reflects on the actions of Saro-Wiwa's characters, one cannot help but surmise that they are fighting other people's wars, which is the source of much of the humour. As Saro-Wiwa writes in his poem "Thoughts in Time of War," "at the front, young men / Clubber one another" to death, in an orgy of technology-facilitated violence, "For a cause they barely understand" (*Songs* 24). The opacity of the war at the centre of *Sozaboy* underscores that, in many ways, it is a distraction, preventing the people of Dukana from addressing their more tangible problems. It hardly seems a coincidence that Sozaboy is handed over to the enemy at the refugee camp, at the instigation of his own chief, after he has learned that powerful figures like Birabee and Barika are stealing food provided to the refugees by the Red Cross. Their behaviour demonstrates to him why "Barika and Birabee...are very fat like pig," whereas "the Dukana people are thin and hungry" (158). Needless to say, with Sozaboy forced out of the kingdom, it is not likely that much will change anytime soon.

The portrayal of social relations in Dukana reveals that, despite his unwavering Ogoni nationalism, Saro-Wiwa is far from being an apologist for nationalism, even of the minority kind. What also becomes apparent is that, whatever else may compel Saro-Wiwa to fight so passionately for the rights of small groups like the Ogoni, it is not the desire to help them return to some Arcadian past. In *Sozaboy*, while Mene can boisterously sing the praises of his hometown, he concedes that Dukana is not exactly utopia. Not only is it a distance from any sizable city, but all its dwellings "are made of mud. There is no good road or drinking water. Even the school is not fine and no hospital or anything." The inhabitants themselves, who are fishers and farmers, "no know anything more than fish and farm. Radio sef they no get. How can they know what is happening?" (Saro-Wiwa, *Sozaboy* 4). Dukana may be a place where "time does not matter," as Saro-Wiwa writes elsewhere (*Forest* 5), but this should be construed as neither a source of solace nor a virtue.

Moreover, Saro-Wiwa, can be critical not only of the material conditions in Dukana but also of the cultural or spiritual ones. In "The Inspector Calls," the second story in his collection *A Forest of Flowers*, the narrator notes that town meetings scheduled to start in the morning often did not begin until nightfall. More germane, because of the reverence for the oral tradition, "no records [were] kept of meetings; each member could be trusted to remember what the others said at previous meetings. Reading and writing were the pastimes of the children at Dukana's school. The elders could not indulge in such child's play" (*Forest* 14–15). The result is that "a lot of time was spent recalling and recapitulating what each and every one had said on previous occasions. And as might be expected, this led to misunderstandings, disagreements, and outright quarrels" (15), suggesting the author might not be too unhappy to see some of those revered traditions give way to more empirically tested practices.

Other traditions are presented as being even less defensible. This is evident in the opening piece in *A Forest of Flowers*, "Home Sweet Home," which depicts an unnamed young woman's return to Dukana to be a teacher at her old school. One of the reasons the protagonist is pleased to return to Dukana is that, besides her mother, her best friend Sira also lives there. The two young women have been close since childhood and the last time they saw each other, Sira already "had four children and was again pregnant" (*Forest* 1). The protagonist is surprised that Sira is not at her homecoming, and when she asks Sira's mother about her, the older woman is evasive, saying only that Sira has "'travelled'" (9). The protagonist becomes concerned about her friend and, after all the visitors leave, asks her own mother if Sira is dead. Her mother too is vague, beyond assuring her that Sira is not dead, or ill. When the protagonist persists, her mother finally confides that Sira "had twins. She could not stay in the town anymore. She went away across the river." The protagonist's mother then repeats that Sira is "not dead," but says that she believes the twins died, and orders her daughter not to "ask [her] any more questions" (10), putting an end to the conversation.

Similarly, in *Sozaboy*, when the people of Dukana become convinced that Sozaboy wants to avenge the deaths of his mother and Agnes by obliterating all of them, their juju tells them that the only way they can kill Sozaboy's "ghost" is by providing the juju with "money and seven white goats and seven white monkey *blokkus* and seven alligator pepper and seven bundles of plantain," as well as "seven young girls" (*Sozaboy* 180). Saro-Wiwa has been known to make light of his treatment of shamanism in his work, telling his Irish confidante Majella McCarron not to worry about his depiction of Ogoni jujus, since their inclusion was merely "meant to frighten the Nigerian soldiers" ("Letters and

Poems" 87). But in *Sozaboy* there is no indication that anyone in Dukana finds the idea of sacrificing girls any more ethically questionable than that of sacrificing goats or anything else, intimating that the practice must not be that exceptional.[6]

It is perhaps because of the ubiquity of such ambiguous portrayals that Ken Wiwa asserts that his "father had a love-hate relationship with Ogoni. Although he was proud of his roots, he despised the slavish mentality and our poor reputation" (65). In his non-fiction, in particular, there is ample proof that Saro-Wiwa felt that his people were oblivious to the multitude of forces that menaced their very existence. As he writes in *A Month and a Day*, with a fair dose of Messianism, the Ogoni "had been sleepwalking their way towards extinction, not knowing what internal colonialism had done and was doing to them. It had fallen to me to wake them up from the sleep of the century" (16). Saro-Wiwa implies that it is because of the lack of political consciousness among the Ogoni, that he is forced to become their self-elected saviour, their *"protector"* (qtd. in Wiwa 133), a sentiment that is echoed in many Ogoni praise songs written about him (Ngaage 148–49). Thus, when Saro-Wiwa writes the Ogoni anthem, "Ogoni Hymn," and asks the Ogoni Creator, "Give us thy wisdom and the strength / To shame our enemies" (*Month* 143–44; "Letter and Poems" 145), he is probably addressing the Ogoni as much as their foes. Yet, whatever misgivings he may have about the Ogoni, there is no question that he believes passionately they have the right to control their destiny—including the right to make wrong decisions about what is best for themselves.

Throughout his writings, Saro-Wiwa raises a series of pivotal issues about collective identity, in the process highlighting the fact that "there can be more than one nation in a nation-state, and consequently more than one national literature" (Braz 16). Not surprisingly, his fervent championing of the Ogoni is not always unproblematic. Even some of his most steadfast supporters are troubled by his failure "to condemn...in the most rigorous language" the killings of the four Ogoni leaders by young MOSOP militants that led to his final arrest, feeling that he "could be assailed with a measure of *moral* responsibility" (Soyinka, "Foreword" xi). That said, the Nigerian government's subjugation of both Saro-Wiwa and the Ogoni vindicates his belief that the reason the Ogoni are so vulnerable is that they have yet to realize that, "no matter the system of government, unless a people take their destiny into their own hands, no improvement will come to them" (Saro-Wiwa, *Month* 41). As he charged during his last address to the military tribunal that sentenced him to death, "Any nations [*sic*] which can do to the weak and disadvantaged what the Nigerian nation has done do the Ogoni people, loses a claim to independence and to freedom from outside influence" (173–74). In other words, when a nation-state treats a segment of its populace as non-citizens, it relinquishes any right to their loyalty.

Significantly, Saro-Wiwa appears to have a more positive perception of the Nigerian nation-state than do some contemporary pundits, such as the literary scholar Pius Adesanmi. Although a professed champion of "Project Nigeria," Adesanmi is dubious about the country's viability, or at least of its legitimacy as a political entity. He contends that each genuine nation must have "a foundational national myth," in the way that the United States has "the American dream" and France has "*l'oeuvre nationale* or *l'oeuvre de la République*" (200, 201). This is purportedly an inspiring narrative that Nigeria lacks, possessing nothing more than "'the national cake,'" a "dessert" that it then denies to most of its citizens (201, 202). The journalist and biographer Richard Gwyn avers that Canada has demonstrated that "a 'new nationality' could be political rather than ethnic…, composed of values and attitudes rather than of race" (243), but Adesanmi would appear to dismiss such an option. He finds Nigeria wanting as a nation precisely because it does not have the equivalent of the Yoruba *orile ede*, in which a people's mind, language, and land are one (223–26). Therefore, because of its ethnonational diversity, Nigeria was doomed to fail, a heterogeneous nation supposedly being a contradiction in terms.

Rather than contesting that Nigeria is a multinational nation-state, or dreaming that it were otherwise, Saro-Wiwa just desires that it grant all its component parts their collective rights. His conundrum is that the Ogoni are a peripheral culture, a numerically negligible group that is easy to ignore. One may appreciate the sentiments expressed by Chinua Achebe when he writes, as he does in the passage that serves as the epigraph to this chapter, that nobody should "suggest to another person, Please drop your culture; let's use mine" (60). At the same time, it is telling that the celebrated Igbo author also remarks that he is "aware that there are people, many friends of mine, who feel that there are too many cultures around. In fact, I heard someone say that they think some of these cultures should be put down, that there are just too many" (60). This is the reality faced by Saro-Wiwa and the Ogoni, whose resistance to the despoliation of their territory culminated in what Soyinka terms "the first Nigerian experimentation with 'ethnic cleansing'" (*Open* 6). Like the rulers of other multinational states who act as if they lived in unitary ones, Nigeria's political leaders deduced that it was more expedient to pretend that members of a small ethnonational group did not exist than to listen to them, even if their silence could only be achieved by physically eliminating them.

The political scientist Scott Pegg posits that "Saro-Wiwa was hanged because he was the only Nigerian and arguably the only writer in the world capable of bringing tens of thousands of people out in the streets" (704). But I do not think we should discard the possibility that he was sacrificed because he belonged to a small ethnonational group without much power and thus whom the federal elites could afford to alienate without significant risk. One just has to contrast Nigeria's treatment of Saro-Wiwa with that of the Igbo leader Odumegwu Ojukwu. Even though Ojukwu initiated Biafra's secession, not only was he not executed for his transgressions, he was not even tried. As Soyinka notes, Ojukwu was later allowed to hold "a chieftaincy title, the Ikemba of Nnewi," or as "many Nigerians find it more appropriate these days to refer to him as the Reversible Ikemba" (*Open* 45).[7] Saro-Wiwa, in contrast, was ritualistically hanged for exposing the Nigerian government's systematic failure to respect the rights of one of the many collectivities that make up the federation, becoming the most famous victim of a protracted civil war that the country still has to acknowledge.

Yet, in the end, one thing that is evident about Saro-Wiwa is that his enemies have not managed to defeat him, as his extraordinary presence in contemporary Nigerian literature testifies. In one of his newspaper columns, Saro-Wiwa lamented "what little effect" his writings had "had on the nation" (*Similia* 69). But this is no longer the case. At least since his execution in 1995, it has become impossible to imagine the Niger Delta struggle without him. Some writers explore how Saro-Wiwa's campaign for minority rights has been used by an ever-growing army of kidnappers, who feel this is the only way they can "share in...the economic life of their communities" (Ojaide 50), since "our people have a right to partake in the spoils from the on-going plunder of their lands" (Garricks 173; see also 294). Other writers examine the cost exacted by his activism and ponder if anyone today would be willing to pay the price "to be the next Ken Saro-Wiwa" (Agary 138).[8] Still others, dramatize his story to bare Nigeria's "endless pleasure in inflicting pain" on its own people (Ogezi 10). All testify to the way Saro-Wiwa gained legitimacy for the discourse on minority rights, by illustrating the consequences when nation-states exclude ethnonational groups from the national family. Indeed, it is largely thanks to the writings of Ken Saro-Wiwa that the plight of the Ogoni (and the other micro-minorities of the Niger Delta) continues to have major repercussions for the whole country. One suspects that it will do so until Nigeria comes to accept that it is composed not just of three ethnonational groups but of a multitude of them.

NOTES

1. The Ogoni have been termed a "micro-minority," since at 500,000 people in the mid-1990s they comprised about "0.4 percent" of Nigeria's population (Nixon 105, 106). However, there is no agreement on what constitutes a micro-minority. Saro-Wiwa, for one, dismissed the assertion by the Ibibio environmental activist and writer Nnimmo Bassey that he too belonged to "a minority ethnic nation...because, with a population of close to three million, the Ibibio could not claim the minorities tag" (Bassey xii).
2. This is the best known version of his name, and Saro-Wiwa himself joked that during a visit to the United States alone, he heard his surname rendered as "Sora-Wawo..., Sira-Wawa..., and Saro-Wee-wee. Uncomfortably close to the toilet, you might say" (*Similia* 60).
3. The observation appears in a newspaper column titled "A Cannibal Rage" and Saro-Wiwa is alluding to the fact that even prominent Nigerians openly admit that they avoid travelling to his "Ogoni homeland because the people there are all cannibals" (*Similia* 166).
4. Presumably for political reasons, in *On a Darkling Plain* Saro-Wiwa often does not capitalize Biafra.
5. Ken Wiwa agrees with his father's assessment, stating that "the Nigerian civil war was a battle for control of the vast and largely untapped oil fields of the Delta" (37–38).

6. The tradition of sacrificing girls is probably not unrelated to the fact that, as Sozaboy points out, "Women do not talk in Dukana meeting. Anything the men talk, the women must do. Dukana people say woman does not get mouth. And it is true" (Saro-Wiwa, *Sozaboy* 8).
7. The nature of the relationship between the Igbo and Saro-Wiwa remains polemical. According to Ken Wiwa, "There are suggestions even today that his execution was the revenge of the Igbo for his siding with the federalists. I'm not sure about this, but my father was never their favourite Ogoni" (38).
8. In the acknowledgements to her novel *Yellow-Yellow*, Kaine Agary writes, "I owe this effort to Ken Saro-Wiwa whose book *A Month and Day: A Detention Diary* inspired me to write fiction" (179). Similarly, Tanure Ojaide dedicates *The Activist* to the "memory of Ken Saro-Wiwa."

WORKS CITED

Achebe, Chinua. *There Was a Country: A Personal History of Biafra*. Penguin Press, 2012.

Adesanmi, Pius. *You're Not a Country, Africa: A Personal History of the African Present*. Penguin Books, 2011.

Agary, Kaine. *Yellow-Yellow*. Dtalkshop, 2006.

Bassey, Nnimmo. "Foreward [sic]: Silence Is Treason." Corley, Fallon, and Cox, pp. ix–xvii.

Boyd, William. Introduction. Saro-Wiwa, *Sozaboy*.

Braz, Albert. "Federal Literatures: Toward a Theory of Literary Intranationality." *Theoretical Studies in Literature and Art*, vol. 38, no. 5, 2018, pp. 14–25.

Brooke, James. "Enugu Journal; 30 Million Nigerians Are Laughing at Themselves." *New York Times*, 24 July 1987, https://www.nytimes.com/1987/07/24/world/enugu-journal-30-million-nigerians-are-laughing-at-themselves.html?pagewanted=2&src=pm.

Cohen, Patricia. "A Writer's Violent End, and His Activist Legacy." *New York Times*, 4 May 2009, https://archive.nytimes.com/www.nytimes.com/2009/05/05/books/05wiwa.html.

Corley, Íde, Helen Fallon, and Laurence Cox, eds. *Silence Would Be Treason: Last Writings of Ken Saro-Wiwa*. Council for the Development of Social Science Research in Africa and Daraja Press, 2013.

Garricks, Chimeka. *Tomorrow Died Yesterday*. Paperworth Books, 2016.

Gwyn, Richard. *Nation Maker: Sir John A. Macdonald: His Life, Our Times, vol. 2, 1867–1891*. Vintage Canada, 2012.

Herder, Johann Gottfried. *J.G. Herder on Social and Political Culture*. Edited and translated by F.M. Barnard, Cambridge University Press, 1969.

Jameson, Fredric. "Third-World Literature in the Era of Multinational Capitalism." *Social Text*, no. 15, 1986, pp. 65–88.

Kundera, Milan. *The Art of the Novel*. Translated by Linda Asher, Perennial Classics, 2003.

Neame, Laura. "Saro-Wiwa the Publisher." *Ken Saro-Wiwa: Writer and Political Activist*, edited by Craig W. McLuckie and Aubrey McPhail, Lynne Rienner Publishers, 2000, pp. 153–73.

Ngaage, Barine Saana. "'The Star of the Morning': Ogoni Praise Songs of Ken Saro-Wiwa." *Research in African Literatures*, vol. 34, no. 3, 2003, pp. 148–58.

Nixon, Rob. "Pipedreams: Ken Saro-Wiwa, Environmental Justice, and Micro-minority Rights." *Slow Violence and the Environmentalism of the Poor*, Harvard University Press, 2011, pp. 103–27.

Ogezi, Isaac Attah. *Under a Darkling Sky*. Hybun Publications International, 2012.

Ojaide, Tanure. *The Activist*. 2006. AMV Publishing, 2010.

Okome, Onookome. "Ken Saro-Wiwa, a Man of Many Tall Parts: Literature, Nationhood and Dissent." *Before I Am Hanged: Ken Saro-Wiwa, Literature, Politics, and Dissent*, edited by O. Okome, Africa World Press, 2000, pp. ix–xxxii.

Pegg, Scott. "Ken Saro-Wiwa: Assessing the Multiple Legacies of a Literary Interventionist." *Third World Quarterly*, vol. 21, no. 4, 2000, pp. 701–08.

Sainte-Marie, Buffy. "Universal Soldier." 1964. *An Anthology of Canadian Native Literature in English*, 3rd ed., edited by Daniel David Moses and Terry Goldie, Oxford University Press, 2005, pp. 166–67.

Saro-Wiwa, Ken. *A Forest of Flowers*. Longman, 1995.

———. "The Language of African Literature: A Writer's Testimony." *Research in African Literatures*, vol. 23, no. 1, 1992, pp. 153–57.

———. "Letters and Poems." Corley, Fallon, and Cox, pp. 41–162.

———. *A Month and a Day & Letters*. Ayebia Clarke Publishing, 2005.

———. "Notes of a Reluctant Publisher." *The African Book Publishing Record*, vol. 22, no. 4, 1996, pp. 257–59.

———. *On a Darkling Plain: An Account of the Nigerian Civil War*. Saros International Publishers, 1989.

———. *Similia: Essays on Anomic Nigeria*. Saros International Publishers, 1991.

———. *Songs in a Time of War*. Saros International Publishers, 1985.

———. *Sozaboy: A Novel in Rotten English*. 1985. African Writers Series, 1994.

Soyinka, Wole. "Foreword: Flight from Auckland—November 1995." Saro-Wiwa, *Month*, pp. vii–xiv.

———. *The Open Sore of a Continent: A Personal Narrative of the Nigerian Crisis*. Oxford University Press, 1997.

Wiwa, Ken. *In the Shadow of a Saint*. Alfred A. Knopf Canada, 2000.

10

"Write Only the Truth"
(Re)contesting the Nigerian Nation in Chimeka Garricks's *Tomorrow Died Yesterday* and Helon Habila's *Oil on Water*

UCHECHUKWU PETER UMEZURIKE

THE NIGERIAN WRITERS Chimeka Garricks and Helon Habila challenge the homogeneity of national identity by articulating narratives that demonstrate the multinational character of Nigeria. Their novels *Tomorrow Died Yesterday* (2010) and *Oil on Water* (2011) depict the contestations of the Nigerian nation-state by the inhabitants of the Niger Delta. Garricks and Habila emphasize the ties between the national and the oil-rich region as one of centre-periphery underpinned by terror and violence. The military, fighting on behalf of the Nigerian state, and the militants, asserting their Niger Deltan identity against the state, comprise the key actors in this asymmetrical relation. Each group communicates "nationness" in ways adversarial to the other that reinforce aggressive patriotism rooted in ethnonationality (militants) or federal nationalism (military). In Garricks's and Habila's work, Nigeria is constructed as a conflictual space that constitutes citizenship around conceptions of "us" versus "them," thus reinstating solidarities along refractory ethnic and national lines. Garricks and Habila underscore the human costs behind the idea of reifying national identity—what terror and counter-terror underwrite in the name of social order, justice, and unity.

Both novelists delineate the forces, processes, and rationalizations that legitimize deployments of violence against human and non-human lives. They question the singularity of national identity by emphasizing the multinational character of Nigeria. In their narratives, the Nigerian nation-state is riven by conflicts and atrocities and its claim to a unitary sovereign space is constantly being challenged from within. By dramatizing various ways that ethnic loyalties are enunciated and asserted, the texts stage a critique of "the idea of the nation as a continuous narrative of national progress" (Bhabha 2). Garricks and Habila further dramatize the struggle over the ownership of oil, thereby "making sovereignty an object of contestation" (Obi 147). *Tomorrow Died Yesterday* and *Oil on Water* not only narrate the deadly epidemic of hydrocarbon capitalism that has transformed the Niger Delta into an implacable, restive place, but also participate in the representation of petromodernity by documenting the ecocide in the region and the transnational movement of capital through an assemblage of actors, agents, and processes (Guyer 239). The texts also participate in the representation of the "politics of truth" by illuminating the struggle between state and non-state actors over narrations, significations, and justifications of nationhood.

Furthermore, in their representation of the Nigerian nation, Garricks and Habila point to the difficulty of defining a "national literature" for Nigeria and classifying Nigerian writers from the various ethnonationalities. Nigeria provides an interesting case to think about the tenuousness of national literature as a category. With a neocolonial government that reinforces ethnicity rather than foster nationality, what is the "national" for the major or minor ethnic groups? What is that collective symbol or dream Nigerians aspire to, and how has it inspired and galvanized the Nigerian self-image? *Tomorrow Died Yesterday* and *Oil on Water* offer a means to consider these questions while demonstrating the limits of applying the rubric of a national literature to Nigerian literatures. Even the Niger Delta literature as a category is equally imprecise because the inhabitants—such as the Isoko, the Urhobo, the Ijaw, the Itsekiri, to cite a few—of the Niger Delta are distinct in cultural and linguistic terms. Their shared experience is rooted primarily in the oil economy and ecological destruction—not in culture or language. As such, Garricks and Habila provoke a rethink of reading literature in postcolonial nations under the rubric of the national and suggest a fluid and capacious understanding that recognizes the nation's constructedness or its performative character, especially in this era of increased globalization and neoliberalism.

Adapting Barbara Harlow's ideas in *Resistance Literature*, I argue that Garricks and Habila employ their narratives to interrogate the national identity by presenting Nigeria as a site of competing heterogeneous identities, where force is authorized, legitimized, and deployed to propagate and enforce (ethno)national loyalties. According to Harlow, resistance literature underwrites "the collective and concerted struggle against hegemonic domination and oppression" (29). Moreover, it is "involved in a struggle against ascendant or dominant forces of ideological and cultural production" (28–29). Although Garricks and Habila are not social or environmental justice activists by any means, their novels could serve as resistance narratives in three pertinent ways: first, they uncover the legacies of British colonialism and imperialism in Nigeria; second, they dramatize the contradictions inherent in "nationness" or what Jonathan Kertzer describes as the "volatile inconsistencies within the very idea of nationhood" (95); third, they demonstrate that national identity is often fraught and tenuous and so "unity [must be] effected by means of brutality" (Renan 11). Questions of marginalization, justice, and self-determination are, indeed, central to the social vision expressed in the two texts.

The Colonial Roots of the Nigerian Identity

Modern-day Nigeria is a British creation. The British colonial administration assembled a "loose collection of nations" to form what we now know as Nigeria (Okonta and Douglas 29). This assembly of ethnonationalities composed the administrative units, which the government of Lord Lugard later amalgamated in 1914. I.A. Eteng criticizes "Lugard's forced amalgamation" for instigating the "inter-ethno-religious suspicion, residential segregation and antagonism among various communal groups" (37). The reality in contemporary Nigeria under a democratic government remains much the same as it was in the 1960s, with little collective optimism and contentment, except that there is some semblance of relative political stability. Larry Diamond argues that "to understand why democratic government has repeatedly failed in Nigeria, despite a broad and deeply felt aspiration for it in the country, we must go back to its origins in the waning period of British colonial rule, and its first, ill-fated experience in the 1960s" (3). The legacy of British colonialism, with its disregard for the discrete historical and cultural differences of the indigenous population, is one of the remote causes of the recurrent ethnic and regional conflicts in Nigeria.

The Paradox of Oil

Nigeria is a petrol state, a rentier federation that runs a largely monocultural economy; the Niger Delta is the major revenue earner for the government, accounting for at least "90 per cent of export earnings" (Obi et al. 3). Geopolitically, the Niger Delta comprises nine states in Nigeria: Akwa Ibom, Cross Rivers, Delta, Bayelsa, Rivers State, Edo (south-south), Ondo (southwest), Abia, and Imo (southeast). Except for Cross Rivers, all of these states are oil producing. The Niger Delta exemplifies what Michael Ross famously calls the "resource curse." In *The Oil Curse*, Ross shows that how the government spends its oil income can determine the degree of prosperity or poverty its citizens will experience (5). Some economists also describe the oil curse as the "Dutch disease." The Netherlands discovered and exploited its petroleum resources during the 1960s and 1970s, registering a boom in its economy, but later suffered an economic bust. Paul Collier categorizes some countries as the "Bottom Billion" because billions of the world's poor live in the global bottom, or, more precisely, the Global South. Beset as it is with a leadership deficit, Nigeria offers a model of Collier's exposition of the conflict trap, the natural resource trap, and the trap of bad governance (5). Rob Nixon comments, "the petro-state has given rise, moreover, to a society in which 85 per cent of oil wealth goes to a mere 1 per cent of the populace, almost none of whom belong to the micro-minorities who inhabit, ingest, and inhale the ecological devastation" (106–07). The Nigerian state has not treated the Niger Delta with care and fairness; rather, it has neglected and plundered the people of this region, transforming it into "the world capital of oil pollution" (Vidal). The despoliation has caused its inhabitants to wonder if they belong to Nigeria, if the government considers them as part of its citizenry—or if they are nothing more than an "oil resource" to be exploited for the "national" good.

The current struggle for regional autonomy and resource control in the Niger Delta began with Isaac Adaka Boro and his armed militia in 1966. Boro founded the Niger Delta Republic at the time—a republic within the federal republic of Nigeria. However, the military crushed his dream within twelve days and he died in mysterious circumstances two years later. Prior to his death, Boro was regarded as "an icon of Ijaw nationalism" for fighting on the side of the federal government against the Biafran separatists in August 1967 (Nwajiaku 102). Cyril Obi has argued that "Boro's action was partly to prevent the oil in the Niger Delta that was part of the Eastern region from falling into the hands of the dominant Igbo elite, and to assert Ijaw 'sovereignty' over its ancestral territory" (157). Acclaimed novelist and playwright Ken Saro-Wiwa would carry on the agitation against the government and its transnational allies. He co-founded the Movement for the Survival of the Ogoni People (MOSOP), a nonviolent social movement, to advocate for environmental justice and "a greater say in future oil exploration" (Junger). Deaf to the international outcry and appeals, the military government of General Sani Abacha rounded up Saro-Wiwa and eight others and had them hanged on November 10, 1995. In their texts, Garricks and Habila show that insurgency is a result of the decimation of the Niger Delta by the state and the oil companies.

Fictionalizing the Niger Delta

Garricks is a practicing lawyer in Lagos, although he is from Rivers State. *Tomorrow Died Yesterday* is the only novel he has published. He has also published a collection of short stories, *A Broken People's Playlist*. Habila is a professor at George Mason University in the United States and author of several fiction and non-fiction texts. *Oil on Water* is his third novel. He is from Gombe State, in the northeastern part of Nigeria. Before moving aboard, Habila worked as a journalist with a national daily in Lagos. Unlike Garricks, who is a relatively new writer, Habila has long been regarded as a member of the Third Generation of Nigerian writers, that is, writers who were born right before or after independence in 1960 and were active in literary activism during the military eras of 1980s and 1990s (Adesanmi and Dunton; Sule; Umezurike). Both writers come from multi-ethnic states that reflect the multinational complexity of Nigeria. Garricks's and Habila's work is part of the body of literature that portrays the struggle of nation-building in postcolonial Nigeria. Similarly, by revealing the anthropogenic impact of oil capitalism on the country, their work is part of the growing literary representations of the Niger Delta. Some of the fictions that have also taken up the theme of regional and national struggle over oil and its repercussions include Gabriel Okara's *The Voice*, Isidore Okpewho's *Tides*, Kaine Agary's *Yellow-Yellow*, Tanure Ojaide's *The Activist*, and Promise Ogochukwu's *Outrage*.

In *Indigeneity, Globalization, and African Literature*, Ojaide discusses the scope of Niger Delta literature. In a chapter titled "Defining Niger Delta Literature: Preliminary Perspective on an Emerging Literature," he clarifies, "the terms Literature of the Niger Delta and Niger Delta Literature are used interchangeably in this study to mean works of literature that have been produced by both indigenes of the Niger Delta and outsiders about the region. These literary works are either set in the Niger Delta or take their themes from the experiences of the people of the region" (56). Ojaide argues that "it is important to state then that literary works can be classified as Niger Delta literature that remain Nigerian, albeit African, literature" (56). He writes that Helon Habila and Ahmed Yerima are two "nonindigenes of the area" who "have written sensitively about the Niger Delta" (56). Ojaide expresses a capacious understanding of Niger Delta literature that accommodates any work whose theme or setting reflects the Niger Delta. Therefore, one does not have to be from that region to have one's work read as belonging to the corpus of writing on Niger Delta. Habila's *Oil on Water* is as much Niger Delta literature as it is Nigerian literature. The novel depicts the Niger Delta experiences of despoliation and oppression and the Nigerian state's oppression of its citizens. The perspective Habila employs emphasizes his ideological affinity with the plights and struggles of the Niger Deltans. He is a minority by ethnicity (Kaltungo) and religion (Christianity) in the Muslim-dominated north; however, he characterizes the militants with remarkable sensitivity such that one can readily side with their resistance against the Nigerian state. Moreover, the imagery he uses to describe the environmental degradation of the Niger Delta is graphic and gloomy. In short, he paints a landscape of death engineered by the Nigerian state and its transnational partners.

Tomorrow Died Yesterday: The Nation, Its Bloodsuckers, and Monsters

Garricks's novel tells the story of four childhood friends—Doye Koko, Kaniye Rufus, Amaibi Akassa, and Joseph Tubo—and how their lives interconnect in the Niger Delta. Doye (aka Doughboy) is the leader of the Asiama Freedom Army; Amaibi is a university professor and environmental activist; Kaniye is a lawyer-cum-restaurateur; and Tubo is a shady executive with Imperial Oil. The novel's themes encompass love, betrayal, friendship, violence, avarice, and corruption. The story takes place in Asiama River, Asiama Town, and Port Harcourt, all in the Niger Delta (south-south) and in Lagos (southwest)—Nigeria's largest city and commercial capital. The narration is driven by multiple narrators—Doye, Tubo, Kaniye, Amaibi, and Deola—and revolves primarily around Doye's kidnapping of Brian Manning, an American engineer working in the Niger Delta, and the attendant consequences. Garricks portrays the region as a "war zone," a place of "dead fish" and "haunted faces," and "lifeless river" clogged with "black oil" (353).

Doye, the militant leader, knows that neither the government nor the oil companies have the interests of his community at heart and exhibits no qualms in renouncing any form of identification with Nigeria. Doye dramatizes this after he seizes the soldiers dispatched to attack him and begins to interrogate them. One of the soldiers appeals to him: "We all be Nigerians. *Abeg*, we all be brothers. We be one people," but Doye counters, "Who said we are brothers?" When the soldier finally answers, Doye asks, "Where are you from?" The soldier starts to say, "Nigeria, sir..." but Doye shakes his head, and the soldier clarifies, "Sorry sir, Kano State, sir" (5–6). Doye lowers his voice at this point to mask his anger: "How can you, a Hausa man, be my brother? When your people were stealing our oil money all these years, was I your brother then?" (6). He promptly disassociates himself from the Hausa soldier whose people he labels as thieves. Doye then turns to another soldier and asks, "Hey, you! Where are you from?" The soldier is afraid to look at Doye, though he manages to reply, "Eh...eh...Ekiti State, sir." Doye asks, "Yoruba man, are you my brother?" but the soldier does not reply, and Doye reprimands him: "My people have the oil, yet it is your people who have all the jobs in the oil companies. Your people refuse to employ my people. They say we are not qualified. Yoruba man, answer me—are my people not qualified?" (7). Doye chafes at this appeal to brotherliness that is predicated on a pan-Nigerian nationality. He therefore distances himself from the Yoruba soldier as well, whose people he sees as nepotistic. While Kano is in the north, Ekiti is in the southwest of Nigeria. By refusing to be interpellated by expressions of oneness, Doye rejects the sentiments that equate nationality with fraternity, on one hand, and affirms nationality with fraternity, on the other. He rejects fraternity with the majority ethnic groups, while affirming fraternity with the other minorities in the Niger Delta. He contests the idea that the Hausa and the Yoruba could be brothers to the Niger Delta indigene since both are involved in the "ongoing plunder of [his] land" (236). Oil makes it difficult for such filiations to exist, Doye seems to suggest.

Jeremiah Dibua argues that "no matter how long a person from an ethnic group, community or state has lived in...another community or state and regularly fulfilled his or her civic obligations, the person remains a stranger" (7). Doye's attitude exemplifies the link between resource control and citizenship rights. He views his people as victims of the collaboration between the Hausa and Yoruba (along with the Igbo), who enjoy hegemonic positions in the body politic and therefore fail to recognize the citizenship rights of the Niger Delta people. In this vein, he refuses to also recognize them as fellow citizens of Nigeria and instead regards them as "bloodsuckers" that "loot our oil" (Garricks 322). In addition, he contends that Hausa and Yoruba are complicit with the state in "persistently brutalising and sodomising [his] people" (323). By deploying such divisive statements as "my people" and "your people," Doye embraces the notion of "us" versus "them" and asserts a politics of difference that ignores the national anthem's promise of "one nation bound in freedom, peace and unity." This politics of ethnic distinction informs his rejection of social affiliations on multiple levels: citizenship, kinship, and humanity. There is no "one people" or commonality between the other ethnic groups and his. That various ethnic nationalities inhabit the same territory does not make them "brothers." Further, Doye positions the Niger Delta indigene as an Other in the body politic. Oyeniyi

Okunoye suggests that "the people of the Niger Delta consciously define themselves as the 'Other' within Nigeria" (415). According to Okunoye, the condition of otherness compels the Niger Delta people to imagine themselves as marginal and alienated from the bonds of nationhood and so they work to construct a "Pan-Niger Delta identity." Okunoye links the origin of this "Pan-Niger Delta identity" to "the shared agony of the people based on perceived neglect and exposure to the ecological disasters that result from oil exploration" (421). Pan-Niger Delta identity is what Doye articulates against majority domination, which, in turn, frames his opposition to ideas of Nigerianness.

Doye suggests that the government is only invested in the Niger Delta because of its oil. He believes that, regardless of the official discourse, "Everyone is milking our oil" (Garricks 234). The Niger Delta is being subjected to "a never-ending gang rape" (235). In an interview with the press, Doye emphasizes the complicity of the government in the degradation of his community and declares that "Mr. President, himself... contributed to the oppression and killing of my people" (327). He complains that "all Mr. President does is shit in and drill oil from my river" (235). His use of the possessive "my river" underlines his disavowal of the state's territorial sovereignty. He sees the river as belonging not to the country but to his people. The "shit" here is not to be taken literally because it figuratively implies the pollution (the slick arising from oil drilling) to which the region is exposed. To "shit" in this sense means polluting the source of sustenance for the people. The president's treatment of such communities is toxic, as is his antipathy to its devastation. When Kaniye reminds Doye that "all land and oil belong to the federal government. That's the law," Doye becomes angry and smashes his left fist into his right hand. He asks Kaniye whether the president eats "the rotten fish from Asiama River? Does his wife drink the contaminated water? Do his grandchildren play next to gas flares and pipelines? So how the hell can he own my river?" (235). Doye is infuriated by the fact that "there is no future for the children of the Niger Delta. Their tomorrow is already dead. It died yesterday" (236). He rationalizes his resort to armed resistance, declaiming it as a strategy since violence is integral to the grammar of nationalism.

In Doye's view, "the Niger Delta struggle is essentially a fight for oil, or the control and use of the resources from oil. No one fights for oil for purely philanthropic purposes" (323). This is why he thinks it necessary to terrorize and kidnap expatriates—because "violence is the only thing that the government and the oil companies respond to" (238). Garricks sets up Doye as "the face of the struggle" to challenge the idea of Nigeria, yet presents him as a complex character who also takes part in the "rape" of his "oil, river, and land" (235). When Kaniye queries him about his illegal activities such as oil bunkering, Doye argues that the Niger Delta appears irredeemable. The rot is so systemic that its roots extend deeper than either of them can comprehend. Doye remarks, "The government has already sold the oil that will be drilled in the next decades. The politicians and military boys have shared oil blocks among themselves" (235). Doye implicates the whole oil assemblage—the political class, or "the big-bellied bastards in government," the military, the multinational oil corporations, and the marketers—in the despoliation of the Niger Delta. However, Garricks problematizes Doye's ideology of liberation by having Kaniye chastise Doye: "You are no different from all the people you complain about, Doye. You are a mercenary, a vulture." Doye does not mind being labelled as such because he believes that "this is the land of the vulture" (235) and he is "just taking [his] share of oil money" (234). Doye is not apologetic about joining in the rape of the Niger Delta since he believes that his "people have a right to partake in the spoils from the ongoing plunder of their land" (236). His conversation with Kaniye presents him as an opportunist, and his motto about "fighting for the people of Asiama and the Niger Delta is just nonsense," as Kaniye argues (236). Kaniye provides us with a way to appreciate the problematics that sometimes characterize liberation struggle and the ideology that usually animates it.

Doye is a "frightening menace" to the state and the oil companies (324), but his community nonetheless appears to revere him. He carries himself as a "king" and "role model." He boasts to Kaniye that "these people believe in me and the justice of my fight. To them, I'm more than a hero, I'm an ideology. Most of their children and young men either beg to join me, or imitate me" (238). Kaniye refutes him: "You are not the role model you think you are, Doye. You've only created monsters that have disfigured the Niger Delta" (238). Ironically, his statement is negated in the wake of Doye's death at the hands of the military. As Kaniye observes, "[Doye] was mourned publicly by everyone, friends, enemies and strangers" (398). The media and masses valorize him, calling him "a revolutionary," "a freedom fighter," "a patriot," and "the Che Guevara of the Niger Delta." Doye is even "mentioned in the same breath as Isaac Boro and Ken Saro-Wiwa" (398). Perhaps because he is murdered by the state, his people venerate him, extolling him as a martyr. Kaniye sums up Doye's martyrdom thus: "If Doughboy was famous in life, he achieved cult status in death" (398). In *Tomorrow Died Yesterday*, Garricks shows how the Nigerian state treats the Niger Delta as a material resource rather than as a living community. He insinuates that the state's propensity for unbridled use of force against youth restiveness in the region and its consequent failure to remediate "the tragic destruction of families, the murder of dreams, and the irreparable damage to the collective psyche of the people" (377) have generated ruptures through which ethnonational solidarities challenge the national idea. Tellingly, Garricks implicates both the Nigerian government and the militants in the violence wreaked on the oil-rich region.

Oil on Water: The Nation, Its Rebels, and the Politics of Truth

Habila's novel is centred on Zaq and Rufus, two journalists who journey through the treacherous, "barren landscape" of the Niger Delta (8), in a bid to ascertain the truth behind the kidnapping of Isabel Floode, the wife of a British oil worker. On the journey, they meet an old man and his son, who ferry them in their boat across the water. The journey, however, brings Rufus face to face with the other side of truth—that is, the truth of nationhood, or how "nations are built," as Zaq says (57). The novel is told from the first-person point of view by Rufus, a neophyte journalist accompanying the veteran alcoholic Zaq. The narrative is nonlinear; it flashes back and forth, mirroring their labyrinthine (mis)adventures through the swamps and mangroves. Snatches of memories are recollected and mediated by Rufus. Like Garricks, Habila examines themes of love, betrayal, avarice, corruption, and kidnapping against the backdrop of militancy. Habila likewise portrays the devastated region as a "war zone." *Oil on Water* is set in Lagos, Port Harcourt, and the riverine hinterlands of Rivers

State. The parties in this conflict are the Major (representing Nigeria) and the Professor (representing the Niger Delta). The former claims to be fighting off the militants in order to "keep the country safe and united" (150), while the latter claims to be "fighting to protect their environment from greedy multinational oil companies" (135).

The opening paragraph foreshadows the tragedy that has become the Niger Delta due to the oil war between the militants and the military. Habila attributes the resurgence of militancy to the endemic destruction of human and non-human lives in the region caused by the transnational forces of capitalism. As Ike Okonta and Oronto Douglas remark, "Historically, the people of the Niger Delta have always been at the mercy of greedy outsiders who plunder their natural resources without giving them anything in return, from days of slavery to the present day" (19). Habila's narrative affirms that "greedy outsiders"—as the oil communities tend to call other Nigerians and the Europeans—have continued to pillage their riches. He shows that oil, more than national interest, is what is at stake here. National unity is threatened by the militants only because it is tied to the oil resource. Both parties are fighting over the control of oil: the mainstay of national identity. It is oil that unites the "multination." Yet it is also the source of disunity and brutalities.

The Niger Delta is described as a place where "all one sees and feels around is death" (Nixon 111). A terrain long despoiled by oil capitalism and state apathy; a "barren landscape" where chickens are "dead and decomposing," "maggots trafficking" in carcasses, "dead birds draped over tree branches," and "dead fishes bobbed" (8, 9). The water is "foul and sulphurous" and emits "rank smell"; "the patch of grass" is "suffocated by a film of oil" (9). Almost all the land and its fauna and flora have been contaminated by "the unmistakable smell of oil" (9). The region is also a site of putrefaction, of death. The funereal atmosphere is amplified in some villages Rufus and Zaq happen to visit. They are confronted by stomach-churning sights of "a dead fowl, a bloated dog belly up with black birds perching on it, and a human arm severed at the elbow bobbing away" (34). By depicting the desolation in graphic detail, Habila suggests that the militants have legitimate reasons to fight over what is left of their devastated land.

What is most striking about *Oil on Water* is that Habila demonstrates a critical understanding of the role the press plays in the articulations of national consciousness. He foregrounds the connections between narration and nation to underscore the nationalist discourses at work in the construction and dissemination of narratives of progression (Bhabha 1). Habila positions Rufus, in particular, as a journalist to interrogate the official discourse of "truth" that figures the militants as "rebels, terrorists, kidnappers" (96). Rufus's journey down the oil-rich communities provides him with a rare opportunity to apprehend the counter-discourse, which posits the country as "so corrupt, only a few had access to that [oil] wealth" (107). Rufus is made to bear witness to all of this, even the atrocities carried out in the name of justice and unity.

John L. Mcmullan and Melissa Mcclung argue that the press functions as an important site for the production and dissemination of "truth" (69). The press operates as one of the "apparatuses of truth," and so the public rarely takes its credibility for granted. Michel Foucault, in *Fearless Speech*, refocuses our attention on "who is able to tell the truth, about what, with what consequences, and with what relation to power" (170). In Habila's novel, there is a struggle over (the representation of) truth between the militants and the military. In a memorable scene, Zaq asks his colleague, "Tell me, Rufus my friend, what do we seek?" Rufus replies that it is the kidnapped woman they seek. Zaq corrects him: "I said 'what,' not 'whom'" (5). Zaq makes clear that it is not the "whom" but the "what" that matters in the truth of nationhood. He underlines its importance when he tells Rufus, "Forget the woman and her kidnappers for a moment. What we really seek is not them but a greater meaning" (5). This cryptic speech mystifies Rufus because he has yet to fathom the meaning behind the kidnapping of the British woman. As he muses to himself, "I have no idea what he meant about the story and its meaning, but perhaps I would find out before this trip was done" (6). Zaq's dismissal of the kidnapping as the "greater meaning" is reiterated by Henshaw, a militant. When Rufus quizzes him about the woman's whereabouts, Henshaw retorts, "Who is she in the context of the war that's going on out here, the hopes and ambitions being created and destroyed? Can't you see the larger picture?" (148). Rufus begins to appreciate the picture only when he encounters the conflicting narratives about identities and loyalties, as played out in the country's backwaters.

In *Imagined Communities*, Benedict Anderson points to the ways that print capitalism helped to facilitate the formation of a nationally imagined community (57). In Habila's text, Zaq restates this fact to Rufus: "Journalism shows you firsthand how nations are built, how great men achieve their greatness" (57). The picture—the story's significance, which Rufus at first fails to apprehend—has to do with the brutalities of the state. Zaq reveals that journalism has offered him a chance to see "children snatched away from their mothers, never to be reunited..., grown men flogged by soldiers in front of their kids" (60). Likewise privileged by the same profession, Rufus is assigned the responsibility to serve as "witness for posterity" (55) and to document the "greater meaning" behind the liberation struggle. Journalism propels him into a historical space where he is able to critique the idea of the nation. Rufus then comes to see that the nation appears predatory and will ultimately discover: "That's how history is made, and it's [his] job to witness it" (60).

Watching the Major torture the captured militants, Rufus recognizes that his role as a witness to how national ideals are constructed and legitimized by violence is made even more urgent when he realizes that the Major has no interest in issues of human rights due to his warped sense of justice. The Major prescribes and dispenses justice on his own terms; he rebukes Rufus for even speaking about "human rights and justice," which to him is "all nonsense." He would rather shoot the militants because "there are no human rights for people like them" (97). The preoccupation with shooting the militants bears out his "volatile, unpredictable" personality and investments in extra-judicial procedures. In "Abu Zubaydah and the Caterpillar," Neel Ahuja discusses how the CIA uses various biopolitical means of torture to exact "truth" from prisoners deemed terrorists. Ahuja highlights the use of insects as part of "torture-as-animalization" regime of "truth-telling" (133). Habila approximates something close to this in his narrative, evident in how the Major treats his prisoners as animals and dehumanizes them. Every morning he has the militants lined up, and then bathes them in petrol (58). The Major alone decides "who is a criminal and who is not" (54). When Rufus intercedes on behalf of their guides, the old man and his son, asking that they be set free because of their innocence, the Major threatens to shoot him and "throw [him] into the swamp" (59).

Despite the grand narrative of the state, Rufus discovers another side to "who is able to tell the truth, about what, with what consequences, and with what relation to power" (Foucault 170). This is an instance of how truth is represented and the politics animating its representation. As Henshaw mentions to him, "We are not murderers, my friend, regardless of what you guys write about us" (148). The Professor, known as the leader of the militants, echoes similar views: "We are not the barbarians the government propagandists say we are. We are for the people. We are for the people. Everything we do is for the people, what will we gain if we terrorize them?" (208). His counter-narrative demonstrates that he understands the "politics of truth" and how propaganda operates in the polity. The Professor also appreciates the authority of the press in truth-making as well as in authenticating truth. This is why he tells Rufus, "Write only the truth. Tell them about the flares you see at night, and the oil on the water. And the soldiers forcing us to escalate the violence every day. Tell them we are hounded daily in our own land. Where do they want us to go, tell me where? Tell them, we are going nowhere. This land belongs to us. This is the truth, remember that" (209–10).

The truth, as the Professor elucidates, includes not only the toxicity of gas flares and "dead fish on oil polluted water" (6), but also how the inhabitants of the Delta "are hounded daily in [their] own land" (209). Though the Professor knows that the military would keep hounding them, he pressures Rufus to remember the truth. This encounter with the Professor climaxes with Rufus avowing that "I will write only the truth" (209). At this point, he has seen "the larger picture" and now understands that the nation is built on the oppression of its other constituent members in the polity. The business of consolidating the foundation of the Nigerian nation requires terror and violence. As the Major mentions to Rufus, "I know these people. I'm the one who can handle them, the only one. They understand only one language: Force. That's all" (97). Force is all that is necessary to contain the "insurgents" within the "multination." Though the Major believes that the unity of Nigeria is non-negotiable and absolute, Habila shows that it would often be undermined by contestations and repudiations from within its boundaries.

The Niger Delta poet G'Ebinyo Ogbowei writes in *marsh boy and other poems*, "communities can't coalesce into a nation / tribes can't be welded into a state" (58). Implicit in this couplet is that no matter how much force is used, it rarely confers a feeling of oneness on people drawn from distinct ethnic and cultural backgrounds. This speaks to the limits of state violence. Perhaps it is the recognition of this "truth" that inspires Henshaw to assert, "We'll outlast them…This land is ours, after all" (150). How much longer can he and his fellow militants hold out? How many "sacrifices more" would have to be made in this bloody impasse and struggle over the land? These are questions the text fails to address, but which it invites its readers to ponder. Habila insinuates that the communities that are likely to survive state terror and probably attain some peace would be those that know how "to pretend to be deaf and blind" (33).

Conclusion

Obari Gomba, another Niger Delta poet from Ogoniland, writes in "Confession of an Oil-Thief," "If they take the oil, they take the money / Oil is money. Money is oil" (12). Gomba's poem, like the novels examined here, emphasizes the centrality of oil to both Nigeria and the Niger Delta. Oil is the core of state-imposed unity; without it, there is apparently no unity. To secure oil means securing unity by any means. Consequently, to secure unity entails securing the oil, regardless of human and environmental costs. As Clifford Geertz notes, "To an increasing degree national unity is maintained not by calls to blood and land but by a vague, intermittent, and routine allegiance to a civil state, supplemented by a greater or lesser extent by governmental use of police powers and ideological exhortation" (260). This chapter has examined how the Nigerian nation is (re)contested in relation to the Niger Delta in *Tomorrow Died Yesterday* and *Oil on Water*. Chimeka Garricks and Helon Habila depict the region's struggle for liberation against hegemonic national forces. Their narratives illustrate the extent to which the idea of national homogeneity is challenged by ethnonational identifications, thus underscoring the obduracy of multinational interests within Nigeria. Drawing on postcolonial insights, particularly from Barbara Harlow, I have argued that Garricks's and Habila's texts critique the official discourse of nationness constellated as "truth" by the Nigerian state to overwhelm the counter-discourse of the Niger Delta. Both writers demonstrate an understanding of the dynamics between narrating the (Nigerian) nation and living in the nation. But, more importantly, they signpost how terror and violence operate in the service of preserving or subverting national unity. Their texts, perhaps, can serve as narratives of resistance.

WORKS CITED

Adesanmi, Pius, and Chris Dunton. "Nigeria's Third Generation Writing: Historiography and Preliminary Theoretical Considerations." *English in Africa*, vol. 32, no. 1, 2005, pp. 7–19.
Agary, Kaine. *Yellow-Yellow*. Dtalkshop, 2006.
Ahuja, Neel. "Abu Zubaydah and the Caterpillar." *Social Text*, vol. 29, no.1, 2011, pp. 127–49.
Anderson, Benedict. *Imagined Communities*. New Left Books, 1991.
Bhabha, Homi. "Introduction: Narrating the Nation," edited by Bhabha, *Nation and Narration*, Routledge, 1990, pp. 1–7.
Collier, Paul. *The Bottom Billion: Why the Poorest Countries Are Failing and What Can be Done About it*. Oxford University Press, 2008.
Diamond, Larry. *Class, Ethnicity, and Democracy in Nigeria: The Failure of the First Republic*. Palgrave Macmillan, 1988.
Dibua, Jeremiah. "Citizenship and Resource Control in Nigeria: The Case of Minority Communities in the Niger Delta." *Africa Spectrum*, vol. 40, no. 1, 2005, pp. 5–28.
Eteng, I.A. "Ethnicity, Ethno-class Relations and Crisis of Nigeria's Enduring 'National Question' and Political Instability.'" *Nigeria and Globalization: Discourses on Identity Politics and Social Conflict*, edited by Duro Oni, et al., CBAAC, 2004, pp. 37–81.
Foucault, Michel. *Fearless Speech*, edited by Joseph Pearson. Semiotext(e), 2001.
Garricks, Chimeka. *A Broken People's Playlist*. Masobe Books, 2020.
——. *Tomorrow Died Yesterday*. Paperworth Books, 2010.
Geertz, Clifford. *The Interpretation of Cultures: Selected Essays*. Basic Books, 1973.
Gomba, Obari. *Pearls of the Mangroves*. Hybun Publications, 2009.
Guyer, Jane I. "Oil Assemblages and the Production of Confusion: Price Fluctuations in Two West African Oil-Producing Economies." *Subterranean Estates: Life Worlds of Oil and Gas*, edited by Hannah Appel, et al., Cornell University Press, 2015, pp. 237–52.
Habila, Helon. *Oil on Water*. Penguin Books, 2011.
Harlow, Barbara. *Resistance Literature*. Methuen, 1987.
Junger, Sebastian. "Blood Oil." *Vanity Fair*, Feb. 2007, https://www.vanityfair.com/news/2007/02/junger200702.
Kertzer, Jonathan. *Worrying the Nation: Imagining a National Literature in English Canada*. University of Toronto Press, 1998.

McMullan, John L., and McClung, Melissa. "The Media, the Politics of Truth, and the Coverage of Corporate Violence: The Westray Disaster and the Public Inquiry." *Critical Criminology*, vol. 14, no. 1, 2006, pp. 67–86.

Nixon, Rob. *Slow Violence and the Environmentalism of the Poor*. Harvard University Press, 2011.

Nwajiaku, Kathryn. "Memory and Oblivion: Isaac Boro and the Trends of Contemporary Ijaw Nationalism." *African Politics*, vol. 103, no. 3, 2006, pp. 106–26.

Obi, Cyril. "Transnationalism, Africa's 'Resource Curse' and 'Contested Sovereignties': The Struggle for Nigeria's Niger Delta." *Africa and International Relations in the 21st Century*, edited by Scarlett Cornelissen, et al., Palgrave Macmillan, 2012, pp. 147–61.

Obi, Cyril, et al. *Oil and Insurgency in the Niger Delta: Managing the Complex Politics of Petroviolence*. Zed Books, 2011.

Ogbowei, G'Ebinyo. *marsh boy and other poems*. Kraft Books, 2015.

Ogochukwu, Promise. *Outrage*. Bookcraft, 2016.

Ojaide, Tanure. *The Activist*. Farafina Press, 2006.

——. *Indigeneity, Globalization, and African Literature*. Palgrave Macmillan, 2015.

Okara, Gabriel. *The Voice*. Africana Publishing, 1970.

Okonta, Ike, and Oronto, Douglas. *Where Vultures Feast: Forty Years of Shell in the Niger Delta*. Sierra Club Books, 2001.

Okpewho, Isidore. *Tides*. Longman, 1993.

Okunoye, Oyeniyi. "Alterity, Marginality and the National Question in the Poetry of the Niger Delta." *Cahiers d'études africaines*, no. 191, 2008, pp. 413–36. https://journals.openedition.org/etudesafricaines/11742.

Renan, Ernest. "What Is a Nation?" *Nation and Narration*, edited by Homi Bhabha, Routledge, 1990, pp. 10–22.

Ross, Michael. *The Oil Curse: How Petroleum Wealth Shapes the Development of Nations*. Princeton University Press, 2012.

Sule, E.E. *Nation, Power and Dissidence in Third-Generation Nigerian Poetry in English*. African Humanities Program, 2014.

Umezurike, Uchechukwu P. "Self-Publishing in the Era of Military Rule in Nigeria, 1985–1999." *Journal of African Cultural Studies*, vol. 32, no. 2, 2020, pp. 212–30. https://doi.org/10.1080/13696815.2019.1627186.

Vidal, John. "Nigeria's Agony Dwarfs the Gulf Oil Spill. The US and Europe Ignore It." *The Guardian*, 30 May 2010, https://www.theguardian.com/world/2010/may/30/oil-spills-nigeria-niger-delta-shell.

Contributors

SABUJKOLI BANDOPADHYAY holds a PHD from the University of Alberta. Her research focuses on interwar world literature, postcolonial theory, and intersectionality. Her scholarly contributions include "Diversity, Inclusion, Critical 'Othering': Methodologies for Comparative Literature," "British Culture and Identity in 1930s Anglophone Literature from Australia, Canada and India," "Subaltern's Resistance against Rape and Sexual Assault: An Aporia?," and "Contextualizing the Idea of the British Working-Class: A Reading of Mulk Raj Anand's *Coolie*." Forthcoming publications include a chapter on 1950s Bengali women's writing, a piece on the "lumpenproletariat," and another chapter on tyranny in George Orwell's novels. She teaches courses in English literature and gender studies.

ALBERT BRAZ is a professor emeritus of comparative literature and English at the University of Alberta. He is the author of *The False Traitor: Louis Riel in Canadian Culture* (2003) and *Apostate Englishman: Grey Owl the Writer and the Myths* (2015) and the co-editor of an issue of the *Canadian Review of Comparative Literature* on Comparative Canadian Literature (2009) and of an issue of *CLC Web: Comparative Literature and Culture* on Indigenous Literatures (2011). A former president of the Canadian Comparative Literature Association, Braz is completing a book on the Canadianization of Louis Riel.

MATTHEW CORMIER is an assistant professor in the English Department at the Université de Moncton. His current research intersects the digital humanities, memory studies, affect theory, and contemporary apocalyptic writing in Canada. The author of *Sieve Reading Beyond the Minor* (forthcoming University of Ottawa Press 2023), his diverse work has appeared in several books as well as in journals such as *Studies in Canadian Literature, English Studies in Canada, Canadian Review of Comparative Literature, Canadian Poetry, American, British and Canadian Studies*, and *Canadian Review of American Studies*.

DORIS HAMBUCH is an associate professor in the Department of Languages and Literature at United Arab Emirates University in Al Ain. She is a contributor to the Greenwood *Encyclopedia of Postcolonial Studies* (2001) and the Routledge *Who's Who in Contemporary Women's Writing* (2001). Hambuch edited a special issue of *Imaginations: Journal of Cross-Cultural Image Studies* (6.2) on Caribbean cinema. She is currently president of the Canadian Comparative Literature Association. Her poetry has appeared in *All That Depends* (2019) and *Monsters* (2021).

CLARA A.B. JOSEPH is a professor in the Department of English and an adjunct in the Department of Classics and Religion at the University of Calgary. She is the author of *The Agent in the Margin* (2008), *The Face of the Other (A Long Poem)* (2016), *Dandelions for Bhabha* (2018), and *Christianity in India: The Anti-Colonial Turn* (2019). Her co-edited collections include two special issues—"The Postcolonial and Globalisation" and "Rethinking the Postcolonial and Globalisation"—for the journal *World Literature Written in English*, and *Global Fissures: Postcolonial Fusions* and *Theology and Literature: Rethinking Reader Responsibility*.

PAUL D. MORRIS is a professor of English and the current director of the master's program in Études canadiennes et interculturelles at the Université de Saint-Boniface. His varied research interests are focused in comparative literature and, more specifically, Canadian, American, and Slavic literatures. The translator of various texts from German, French, and Russian, he has also authored, edited, and co-edited a number of book-length studies and collections. His most recent book publications have been *Vladimir Nabokov: Poetry and the Lyric Voice* (authored, 2010) and *Le Canada: Une culture de métissage / Transcultural Canada* (edited, 2019).

ASMA SAYED is the Canada Research Chair in South Asian Literary and Cultural Studies in the Department of English at Kwantlen Polytechnic University. Her interdisciplinary research focuses on Indian Ocean studies, postcolonial studies, feminist and critical race studies, and the South Asian diaspora in Canada. Her publications include five co-/edited books and numerous articles in a range of periodicals, anthologies, and academic journals.

MATTHEW TÉTREAULT has a PHD in English and Film Studies from the University of Alberta. He is Métis and French Canadian from Ste. Anne, Manitoba. A creative writer and scholar, he is the author of *What Happened on the Bloodvein*, a collection of short fiction (2016). His novel, *Hold Your Tongue* is forthcoming with NeWest Press (spring 2023). He is also the author of "Reading Scofield through Riel: *Louis: The Heretic Poems* as Dissonance" (2020). His current research investigates Métis literary history, with particular attention to language use and expressions of national identity.

UCHECHUKWU PETER UMEZURIKE is an assistant professor of English at the University of Calgary. He holds a PHD degree from the University of Alberta, Canada. An alumnus of the International Writing Program (USA), Umezurike has published his critical writing in *Men and Masculinities, NORMA: Nordic Journal for Masculinity Studies, Journal of African Cultural Studies, Postcolonial Text,* and *Cultural Studies*. He is the author of *Double Wahala, Double Trouble* (2021) and *Wish Maker* (2021), and a co-editor of *Wreaths for Wayfarers* (2020). His poetry collection, *there's more*, is forthcoming from the University of Alberta Press in 2023.

JERRY WHITE is a professor of English at the University of Saskatchewan. His articles on Catalan cinema, literature, and politics have appeared in *Comparative Literature, Screen, CineAction, Cinema Scope, Dalhousie French Studies* (for whom he edited a special section on the Catalan language in France), *European Review*, *Aboriginal Policy Studies*, and *Sjani: Journal of Literary Theory and Comparative Literature* (Tbilisi). His book reviews and op-eds on Catalan topics have appeared in *Le Devoir* and the *Irish Times*.

Other titles from University of Alberta Press

All the Feels / Tous les sens
Affect and Writing in Canada /
Affect et écriture au Canada

Edited by MARIE CARRIÈRE, URSULA MATHIS-MOSER & KIT DOBSON

Essays in French or English use affect as a lens for reading contemporary Canadian literatures.

Narratives of Citizenship
Indigenous and Diasporic Peoples
Unsettle the Nation-State

Edited by ALOYS N.M. FLEISCHMANN, NANCY VAN STYVENDALE & CODY MCCARROLL

Thirteen essays examine literature, film, music, etc. to conceptualize citizenship as a narrative construct.

Countering Displacements
The Creativity and Resilience of Indigenous and Refugee-ed Peoples

Edited by DANIEL COLEMAN, ERIN GOHEEN GLANVILLE, WAFAA HASAN & AGNES KRAMER-HAMSTRA

This collection of essays forges compelling linkages between cultural experiences of refugees and Indigenous peoples worldwide.

More information at uap.ualberta.ca